A FALCON GUIDE®

D0547454

Hiking the Redwood Coast

Best Hikes along Northern and
Central California's Coastline

Dan Brett

FALCON®

GUILFORD, CONNECTICUT
HELENA, MONTANA

AN IMPRINT OF THE GLOBE PEQUOT PRESS

A FALCON GUIDE ®

All photographs by the author
Maps by XNR Productions, Inc. © The Globe Pequot Press
The author used MapTech software to produce some
source maps.

ISSN 1548-422X
ISBN 0-7627-2582-6

Manufactured in the United States of America
First Edition/First Printing

Contents

The Redwood Coast

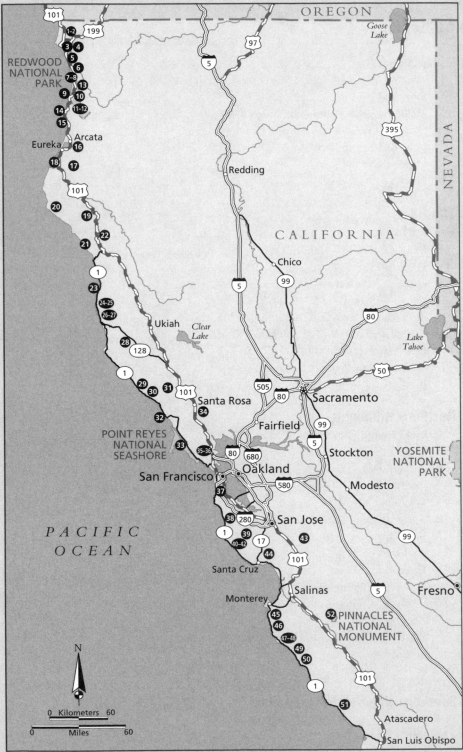

Introduction

Among out-of-staters, California is probably best known for its movie stars, wacky politics, and a few iconic landmarks such as Hollywood and the Golden Gate Bridge. With all of the glitz and hype, it is easy for outsiders to forget that California is also a natural wonderland, full of rich and varied landscapes—much of which is still largely undeveloped. As the last stop in America's westward expansion, much of California came late to modern civilization, and vast tracts of the Wild West's final frontier were not "tamed" until well into the twentieth century. More than a few places were never tamed at all. This land's history is still fresh, and traces of it are everywhere.

Nowhere is this more true than along the Golden State's Redwood Coast. Almost every hike in this book has a fascinating tale to tell, and it was often difficult to squeeze it all into this small space. For those who wish to learn more, Web links and further reading suggestions are provided.

Of course, it is the land itself that provides the greatest attraction for hikers, and the Redwood Coast has a lot to offer. Whether you like it wet, dry, high, low, perfectly level, or very nearly vertical, there is something here for you. These trails will take you to rocky spires, silent glades, and wave-battered shores. They will show you bare ridgetops with 100-mile views, and deep verdant forests where ferns grow head-high and colossal trees stand like pillars holding up the sky. And they will consistently bring you to places where the traces of history seem tangible and close enough to touch.

The purpose of this guidebook is to offer readers an opportunity to explore the Redwood Coast's many facets. Rather than just throwing together a collection of pleasant hikes, the intent of the author and publisher has always been to present excellent hikes that do the history, natural diversity, and character of this region justice. What you have in your hands is a guidebook to the Redwood Coast—by trail. There are hikes here for every level of experience, and three of them are at least partially wheelchair accessible.

Weather

As you might expect, weather patterns along the Redwood Coast are influenced greatly by the whims of the Pacific Ocean next door. A permanent current, known as the North Pacific Gyre, flows in a clockwise direction around the edge of this vast body of water. The eastern portion of the ring, flowing just offshore of western North America, is known as the California Current. As it flows southward, it brings cool, low-salinity water down from the Arctic, creating special weather patterns in the coastal regions within its reach. The result for the Redwood Coast is mild, wet weather that for eons has sustained the temperate redwood rain forests. While the

Bridge in a riparian forest

loss of much of this forest has noticeably altered weather patterns in the past fifty years, it is still known for wet winters and foggy summers. Generally speaking, you are more likely to get rained on in the winter, and seasonal bridges will all be removed at this time of year, since creeks and rivers tend to swell dramatically with the rains. At times the precipitation may seem extreme. Along the Lost Coast, for example, precipitation averages more than 100 inches per year, with up to 200 inches in "wet" years.

The trade-off for all this wetness are the mild winters. Snow is rare along the coast, except at higher elevations, and T-shirt weather in January is not uncommon. In between the rains, sunny days are common enough that it is easy to forget what time of year it is. This feeling is encouraged by the thick fog that often blankets the coast in summer, especially in early morning. The fog and prevalent offshore breezes prevent temperatures from climbing much above about 70 degrees Fahrenheit most of the time. The average temperature in San Francisco hovers between 50 and 60 degrees, year-round.

A string of mountains stretches nearly unbroken the length of the Redwood Coast, and these mountains tend to create a natural barrier for the Pacific's weather influence. East of the range, summer temperatures can easily soar into the 100s, and winters are a little harsher than directly on the coast.

Flora and Fauna

The obvious star of the Redwood Coast is *Sequoia sempervirens,* better known as the coast redwood—tallest living thing on earth. Under the thick, emerald canopies of these giants, sword ferns carpet the forest floor, occasionally making room for clover-like redwood sorrel, and shade-tolerant tan oak, big-leaf maple, and pungent California laurel. The coast redwood is not to be confused with its close relative, the giant sequoia *(Sequoiadendron giganteum),* which is confined to several isolated groves on the western slopes of the Sierra Nevada.

The scope of this book falls largely within the historic range of the world's only surviving redwood forests. When the first Europeans arrived in California, these magnificent trees stretched in a broad strip from just north of the modern Oregon border south to southern Monterey County. Of the estimated two million acres of old-growth redwood existing at the time of European contact, only around 3 percent survive.

Although old-growth or second-growth redwoods can be found all along the Redwood Coast, the wild lands between Del Norte and Monterey Counties are hardly homogenous. Interspersed and adjoining redwood-favored zones are a wide variety of habitats, largely influenced by geological, geographical, and climate factors. In the north the redwoods occupy a solid swath of land between 20 and 40 miles wide. On the east these forests gradually give way to more drought-tolerant

Trillium

mixed forests, with red and Douglas fir, Sitka spruce, incense cedar, Port Orford cedar, sugar pine, and several oak species sharing the space with manzanita, madrone, and wildflower-filled, grassy meadows. In the Siskiyou Mountains of Del Norte County, special soil types encourage even greater diversity. In one small area, seventeen *conifer* species are found growing side by side, creating an astounding pool of diversity that includes several endemic plant species.

Directly on the coast, salt-sensitive redwoods leave a narrow strip to hardier plants such as Monterey cypress. Sandy dunes and beaches are home to the coastal scrub community, while windswept headlands are dominated by grasses.

As you move south the redwoods become restricted to moist valleys that receive lots of coastal fog. Larger portions of the coast are covered with brushy chaparral and coastal scrub. The drier upper slopes and ridgetops are given over to sparse oak forests and golden grasses. About half of the twenty or so oak species native to California are endemic to the state, and—unlike oaks in general—all but four of them are evergreens. The acorns from these oaks were once a primary source of food for California Indians, prior to the influx of European-American settlers.

By the time you arrive in the Big Sur regions, the redwoods have become downright scarce, with grassy rangeland, scruffy oak forests, and thick coastal scrub dominating.

Wildlife in the region is easily as impressive as the flora. Half of the insects and invertebrates in the state are endemic, as are 65 of the more than 1,000 native vertebrates. Many of these species have adapted to specific environments. The marbled murrelet and spotted owl, for example, are limited to old-growth forests on the north coast. Wetlands, scattered along the coast and around the San Francisco Bay Area provide important feeding and breeding grounds for migratory birds, including sandhill cranes, snow geese, and American coot. Osprey nest in the broken tops of tall trees near the rivers where they fish.

Roosevelt elk, once numbering in the tens of thousands, were hunted to near extinction before being protected. Small herds now survive in the forests and mountains of the north coast, particularly around Prairie Creek Redwoods State Park. Grizzly bears—symbol of the state and once widespread—have been extinct here since the 1920s, but their smaller cousin the black bear is well represented. Mountain lions, seldom seen, roam throughout the state, wherever deer are abundant. Bobcats, coyotes, ravens, raccoons, and skunks are also common. Several members of the weasel family are found in these forests, including weasels, marten, fisher, and badger. River otter and the larger sea otter play and hunt in secluded forest waterways and along the coast, respectively.

Seals and sea lions are a common sight along the coast and in coastal estuaries. Harbor seals are the most often seen, but California sea lion and northern sea lion are also abundant. Largest of the lot, northern elephant seals can be seen on the coast at Point Reyes and Año Nuevo Point, where they breed. Whale watchers can observe the yearly migrations of the gray whale from any high spot along the coast. Point Reyes, Bodega Head, the cliffs of Big Sur, and Patrick's Point are all good locations for this.

While threatened by logging, agricultural runoff, dams, and overdevelopment, California's rivers still host impressive seasonal salmon runs. Sockeye, coho, and chinook are some of the monsters that make their way from the ocean up rivers and streams to spawn in the headwaters where they were born.

Wilderness Restrictions and Regulations

The Redwood Coast has literally dozens of state parks, beaches, and reserves, as well as a national park, a national seashore, two national forests, and two national recreation areas. These lands are maintained as reserves of undeveloped land with important biological, cultural, economic, and recreational value. The trick for the agencies managing them is to balance human use without compromising the health and wild character of the parks. Permits, access quotas, and fees are part of this effort.

Rules and regulations vary dramatically from park to park, generally becoming stricter with increased use—and consequent potential damage—of the resource. Out of the way or undeveloped areas such as the Smith River National Recreation Area or Garrapata State Park often don't require day-use fees, while the highly sensitive wildlife at Año Nuevo State Reserve has led to fees and permits for walking in half of the park, even closing the area entirely for part of the year. Almost all areas require permits and/or fees for overnight use. Due to the ever-present fire danger, campfire permits are required on most public land throughout the state.

Before heading off on an overnight hike, call the land management agency responsible for your destination and inquire about permits and regulations that may apply. Staff will often make recommendations about human waste disposal, bear behavior, and campsites that will minimize any negative impact you may have on the resource. Please heed this advice, follow regulations, and get required permits. It may seem like a pain, but with six billion people on the planet, open space is becoming an increasingly precious commodity. Help keep the wilderness wild.

Redwood Coast Hike Index

I've grouped the hikes covered in this book into categories, so you can quickly find the type that interests you.

Beach Hikes

5: Damnation Creek Trail
6: Coastal Trail: Yurok Loop to Hidden Beach
13: Skunk Cabbage Trail
20: Mattole Beach Trail
23: Ten Mile Beach Trail
29: Fisk Mill to Stump Beach Trail
42: Año Nuevo Point Trail
47: River/Ridge Loop
D: Stone Lagoon Trail
J: Jepson/Johnstone Loop
L: Asilomar Beach Trail

Coastal Bluffs Hikes

3: Crescent Beach Trail
6: Coastal Trail: Yurok Loop to Hidden Beach
13: Skunk Cabbage Trail
14: Rim Trail Loop
15: Trinidad Head Loop
21: Lost Coast Trail
23: Ten Mile Beach Trail
24: Ecological Staircase Trail
26: Mendocino Headlands Loop

View of the bluffs at the mouth of Whale Gulch

Hikes for Peak Baggers and Ridge Runners

Waves on the rocks

5: Damnation Creek Trail
7: James Irvine/Miner's Ridge Loop
9: Trillium Falls Trail
10: Ladybird Johnson Grove Trail
11: Tall Trees Grove Trail
12: Dolason Prairie Trail
13: Skunk Cabbage Trail
19: Bull Creek Flats Loop
22: Toumey Trail
28: Big Hendy Long Loop
31: Two Ridge Loop
40: Berry Falls Loop
 B: Boy Scout Trail
 C: Zig Zag Trail
 F: Big Tree Loop

Hikes for Waterfall Lovers

1: Myrtle Creek Trail
9: Trillium Falls Trail
25: Russian Gulch Double Loop
29: Fisk Mill to Stump Beach Trail
39: Castle Rock Double Loop
40: Berry Falls Loop
48: Valley View Loop

Hikes for History Buffs

1: Myrtle Creek Trail
8: Fern Canyon Loop
12: Dolason Prairie Trail
15: Trinidad Head Loop
20: Mattole Beach Trail
23: Ten Mile Beach Trail
26: Mendocino Headlands Loop
30: Cemetery Trail
36: Railroad Grade Trail
37: Sweeney Ridge Trail
44: Loma Prieta Loop
45: Whalers Knoll Loop
47: River/Ridge Loop
49: Partington Point Trail
50: Limekiln Trail
52: High Peaks Loop
 G: Robert Louis Stevenson Trail

H: Wolf House Trail

I: Olompali Trail

Hikes for Plant Lovers

1: Myrtle Creek Trail

8: Fern Canyon Loop

19: Bull Creek Flats Loop

24: Ecological Staircase Trail

27: Fern Canyon/Logging Road Loop

33: Sky/Laguna Loop

37: Sweeney Ridge Trail

46: Whale Peak Loop

J: Jepson/Johnstone Loop

Hikes for Whale Watchers

14: Rim Trail Loop

15: Trinidad Head Loop

26: Mendocino Headlands Loop

29: Fisk Mill to Stump Beach Trail

32: Bodega Head Loop

33: Sky/Laguna Loop

45: Whalers Knoll Loop

46: Whale Peak Loop

A: Point St. George Trail

Hikes for Birders

14: Rim Trail Loop

18: Hookton Slough Trail

48: Valley View Loop

52: High Peaks Loop

Hikes for Wildlife Viewing

9: Trillium Falls Trail

15: Trinidad Head Loop

18: Hookton Slough Trail

21: Lost Coast Trail

29: Fisk Mill to Stump Beach Trail

33: Sky/Laguna Loop

42: Año Nuevo Point Trail

45: Whalers Knoll Loop

46: Whale Peak Loop

47: River/Ridge Loop

Hikes with Tide Pools

20: Mattole Beach Trail

L: Asilomar Beach Trail

How to Use This Book

Hiking the Redwood Coast was designed to be highly visual and easily referenced. The Redwood Coast has been split into six regions: Del Norte, Northern Humboldt, Southern Humboldt, North Bay/Wine Country, South Bay, and Monterey. Each region begins with an introduction, with a sweeping look at the lay of the land. Following the introduction are each of the hikes featured within that region.

To aid in quick decision making, we start each hike with a hike summary. This briefing gives you a taste of the hiking adventure to follow. You'll learn about the trail terrain and what surprises the route has to offer. If your interest is piqued, read on and learn more. If not, skip to the next hike.

The hike specs are fairly self-explanatory. Here you'll find the quick, nitty-gritty details of the hike: where the trailhead is located, the nearest town, hike length, approximate hiking time, difficulty rating, best hiking season, type of trail terrain, what other trail users you may encounter, trail hotlines (for updates on trail conditions), and trail schedules and use fees. Our Finding the trailhead section gives you dependable directions from a nearby city right down to where you'll want to park. The Hike section is the meat of the chapter. Detailed and honest, it's the author's carefully researched impression of the trail. While it's impossible to cover everything, you can rest assured that what's important won't be missed. The Miles and Directions section provides mileage cues to identify all turns and trail name changes, as well as points of interest. The Hike Information section at the end of each hike is a hodgepodge of information. In it you'll find ideas on where to stay, what to eat, and what else to see while you're hiking in the area.

The Honorable Mentions section details all of the hikes that didn't make the cut, for whatever reason. In many cases it's not because they aren't great hikes, instead it's because they're overcrowded or environmentally sensitive to heavy traffic. Be sure to read through these. A jewel might be lurking among them.

How to Use the Maps

We don't want anyone, by any means, to feel restricted to just the routes and trails that are mapped here. We hope you will have an adventurous spirit and use this guide as a platform to explore the Redwood Coast and discover new routes for yourself. One of the simplest ways to begin this is to just turn the map upside down and hike the course in reverse. The change in perspective is fantastic, and the hike should feel quite different. With this in mind, it will be like getting two distinctly different hikes on each map.

You may wish to copy the directions for the course onto a small sheet to help you while hiking, or photocopy the map and cue sheet to take with you. Otherwise, just slip the whole book in your pack and take it all with you. Enjoy your time in the outdoors and remember to pack out what you pack in.

Elevation Profile: This helpful profile gives you a cross-sectional look at what's in store and accompanies each hike that involves significant elevation gain or multiple ascents and descents. The ups and downs of the route are graphed on a grid of elevation (in feet above sea level) and miles hiked. Elevation is labeled on the left, mileage is indicated on the top. The charts are not meant to be a detailed foot-by-foot account of the route, but serve as a quick glimpse of overall elevation change.

Route Map: This is your primary guide to each hike. It shows the accessible roads and trails, points of interest, water, towns, landmarks, and geographical features. It also distinguishes trails from roads, and paved roads from unpaved roads. The selected route is highlighted, and directional arrows point the way.

Map Legend

84	Interstate
26	U.S. highway
1	State highway
549	Forest road
———	Paved road
━━━	Featured gravel road
———	Gravel road
═══	Featured unimproved road
=====	Unimproved road
■■■■■	Featured trail
- - - - -	Other trail
⊢──⊣	Tunnel
⌒	Bridge
🚌	Bus stop
▲	Campground
†	Cemetery
◦	City
●—●	Gate
🐎	Horse trail
▭	Lodging
🚶	Other trailhead
◻	Overlook/viewpoint
P	Parking
▲	Peak/elevation
🏕	Picnic area
■	Point of interest
—•—	Powerline
▮	Ranger station
🚻	Rest room
◓	Spring
≣	Steps/boardwalk
START 🚶	Trailhead
i	Visitor information
∥	Waterfall
↡	Wetlands

Del Norte

As its name suggests, Del Norte is the northernmost of California's coastal counties, butting up against Southern Oregon at the 42nd parallel. Stubbornly pronounced "Del Nort" by locals, this small county's economy is firmly rooted in the timber and fishing industries, with a hefty boost from the maximum security prison at Pelican Bay. Located far behind the "redwood curtain," Del Norte is sparsely populated and full of wild lands, but its conservative politics have made it slow to take advantage of the latent tourism and outdoor recreation potential of the region. With three state parks, a national forest, a national recreation area, a national park, and one of California's last undammed major rivers, there is certainly potential there.

Crescent City, Del Norte's county seat and largest municipality, has the run-down feel of many former logging towns, and empty storefronts abound. Still, the place has a lot going for it, including a historic lighthouse, fresh seafood, excellent tide pools, whale watching, and Redwood National Park headquarters. Crescent City is a convenient springboard into the outdoor adventures that await on all sides. South and east of town, Redwood National Park, Jedediah Smith Redwoods State Park, and Del Norte Redwoods State Park cover the coastal hills like a patchwork blanket. The dark, brooding redwood forests here are the closest you will likely come to experiencing what the first foreign visitors did, when they first glimpsed these fog-shrouded ancient groves in their natural state. Elsewhere, redwood parks have the air of neatly kept tree museums, but Del Norte's groves seem wilder, and more like the primeval forests they are.

For something completely different, head north of town to the dunes and broad, sandy beaches of Tolowa State Park. Or head northeast, following the sinuous curves of the wild and scenic Smith River, with its strange turquoise green water. The color comes from the unusual serpentine soils of the surrounding mountains—soils that give rise to a number of endemic species and help make this area one of North America's most botanically diverse. Hike the feral river canyons in the Smith River National Recreation Area, and keep an eye open for Bigfoot, said by some to still wander these woods.

1 Myrtle Creek Trail

This is an easily accessible, short day hike with the feel of a backcountry wilderness area. The trail follows the course of a water diversion ditch that was used for a turn-of-the-century hydraulic mining operation. Along the way, interpretive signs explain a little of the history, and a lot of the diverse flora in the surrounding forest, part of the Myrtle Creek Botanical Area.

Start: Myrtle Creek Trail trailhead.
Distance: 2.1 miles out and back.
Approximate hiking time: 1½ hours.
Difficulty: Easy, due to little elevation gain.
Trail surface: Dirt path.
Lay of the land: Riparian forest.
Other trail users: Hikers only.
Canine compatibility: No dogs allowed.
Land status: National recreation area.

Nearest town: Hiouchi.
Fees and permits: No fees or permits required.
Schedule: Open year-round.
Map: USGS map: Hiouchi, CA.
Trail contact: Smith River National Recreation Area, Six Rivers National Forest, Gasquet; (707) 457-3131.

Finding the trailhead: From Crescent City, take U.S. Highway 101 north about 7 miles, then turn onto U.S. Highway 199 at the Grants Pass exit, heading northeast. Follow this 7 miles, past the Hiouchi Visitor Center (Redwood National Park). About a mile past the visitor center, pull off and park at the gravel turnout just south of the Myrtle Creek Bridge. The trailhead is just across the road, at a cut in the rocky bank. *DeLorme: Northern California Atlas & Gazetteer:* Page 22, B3.

The Hike

It is obvious at first glance that the Myrtle Creek area has been touched by man. The old-growth is gone and there are mining scars along the riverbanks and a highway through the valley. Yet for some reason the spot exudes a wildness unmatched by many officially designated wilderness areas. Perhaps it is the sparse settlement in the surrounding area, or the fact that all the major activity came and went rapidly, the last of it already half a century in the past. Maybe it is the untamed rivers flowing past, with their strange gray-green waters and jumbled rocky banks. Or maybe it is the brooding skies and the dubious but persistent rumors that Sasquatch—known to white men as Bigfoot—still roam these woods. Whatever the reason, the Myrtle Creek Trail has a lot more backwoods atmosphere than you would expect from a 2-mile out-and-back with its trailhead located on the shoulder of a highway.

The trail starts at a deep cut in the steep uphill embankment lining US 199. The cut is the result of hydraulic mining that took place during the last gasp of the California Gold Rush. Powerful water cannons blasted away the soil, which was

Myrtle Creek Trail, with hydraulic mining ditch on left

run through sluices to catch any gold deposits. What remained were deep scars like this one, where the topsoil has been completely blasted away, leaving piles of exposed scree and bedrock.

The trail soon climbs up out of the cut and begins contouring around the slope through a lush second-growth mixed forest. Myrtle Creek is located in the transition zone between the coastal forest community, which includes redwoods, rhododendrons, and ferns, and the drier interior region dominated by knobcone pine. The watershed is made even more botanically diverse by the wet riparian habitat near the creek bed and the addition of rare serpentine soils. All these elements interact to create a very diverse range of conditions for plant life, which has lead to the Myrtle Creek area being designated as one of six special botanical areas within Six Rivers National Forest. The trail has been outfitted with nature trail–style guideposts, and each of the fifteen interpretive stops has a small sign explaining a little about the cultural history or interesting flora to be found there. A brochure that goes into greater depth can be picked up at the information center in Hiouchi, or at the National Forest office a few miles upriver in the town of Gasquet.

Myrtle Creek Trail

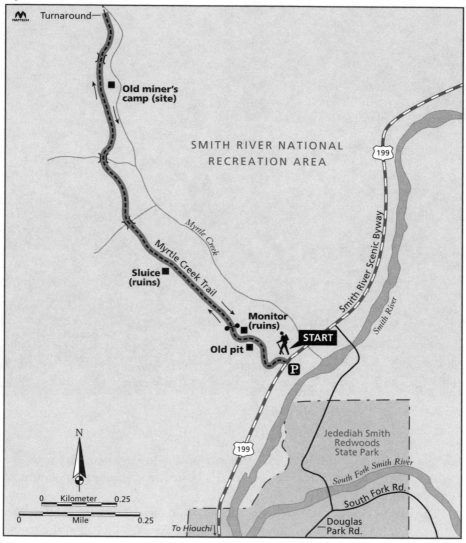

At the third stop on this self-guided tour, the trail begins to parallel a mining-era ditch that was used to channel water down to the big water cannons. The remainder of the trail follows this ditch, ending where the water was originally drawn from the creek, about a mile upstream.

Crescent City investors had good reason to expect a return on their money when they founded the Myrtle Creek Mining Company in 1894. After all, placer mining (panning for gold) during previous years had turned up some impressive nuggets in the drainage. The largest single nugget found in the creek was the size and shape of an ax bit and weighed in at a healthy forty-seven ounces. With the easy

A FEW FACTS ABOUT REDWOODS

- Redwoods can easily exceed 350 feet in height. That's taller than a football field is long. By comparison, the Statue of Liberty (pedestal included) is only 152 feet tall.

- With their great height, redwoods actually influence the local weather. Their highest branches literally comb moisture out of the foggy coastal air. The moisture collects on branches and drips to the ground, increasing moisture levels on the ground by the equivalent of 40 inches of rain per year. By intercepting this moisture, the redwoods leave inland areas drier than they would otherwise be.

- A single redwood tree may weigh up to one million pounds.

- Redwoods commonly reach ages of 500 to 700 years, but some can reach ages of 2,000 years or more.

- Huge knobby growths known as burls often develop on redwood trunks. These growths show a characteristic swirling grain when cut open, sought after by craftsmen. Burls often sprout, creating new redwood shoots.

- When a redwood falls over, new shoots may grow from the root wad of the old tree. Rings of mature trees are often seen growing in a circle around the location of the original tree. Such formations are called "Cathedral Trees."

- When trees grow from sprouts of old trees, they are genetic "carbon copies" of the parent tree. Theoretically, some mature redwoods may be genetically identical to trees that lived millions of years ago.

- A redwood has two kinds of needles. The majority of the needles are about ½-inch long and grow in a flat plane. In the very tops of the trees, however, the needles show in stubby, scalelike patterns around the branches, looking similar to cypress foliage. This adaptation helps them deal with hotter temperatures and drier weather above the forest canopy. These treetop needles can sometimes be seen when they are blown to the ground by storms.

pickings gone, however, the new miners turned immediately to hydraulic mining, which allowed them to extract the tiny deposits left in the sand and soil. For a time the effort paid off, but by the early 1920s the gold had become too expensive to remove profitably, and the mine closed. Today only the ditch, a few pipes and trestle timbers, and the slowly healing scars remain.

From the turnaround point where the trail meets the creek, return the way you came to the trailhead.

Miles and Directions

0.0   Start at the little trail sign on the west side of the road. The trail heads steeply up through a cut in the bank. (FYI: The first few yards of the trail head up through an old hydraulic-mining site, which has washed away all the soil, leaving a sort of rock-lined pit.)

0.1   A small fenced area to the left surrounds an old pit. From this point the trail follows the edge of a ditch once used to channel water to the hydraulic-mining operation.

0.2   To the right of the trail are the remains of a wooden gate and hydraulic monitor pipe.

0.3   At Stop 7 on the nature trail, insectivorous Darlingtonia plants can be seen on the left.

0.4   (FYI: At this point the hill was too steep and rocky for a ditch, so the water ran across a wooden flume, now mostly gone.)

0.5   A simple plank bridge crosses the stream, just above a little waterfall.

0.7   The trail drops a few steps, crosses a stream, and climbs back up on the other side. Shortly after, the trail crosses a 10-foot plank bridge.

0.8   At Stop 10 on the nature trail, a spur trail goes down to the right to what may have once been a miner's camp. The paths converge again 0.1 mile upstream.

1.0   The trail crosses a plank bridge at a small waterfall. The creek is visible below to the right. About 50 feet later, the trail drops to creek level, revealing a nice soaking hole. This is the turnaround point. Return the way you came.

2.1   Trailhead.

Hike Information

Local Information

Del Norte Chamber of Commerce, Crescent City; (800) 343-8300; www.northerncalifornia.net.

Local Events/Attractions

World-Championship Crab Races, held in February, crab feed, kids games, etc., Crescent City; (800) 343-8300; (707) 464-3174.
Aleutian Goose Festival, held the third weekend in March, celebrates the annual gathering of the world's entire population of Aleutian Canada Geese with speakers, seminars, and workshops, Crescent City; (800) 343-8300; (707) 465-0888; www.redwoodlink.com/soar.

Redwood Wild River Run, held in March, Jedediah Smith Redwood State Park; (707) 464-3779.
Gasquet Raft Races, held in mid-July, a fun flotilla of decorated rafts, Gasquet; (707) 457-3064.

Lodging

Hostelling International–Redwood National Park, Klamath; (707) 482-8265; www.norcalhostels.org.
There are several public and private campgrounds upstream in the immediate area.
State park campsite reservations: (800) 444-7275.

2 Hiouchi Trail

An easy hike through some top-notch old-growth redwood forest. As an added bonus, the hike follows the south bank of the jade green Smith River, one of the largest undammed rivers left in the United States. In summer a seasonal bridge links up with the Jedediah Smith Redwoods State Park campground, but in winter you'll have it all to yourself.

Start: At the south end of the Hiouchi Bridge, on the east side of the road.
Distance: 4.2 miles out and back.
Approximate hiking time: 2 hours.
Difficulty: Easy, due to good trails and little elevation gain.
Trail surface: Dirt path.
Lay of the land: Riverside old-growth redwood forest.
Other trail users: None.

Canine compatibility: No dogs allowed.
Land status: State park.
Nearest town: Hiouchi.
Fees and permits: None, if accessed from the highway.
Schedule: Open year-round.
Map: USGS map: Hiouchi, CA.
Trail contact: Jedediah Smith Redwoods State Park, Crescent City; (707) 464-3779; www.parks.ca.gov.

Finding the trailhead: From Crescent City, just before the Smith River Bridge before Hiouchi, pull off and park along the road. Trailhead is next to the highway sign along the bridge. *DeLorme: Northern California Atlas & Gazetteer:* Page 22, B3.

The Hike

Jedediah Smith Redwoods State Park is named for a famous mountain man and explorer of the early nineteenth century. Smith was one of the first white men to visit extreme Northern California, passing by the mouth of the river that bears his name with a party of trappers in 1828. (For more on Jed Smith, see Hike 5: Damnation Creek Trail.) Jedediah Smith Redwoods State Park was created in 1929, a century after Smith's party passed by the area. The 10,000-acre park preserves some of the finest old-growth redwood groves still in existence. The Hiouchi Trail explores some of these, and it also takes in some panoramic views of the Wild and Scenic Smith River along the way.

At the time of Jed Smith's expedition, this land was occupied by the He-nag-gi people, a subgroup of the Tolowa Indians. Living on the riverbanks at the edge of the towering redwood forests, these people subsisted mainly on salmon, wild game, and the acorns of the tan oak tree. Life changed dramatically in the 1850s, as white gold prospectors poured into the area, followed soon by wave after wave of new settlers. For the Tolowa, disease, murder, and the destruction of their traditional way of life were the result. Today only a small community of surviving Tolowa descendants remain to keep the culture alive.

Smith River

The hike begins at the south end of the Hiouchi Bridge, where U.S. Highway 199 crosses the Smith River on its way up to the Oregon border. The trail enters the forest at an unassuming little trail marker and parallels the south bank of the turquoise-colored Smith. The river's unique coloration can be traced back upstream to extensive deposits of serpentine, a rare gray-green mineral that forms the basis for soils in large swaths of the Six Rivers National Forest and Smith River National Recreation Area, which border the park. The serpentine soils are high in metals and low in nutrients such as nitrogen and potassium—crucial for most plants. The result is a hotbed of species diversity, where a variety of plant species have evolved to cope with the difficult conditions, many of which are endemic (found nowhere else). In fact the nearby North Fork Smith River Botanical Area has the highest concentration of endemic plants in North America.

In addition to its unique flora, the Smith River watershed has one more thing going for it. It is the largest completely undammed river system in California. From its mouth to the tiniest trickle in every one of its tributaries, this river is as free-flowing today as it ever was. Not surprisingly, it also has one of the healthiest fisheries of any

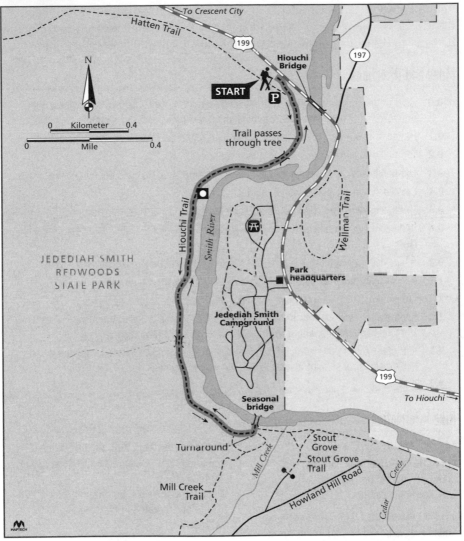

river in the state, a fact not lost on anglers, who flock here to fish for salmon, steelhead, and cutthroat trout. The record chinook salmon caught in the river weighed in at a whopping eighty-six pounds!

In all, 315 miles of the Smith River's main stem and three major forks are officially designated part of the national Wild and Scenic River System. Congress designated the 305,000-acre Smith River National Recreation Area in 1990.

The bulk of the Hiouchi Trail follows the south bank of the Smith, where old-growth redwood specimens tower above the water right at the edge of the low bluffs. The trail builders seem to have had some fun in constructing the trail, running it up to the edge of the bluffs for several dramatic views, and even straight through a hollow redwood stump. The climax of the trail comes at the far end, when it reaches the park's crown jewel, Stout Grove. From here, a seasonal summer bridge heads across the river to the park campground. Return to the trailhead the way you came.

Miles and Directions

0.0 Start at the southwest end of the Hiouchi Bridge, on the east side of the highway. The trail follows the river east, then climbs a short series of steps and a couple switchbacks.

0.1 Hatten Trail merges into our trail from the right. Continue straight on the Hiouchi Trail.

0.2 The trail descends a few steps to a river overlook.

0.3 The trail heads right through an old-growth redwood snag that has been hollowed by fire.

0.4 Cross a side creek via a small footbridge.

0.5 The trail crosses three hand-built stone drain-ways.

0.6 Serious old-growth begins to appear. Trail passes through the first of several memorial groves.

0.8 A nice river overlook has been built here, complete with bench and rail.

1.1 A large boulder looms on the right, covered with droopy green moss.

1.4 Cross a footbridge, and climb a few steps on other side.

1.9 Another river overlook with handrail. Shortly after this, the trail crosses a shallow gully. The forest floor opens, with a thick carpet of ferns and redwood sorrel.

2.1 End of the trail. To the left, a seasonal bridge crosses the river to the campground. The Mill Creek Trail is straight ahead. Return the way you came.

4.2 Trailhead.

Hike Information

Local Information
Del Norte Chamber of Commerce, Crescent City; (800) 343–8300; www.northerncalifornia.net.

Local Events/Attractions
Jammin' at Jed, held in September, an eclectic annual music festival, Jedediah Smith Redwoods State Park; (707) 464–8311.

World-Championship Crab Races, held in February, crab feed, kids games, etc., Crescent City; (800) 343–8300; (707) 464–3174; FAX (707) 464–9676.

Aleutian Goose Festival, held the third weekend in March, celebrates the annual gathering of the world's entire population of Aleutian Canada Geese with speakers, seminars, and workshops, Crescent City; (800) 343–8300; (707) 465–0888; www.redwoodlink.com/soar.

Redwood Wild River Run, held in March, Jedediah Smith Redwood State Park; (707) 464–3779.

Gasquet Raft Races, held in mid-July, a fun flotilla of decorated rafts, Gasquet; (707) 457–3064.

Lodging
Hostelling International–Redwood National Park, Klamath; (707) 482–8265; theredwood hostel@earthlink.net; www.norcalhostels.org. In addition to the Jed Smith campground, there are several public and private campgrounds upstream in the Gasquet area, as well as downstream in and around Crescent City.
State park campsite reservations: (800) 444–7275.

3 Crescent Beach Trail

The trail crosses meadows and alder forests just inland from the broad, sandy shore-line of Crescent Beach. The easy grade and pastoral surroundings make for a very pleasant walk, which culminates with a short climb through denser coastal forest to the overlook above Enderts Beach. From here, hikers can enjoy an excellent view of the Pacific and the scenic shoreline stretching north to Crescent City.

Start: Enderts Beach House.
Distance: 4.2 miles out and back.
Approximate hiking time: 2 to 3 hours.
Difficulty: Easy, due to good trail and little elevation gain.
Trail surface: Dirt path, mowed grass.
Lay of the land: Wet low coastal meadows and alder forest.
Other trail users: None.

Canine compatibility: No dogs allowed.
Land status: National park.
Nearest town: Crescent City.
Fees and permits: None.
Schedule: Open year-round.
Map: USGS map: Sister Rocks, CA.
Trail contact: Redwood National and State Parks, Crescent City; (707) 464-6101; www.nps.gov/redw/.

Finding the trailhead: From Crescent City, take U.S. Highway 101 south 2 miles. Turn right (west) onto Enderts Beach Road. Follow this 0.4 mile, then turn left onto a long driveway leading up to a white house (this is park property). Follow the road for 0.2 mile, parking in the small gravel lot behind the house. The trailhead is on the south side of the house, across from the garage. *DeLorme: Northern California Atlas & Gazetteer:* Page 22, C2.

The Hike

This trail could have easily been named the bridge trail, since it crosses what seems like a dozen small footbridges on its way down the coast. From the historic white ranch house at the trailhead, the path leads across the grassy meadows of former agricultural land—now making the slow transition back to forest as brush and fast-growing alders gradually reclaim the fields. Aside from the many bridges, the trail consists mostly of mown grass. This makes for a nice, cushy walking surface, but it can also lead to a serious case of soggy feet, especially after rain or when morning dew is still fresh on the ground.

For most of its length, the trail keeps to the nearly flat strip of grassland and alder forest that's tucked neatly between the ocean and the coastal range to the east. This changes when the trail reaches Enderts Beach Road, a little more than a mile from the trailhead. Here the trail heads across the road and down to a little picnic area under a massive spruce tree. One last bridge awaits at the creek flowing through the hollow, then a last ascending leg, as the trail climbs the coastal bluffs to the Enderts Beach Overlook and the turnaround point. In the decades before the National Park

View of the Pacific through the trees

Service took over, the parking lot at the overlook served as the local Lover's Lane for Crescent City teenagers, who gave the spot the bawdy nickname "Endert's Knob."

From the overlook the view to the north is of the broad, curving beach that gives nearby Crescent City its name. The town was founded in 1853 by a group of prospectors and settlers who had come down from Oregon after hearing reports that there was a good harbor in the area. The bay did prove to be a good haven for ships, and soon the harbor was handling tons of supplies for the settlers and miners farther inland and carrying off the gold, redwood lumber, and other produce of the region.

Like most of the ports along this treacherous coast, however, Crescent City's harbor was not without danger for passing ships. Offshore rocks in the area claimed sailing vessels even before the city was founded, and within three years of the first settlers' arrival, a lighthouse was being built on a rocky point near the mouth of the harbor (it still stands today). The light was an improvement, but it was not enough to prevent what happened in 1856.

In that year the steamer *Brother Jonathan* sailed up the coast from San Francisco, dangerously overloaded with passengers and freight destined for points north. The

Crescent Beach Trail

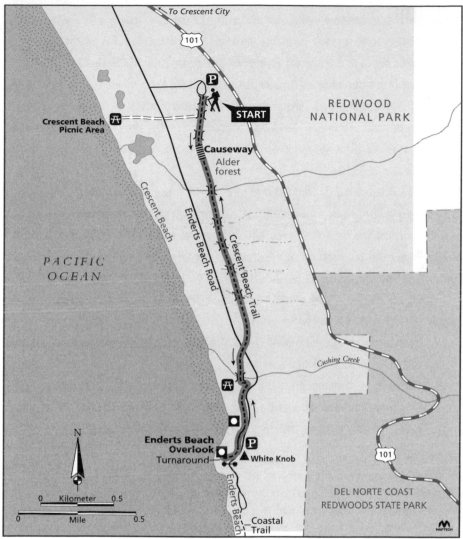

ship arrived safely for a stop in Crescent City on Saturday, July 29, and set off again the next morning, amidst stormy seas. Things soon turned ugly, and the captain of the ship decided to give up and return to the safety of Crescent City's harbor. He never made it.

A few miles north of town, a tongue of land named Point St. George juts out into the Pacific. From it a string of tiny islands and submerged rocks stretches more than 6 miles out to sea, forming a natural hazard known as Point St. George Reef. In the chaos of the tossing waves and gale-force winds, the crew found the dangerously overloaded *Brother Jonathan* difficult to steer as they attempted to return to safe waters. The vessel struck a rock, shattering the hull, and within minutes, it sank

TSUNAMI!

Commonly referred to as a tidal wave, the tsunami—Japanese for "storm wave"—is a destructive force that has struck the California coast more than once within living memory. The most severe of these recent events centered on the town of Crescent City in 1964.

Tsunamis are caused by earthquakes, usually beneath the seafloor. The vibration of the quake and shifting of the earth's crust set in motion a series of waves. On the open ocean, these waves may be just a few inches high, barely noticeable. But they can move at speeds of up to 600 mph, and when the waves reach the shallow water near shore, they may pile up to heights of between 20 and 45 feet.

The 1964 tsunami began in Alaska, when a huge 8.3-magnitude earthquake ripped open the ground and lifted parts of the land 30 feet, causing huge amounts of damage. The wave that resulted swept across the North Pacific, hitting Vancouver Island and Hawaii, as well as Northern California. But the worst damage was in Crescent City, where the tsunami destroyed the entire downtown area, killing 12 people and causing more than $17 million in damage.

While the danger of being caught by a tsunami is pretty slim, there are a few things you should remember when hiking on the coast.

- If an earthquake hits, head uphill or inland as soon as possible; 100 feet above sea level or 2 miles inland is safest.
- There may be more than one wave, and the first is not necessarily the biggest.
- Even if you don't feel the quake, a sudden rise or drop in sea level could signal a coming wave from a distant quake. Take precautionary action immediately.

in the freezing waters. One lifeboat made it to shore, carrying nineteen survivors. The other 200 or so passengers and crew drowned. At the time, it was one of the worst shipwrecks the country had seen, and it led to another lighthouse being built on Seal Rock, far out on the reef. A monument to those lost in the wreck now stands in Crescent City.

Miles and Directions

0.0 Start at the signed trailhead opposite Enderts Beach House's garage. The trail heads into the dense brushy foliage, crossing a bridge over a small stream almost immediately.

0.1 Cross a 12-foot bridge. A few yards later, a spur trail heads right to Crescent Beach Picnic Area. Go straight.

0.2 The trail crosses a 6-foot bridge, then traverses a marshy section via gravel causeway.

0.4 The trail enters a pretty alder forest. (FYI: The first big tree on the right has been scratched up by a bear.)

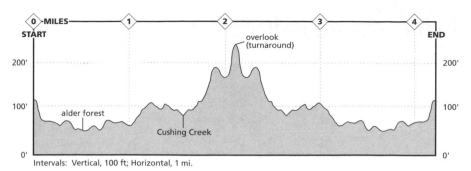

Intervals: Vertical, 100 ft; Horizontal, 1 mi.

0.6 The trail crosses a 22-foot bridge over a small creek, then leaves the alder forest behind.

0.7 The trail crosses a 20-foot bridge and a patch of forest.

0.8 Cross a 12-foot bridge.

1.0 The trail enters another small patch of alders and crosses a 20-foot bridge.

1.1 Cross a 12-foot bridge.

1.3 Enderts Beach Road. Cross the road and continue along the trail on the other side. (FYI: Crescent City can be seen in the distance off to the right.)

1.4 The trail drops into a little hollow with a picnic table under a large spruce tree. Cross Cushing Creek via the 30-foot bridge and continue up the bank on the other side.

1.5 The trail is now under an alder/spruce forest, and begins switchbacking up.

1.7 The trail passes a big old-growth spruce to the right, then climbs a few steps.

1.8 A deep gully opens up to the right, offering an excellent view of distant Crescent City.

1.9 The trail climbs some wooden steps, then pops out onto Enderts Beach Road again. Turn right, heading uphill along the road.

2.0 The trail leaves the road, heading back into the brush on the right.

2.1 The trail reaches the overlook. This is the turnaround point. Return the way you came.

4.2 Trailhead.

Hike Information

Local Information

Del Norte Chamber of Commerce, Crescent City; (800) 343–8300; www.northerncalifornia.net.

Local Events/Attractions

World-Championship Crab Races, held in February, crab feed, kids games, etc., Crescent City; (800) 343–8300; (707) 464-3174.

Aleutian Goose Festival, held the third weekend in March, celebrates the annual gathering of the world's entire population of Aleutian Canada Geese with speakers, seminars, and workshops, Crescent City; (800) 343–8300; (707) 465–0888; www.redwoodlink.com/soar.

Redwood Wild River Run, held in March, Jedediah Smith Redwoods State Park; (707) 464-3779.

Gasquet Raft Races, held in mid-July, a fun flotilla of decorated rafts, Gasquet; (707) 457-3064.

Lodging

Hostelling International–Redwood National Park, Klamath; (707) 482–8265; www.norcalhostels.org.

4 Hobbs Wall Trail and Trestle Loop

A somewhat more adventurous hike around the thickly forested basin of Mill Creek's upper West Branch. The trail heads down through sparse old-growth fragments to the verdant creek-side riparian zone surrounding Mill Creek Campground. From here a short stretch along the access road brings hikers to the wilder, more challenging ups and downs of the return loop.

Start: Just east of the junction between U.S. Highway 101 and the Mill Creek Campground access road.
Distance: 6-mile loop.
Approximate hiking time: 3 to 4 hours.
Difficulty: Difficult, due to elevation gain and steep climbing on the return loop.
Trail surface: Dirt path, paved road (briefly).
Lay of the land: Old-growth and second-growth redwood forest and riparian forest.
Other trail users: Hikers only.

Canine compatibility: No dogs allowed.
Land status: State park.
Nearest town: Crescent City.
Fees and permits: $2.00 day-use fee; $1.00 per person hike/bike.
Schedule: Open year-round. Campgrounds are open April 1–October 1.
Map: USGS map: Childs Hill, CA.
Trail contact: Del Norte Coast Redwoods State Park, Crescent City; (707) 464-6101 ext. 5120; www.parks.ca.gov.

Finding the trailhead: From Crescent City, drive south 4 miles on U.S. Highway 101, then turn left (east) onto the Mill Creek Campground access road. (In winter the gate may be closed. If so, park off the highway and walk down the campground access road to the trailhead.) Park alongside the road just inside the gate. The trail starts at the first bend in the road, on the right side of the road, at a small trail sign marked Hobbs Wall Trail. *DeLorme: Northern California Atlas & Gazetteer:* Page 22, C3.

The Hike

The hike down into the emerald abyss of the West Branch Mill Creek drainage begins just inside the entrance gate to the Mill Creek Campground access road. An unassuming little trail sign marks the spot where the Hobbs Wall Trail crosses the road, just before the first curve in the road. Like the rest of the ridge, this part of the forest is dominated by old-growth redwoods. These living giants survived the logger's ax mainly because of their location—high on the steep slopes of the drainage, where they were much more difficult to remove than those on the rich alluvial flats far below. By the time logging technology advanced to the point where it was economically feasible to log these slopes, far-thinking conservationists had already managed to preserve them within the boundaries of a state park. Established in 1929, Del Norte Redwoods State Park encompasses some 6,400 acres of land, roughly half of which host old-growth redwood groves. This hike

Twin redwood, hollowed by fire

Hobbs Wall Trail and Trestle Loop

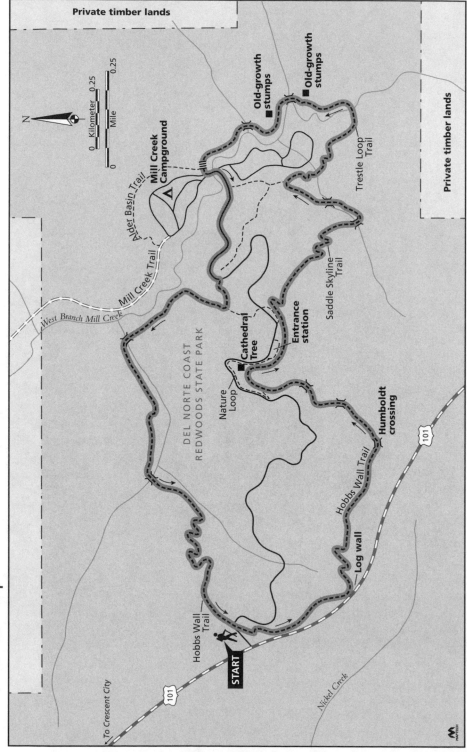

Private timber lands

Private timber lands

Old-growth stumps

Old-growth stumps

Trestle Loop Trail

Mill Creek Campground

Saddle Skyline Trail

Entrance station

Cathedral Tree

Alder Basin Trail

Mill Creek Trail

West Branch Mill Creek

Nature Loop

DEL NORTE COAST REDWOODS STATE PARK

Humboldt crossing

Hobbs Wall Trail

Log wall

Hobbs Wall Trail

START

To Crescent City

Nickel Creek

101

101

N

Kilometer 0.25

0

Mile

0   0.25

circumnavigates the northeastern block of the park, from the ridge down to the creek and back up again near the park's northern boundary.

From the trailhead the hike first contours south along the ridge, soon arriving at a very peculiar structure. To the right of the trail, a massive wall is formed by the exposed ends of hundreds of redwood logs that have been stacked on top of each other and covered with gravel and dirt to form the foundation for US 101, above you on the right. It is unusual, to say the least, that a modern road is built using wood as a foundation. Thanks to the famed rot-resistance of redwood, however, this was a common practice in the area for many years, especially when building logging roads. Instead of building bridges over small creeks and shallow drainages, road-building crews would simply fell several nearby trees and lay the trunks in the depression, piling gravel on top to form a smooth roadbed. These quick-and-dirty ersatz bridges were known as Humboldt crossings.

It is tempting to assume that the Hobbs Wall Trail gets its name from the wall of logs beneath US 101, but in fact the name comes from the nineteenth-century entrepreneurial firm Hobbs, Wall & Co., which had extensive land and timber holdings in Del Norte County from the mid-1800s to the 1940s. The company had a large mill and logging operation set up in the Mill Creek Valley just north of the park. Beginning in 1884 the company ran a short railway called the Crescent City & Smith River Railroad, which ran several miles up the Mill Creek drainage, well into the present park lands.

From the ridge the trail switchbacks down into the canyon, eventually arriving at the scene of this early railroad, on what is now called the Trestle Trail. Although there are a few remnants of the old train trestles, the most visible reminder of the lumber company's presence are the huge redwood stumps that fill the flats at the valley bottom. The railroad allowed easy transportation of even the largest logs, and the best old-growth groves in the watershed fell within a few years of the railroad's arrival. Slender alder trees are pioneering a new forest in the valley, but it will be a very long time before the redwoods have recovered.

After a short jaunt downstream, the Trestle Trail dumps hikers out into the extensive Mill Creek campground, located on the flats around the creek. From here the trail heads left over the bridge and up the access road to a sharp bend. The trail then once again heads into the dense greenery of the forest, this time north of the access road. The final leg of the hike heads first down a steep series of stairs almost to the creek level, then back up in a wide loop to the ridge and trailhead.

Miles and Directions

0.0 Start at the small Hobbs Wall Trail sign on the south side of the entrance road, just inside the gate. The trail plunges immediately into thick second-growth forest.

0.1 The trail switchbacks down into an old-growth redwood forest with lots of rhododendrons. (FYI: Just below the second switchback, there is a big redwood on the right with several burls on it.)

0.3 (FYI: To the right is a double-trunked redwood with a hollow base. Nearby are several stumps that show that someone started logging but didn't get far. Just beyond this on the right is a live tree that had a kerf cut out but wasn't felled. The whole kerf has since healed.)

0.4 The ends of stacked logs form the foundation for the highway (to the right) and also form a wall alongside the trail.

0.5 The trail switches back, heading uphill. A few yards later, it drops again.

0.9 The trail curves east, heading away from the highway and gently down into the valley.

1.0 At this point, the trail seems to be following an old skid road. At the stream crossing, the path crosses a rotten Humboldt crossing (piled logs) over a drainage, then drops and crosses a small stream via a plank bridge.

1.1 The trail crosses a stream over a split-log bridge.

1.2 Descend several steps and cross the creek via a longer footbridge.

1.3 Hobbs Wall Trail ends at a T-junction. Nature Loop heads left to the entrance station, and right to the Saddle Skyline Trail. Go right.

1.4 (FYI: To the left, a circle of redwoods forms a "Cathedral Tree" formation.) The entrance station can be seen through the trees, below to the left.

1.5 At the fork in the trail, veer right, heading uphill on the Saddle Skyline Trail.

1.6 The trail switchbacks uphill.

1.8 The trail heads directly through an old-growth stump.

1.9 Begin descending a series of switchbacks.

2.1 Cross the creek via a 20-foot bridge.

2.2 After descending some steps, the trail switches back and crosses the same drainage via another bridge.

2.3 At the junction, turn right onto the Trestle Loop.

2.4 After dropping a few more switchbacks, the trail crosses the same stream a third time, via another bridge. The vegetation is now riparian.

2.7 The trail comes out onto a large flat creek bed. Cross via the seasonal bridge, or wade if the water level allows during off-season. Continue straight into the forest on the other side.

2.8 Dozens of old-growth stumps line the trail on a wide alluvial flat.

2.9 The trail crosses a side creek via a long footbridge.

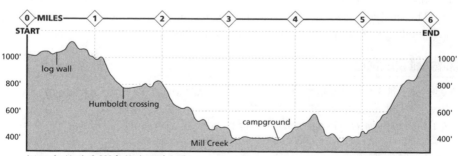

Intervals: Vertical, 200 ft; Horizontal, 1 mi.

3.0 More impressive stumps can be seen alongside the trail.

3.1 The trail crosses another tributary via a bridge.

3.2 The trail heads down several wooden steps.

3.25 The Alder Basin Trail heads up to the right. Continue straight.

3.3 Mill Creek Campground. At the paved road, turn left and cross the bridge. On the other side of the bridge, turn right and follow the park access road (the one with the EXIT sign) uphill.

3.8 The Saddle Skyline Trail crosses the road. Turn right onto the trail and head north into the forest.

3.9 The trail climbs several switchbacks.

4.0 At the junction, continue straight, heading back down into the valley.

4.4 The trail descends a few steps, crosses a stream, and heads back uphill.

4.8 Cross a stream over a footbridge.

5.0 Begin climbing a series of switchbacks.

5.8 The trail levels out at the burned-out old stump and heads south along the ridge.

6.0 Trailhead.

Hike Information

Local Information

Del Norte Chamber of Commerce, Crescent City; (800) 343-8300; www.northerncalifornia.net.

Klamath Chamber of Commerce, Klamath; (707) 482-7165; info@klamathcc.org.

Local Events/Attractions

World-Championship Crab Races, held in February, crab feed, kids games, etc., Crescent City; (800) 343-8300; (707) 464-3174.

Aleutian Goose Festival, held the third weekend in March, celebrates the annual gathering of the world's entire population of Aleutian Canada Geese with speakers, seminars, and workshops, Crescent City; (800) 343-8300; (707) 465-0888; www.redwoodlink.com/soar.

Lodging

Mill Creek Campground, April 1–October 1, sites: $12 per night; (800) 444-7275.

Hostelling International–Redwood National Park, Klamath; (707) 482-8265; www.norcalhostels.org.

5 Damnation Creek Trail

This hike follows a steep but very scenic trail, which offers the best of old-growth redwoods and rugged coastline. In spring the trail is sprinkled with a variety of wild-flowers—most notably the distinctive three-leafed trillium, a showy native flower with white and pink blossoms. The trail ends at a beach next to a small, natural rock arch, carved by waves. Excellent tide pools can be explored at low tide.

Start: From the Coastal Trail turnout.
Distance: 3.4 miles out and back.
Approximate hiking time: 2 hours.
Difficulty: Moderate to strenuous, due to steep, but well-maintained, trail.
Trail surface: Dirt path, asphalt road (closed to cars).
Lay of the land: Old-growth redwoods and coastal scrub, as well as rocky beach.
Other trail users: Cyclists.
Canine compatibility: Dogs not permitted.

Land status: State park.
Nearest town: Crescent City.
Fees and permits: No fees or permits required.
Schedule: Open year-round.
Maps: USGS maps: Childs Hill, CA; Sister Rocks, CA.
Trail contact: Del Norte Redwoods State Park, Crescent City; (707) 464-6101 ext. 5064 or 5120.

Finding the trailhead: From Eureka, take U.S. Highway 101 north for 67 miles. North of the Klamath River the highway briefly skirts the ocean at Wilson Creek and False Klamath Cove before climbing steeply. As the highway veers inland away from the coast, it enters old-growth redwood forest. Park at the first turnout on the right, where the Coastal Trail crosses US 101. Start hiking where the Coastal Trail heads into the forest on the opposite (north) side of the road. *DeLorme: Northern California Atlas & Gazetteer:* Page 22, C3.

The Hike

The dark and secluded Damnation Creek lies entirely within the boundaries of Del Norte Redwoods State Park, one of the three state redwood parks nestled in among the patchwork of lands that make up Redwood National Park. With only 6,400 acres, it is the smallest of the three parks. But what it lacks in size, it makes up for in show: It has some 3,200 acres of old growth and oversees 8 miles of pristine coast-line. The rugged sea cliffs here are tall and inhospitable to humans, a feature that allows easy beach access only via the redwood-lined Damnation Creek Trail and the Footsteps Rock Trail at the southern tip of the park.

It's likely that the creek—and trail—got their intimidating name because of the area's difficult nature. The perilous terrain also kept the Native Americans away prior to European contact: There were no permanent Indian villages along this stretch of coast before Europeans began settling the region. The nearest major settlements

Natural bridge

originally were on Pebble Beach to the north—at present-day Crescent City—and near the mouth of Wilson Creek to the south.

The land south of Wilson Creek traditionally was considered Yurok territory, while the territory north of Wilson Creek, including Damnation Creek, was generally regarded as Tolowa country. The groups shared a number of cultural traits, such as the use of toothlike dentalia shells for currency and the custom of women wearing basket hats. But the Tolowa differed from the Yurok by having clearly defined, politically powerful chiefs. And occasionally there was violent conflict between the two groups, usually in the form of raids.

Both the Tolowa and the Yurok nations have survived, but the Tolowa have been reduced to a tiny fraction of their former numbers and are no longer federally recognized as a tribe. The Yurok have fared better in that sense. With more than 4,000 members, they are considered the largest Native American tribe in California (at the time of this writing).

The first part of the hike follows a piece of the Coastal Trail along a defunct section of the original US 101. If you scrape a few inches of duff off the trail, you'll find the pavement still mostly intact—right down to the yellow dividing line. The

Damnation Creek Trail

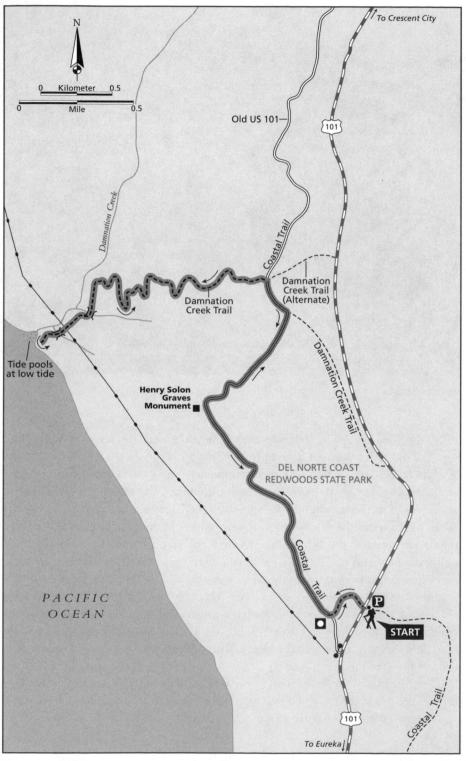

highway was diverted several years ago to avoid the coastline's slow but persistent slide into the ocean. Even today this phenomenon keeps the highway between Wilson Creek and the trailhead in constant need of repair.

The upper portion of the trail roughly follows the footsteps of Northwest California's patron pioneer, Jedediah Smith—one of the most famous nineteenth-century mountain men. In 1827 the thirty-year-old Smith set out from Utah's Great Salt Lake to explore the area in hopes of opening new trade routes and new sources for beaver and otter skins. He survived dangerous river crossings, a battle with Mojave Indians that cost him most of his men and all of his horses, and a trek across the brutal Mojave Desert. He finally arrived in Southern California, only to be taken into custody by Mexican authorities suspicious of American intentions. After placating the Mexican governor, Smith was released and allowed to continue his exploration. He resupplied and made his way up the Sacramento Valley, cutting west along a tributary of the Trinity River and trapping furs as he went. Smith followed the river down to its confluence with the Klamath, and from there he continued downstream to the ocean. Smith and his party headed north from the mouth of the Klamath along the coast, reaching the Damnation Creek area in early June 1828. The difficulties of traveling with large pack animals in Redwood Country were daunting, to say the least. Once you see the jumbles of giant logs and dense vegetation that cover the forest floor here, you'll understand why. The journey was so difficult that the expedition sometimes managed to travel less than 2 miles a day!

From the old highway the Damnation Creek Trail descends steeply through the dense forest that lines the deep Damnation Creek gully. The abundant fog creates an eerie, dramatic backdrop for the hike. As you make your way down through the tangled forest to the seemingly forgotten coastline, leather ferns perch high above the trail in the crooks of wind-twisted spruce and pine trees. The trail ends at a pristine, rocky cove, complete with stone arches and dramatic offshore rocks. At low tide, these rocks reveal tide pools full of marine life. Mussels, sea urchins, anemones, and starfish can all be found clinging to the surf-pounded rocks. In spring, look for a splash of color in the tiny meadow above the beach, as wildflowers come into bloom.

Return the way you came.

Miles and Directions

0.0 Start at the junction of the Coastal Trail and US 101. The trail curves and heads west toward the coast.

0.1 The trail drops down onto an abandoned section of US 101, which is now nearly buried beneath redwood needles and duff. Turn right onto the old highway (now part of the Coastal Trail) and head north.

0.5 (FYI: To the left of the trail is a small boulder inset with a bronze plaque as a monument to Henry Solon Graves, who was a local forester, educator, and administrator in the early twentieth century. Henry's monument was placed here by the Save-the-Redwoods League in 1925.)

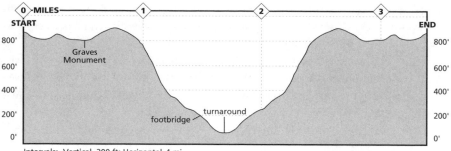

Intervals: Vertical, 200 ft; Horizontal, 1 mi.

0.7 Damnation Creek Trail heads right (0.6 mile) to US 101. Continue straight on the Coastal Trail.

0.8 An alternate fork of Damnation Creek Trail heads right to US 101. The Coastal Trail continues north to Crescent City. Turn left onto Damnation Creek Trail and head downhill.

1.0 Halfway down to the beach, the trail begins a series of sharp switchbacks and descends rapidly.

1.3 As the trail nears the ocean, the forest changes from predominantly redwoods to predominantly spruce and fir, which are more tolerant of the salty sea air. (FYI: Big balls of leather ferns are visible high in the trees to the right.)

1.5 The trail crosses a wooden footbridge over a shallow ravine.

1.6 After crossing another wooden bridge, the trail enters the coastal scrub habitat zone, with low bushes and a grassy meadow that is full of wildflowers in the spring.

1.7 Follow the faint path down to the right and down a series of wooden steps to the beach. The last few steps are rock. (Note: Be careful, because they can be slippery.) This is the turnaround point. Return the way you came.

3.4 Arrive back at the trailhead.

Hike Information

Local Information
Del Norte Chamber of Commerce, Crescent City; (800) 343–8300; www.northerncalifornia.net.

Lodging
Hostelling International–Redwood National Park, Klamath; (707) 482–8265; www.norcalhostels.org.

There is a youth hostel at the mouth of Wilson Creek.

Del Norte Redwoods State Park, Crescent City; (800) 444–7275. Campgrounds open April1–October 1.

6 Coastal Trail: Yurok Loop to Hidden Beach

A scenic hike along the Pacific coast through tunnels of wind-shaped cypress, alders, and dense coastal scrub, with plenty of spectacular views of this rugged and forbidding coastline. The turnaround point for the hike is tiny Hidden Beach, a quiet little cove accessible only by foot.

Start: Yurok Loop trailhead.
Distance: 2-mile reverse lollipop.
Approximate hiking time: 1 to 2 hours.
Difficulty: Easy to moderate, due to a short stretch of steep, slippery trail.
Trail surface: Dirt path.
Lay of the land: Coastal scrub and forest, rocky beach.
Other trail users: Hikers only.

Canine compatibility: No dogs allowed.
Land status: National park.
Nearest town: Klamath.
Fees and permits: None.
Schedule: Open year-round.
Map: USGS map: Requa, CA.
Trail contact: Redwood National and State Parks, Crescent City; (707) 464-6101; www.nps.gov/redw/.

Finding the trailhead: From Crescent City, take U.S. Highway 101 south 14 miles to False Klamath Cove. At the south end of the cove, the highway leaves the coast and heads inland, passing a small picnic area to the south and west of the highway. Turn right into this picnic area (Lagoon Creek) and park. The trailhead is at the west end of the parking lot. *DeLorme: Northern California Atlas & Gazetteer:* Page 22, D2–3.

The Hike

The first part of the trail is named for the native Yurok people, who have lived in this part of California for time immemorial. Although the Yurok's world tradition- ally centered around the lower Klamath River—their name comes from the neigh- boring Karuk language and means "downriver"— there were also numerous Yurok settlements up and down the coast, from False Klamath Cove south to the Little River, near what is now McKinleyville. At the time of European contact, the north- ernmost Yurok village was called O'men-Hipu'r and was located on the north bank at the mouth of Wilson Creek, about 0.75 mile north of the trailhead. A smaller group of homes was located on the site of the modern youth hostel, just south of Wilson Creek. But the main village in this area, and the one with the most history and symbolic importance, was called O'men and sat near the present-day Yurok Loop trailhead.

The hike begins at the Lagoon Creek Picnic Area, near where US 101 leaves the coast at False Klamath Cove and heads inland toward the town of Klamath, 5 miles to the south. The cove gets its name from the seafaring days, when sailors would fre- quently mistake it for the mouth of the Klamath. They were not too far off, since

Looking north over False Klamath Cove

the valley through which the highway now runs was once an ancestral bed for the mighty river, making the cove its original mouth.

From the west end of the picnic area, the trail enters a clump of willows and turns left to cross a footbridge over the lagoon's outlet. Just on the other side of the bridge is where the village of O'men once stood, but the spot is grown over now, and there is little to tell the untrained eye that a village once stood here. A little farther on, the trail forks in a rather dramatic way, with both paths immediately plunging into brush so thick it forms tunnels over the trails. The hike follows the left fork, up around the point to a fine overlook.

Offshore of the overlook, several sea stacks are visible, the largest of which was known to the Yurok as Olr'gr. It is said that there were once five brothers, the youngest of which was transformed into a supernatural being and made his home in that rock. The brother kept a pipe in a weasel-skin bag, which occasionally came to life and went barging in on people while they were eating. For this reason, it was warned never to harm a weasel that came into the home. To do so would be very bad luck.

Coastal Trail: Yurok Loop to Hidden Beach

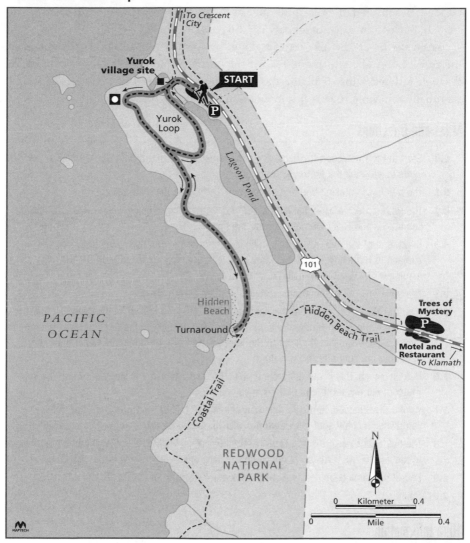

The trail continues around the point, following the coastline from the safety of the forest edge. This is part of the Coastal Trail, a network of trails that stretches up and down the ocean's edge more or less continuously from Oregon to Mexico. The local section of the trail also follows the route of an earlier Indian path, which connected the coastal villages and allowed for trade between settlements and neighboring tribes. About a mile south of the trailhead, the hike veers off to the right, following a steep, narrow path down to Hidden Beach. The small driftwood-strewn cove held little importance to the Yurok, since there were no fish-bearing streams emptying into it, and no good village sites, but for today's hiker, it is a sweet spot.

Hidden Beach offers a quiet little hideaway, far away from busy roads and tourist crowds, but within reach of an easy day hike.

From the beach the hike returns along the Coastal Trail to the southern end of the Yurok Loop. The return trail follows the inland portion of the loop, which passes through lush alder forests before dropping down to the lagoons western edge and eventually returning to that first Y junction near the trailhead.

Miles and Directions

0.0 Start at the Yurok Loop trailhead. Enter the forest on the broad path and turn left a few yards in, crossing the footbridge over the creek.

0.1 The trail forks, marking the start of the Yurok Loop. Take the right fork.

0.2 The path crosses a wide, flat spot that forms a natural overlook. Great view of offshore sea stacks and False Klamath Cove to the north.

0.3 South end of the Yurok Loop Trail. The inland half of the loop heads left, but continue straight, to Hidden Beach. A few yards later, a spur cutoff comes in from the left, also leading to the Yurok Loop Trail. Go straight.

0.5 The trail pops out of the woods, revealing Hidden Beach ahead.

0.9 (FYI: The Monterey cypress to the right has taken the form known as Krummholz.) Just after the cypress, the Hidden Beach Trail heads left, leading to the Trees of Mystery complex. Continue straight. The spur to Hidden Beach heads down steeply to the right. Veer right onto the spur and follow it down.

1.0 Hidden Beach. This is the turnaround point. Enjoy the beach a while, then return the way you came to the south end of the Yurok Loop.

1.7 Yurok Loop Junction. Turn right, following the inland half of the Yurok Loop Trail. A few yards later, a cutoff spur joins from the left. Continue straight.

1.8 The trail heads down a steep slope. At the bottom the lagoon is visible through the trees to the right. A few yards up, a bench on the right offers a nice view of the lagoon.

1.9 End of the Yurok Loop. Turn right and retrace the first part of the trail to the trailhead.

2.0 Trailhead.

Hike Information

Local Information

Del Norte Chamber of Commerce, Crescent City; (800) 343–8300; www.northerncalifornia.net.
Klamath Chamber of Commerce, Klamath; (707) 482–7165; info@klamathcc.org.

Local Events/Attractions

Terwer Valley Fair, held in mid-July, an old-fashioned country fair, Klamath; (707) 482–3713.
Klamath Salmon Festival, held in mid-August, salmon barbecue, Native American arts, crafts, dance, and games, Klamath; (707) 444–0433.
Annual Orick Rodeo, held in mid-July, rodeo and wild horse race; (707) 488–2885; orick@orick.net.

Lodging

Hostelling International–Redwood National Park, Klamath; (707) 482–8265; theredwood hostel@earthlink.net; www.norcalhostels.org. There are also state park, national park, and private campgrounds nearby.

Honorable Mentions

Del Norte

A Point St. George Trail

An easy 2 miles out and back. From the parking lot at the former Coast Guard station, the faint trail heads west to the edge of the cliff, then south along the grassy bluffs to dramatic Point St. George. Return the way you came, or along the parallel-running Radio Road. To reach the trailhead from Crescent City, take U.S. Highway 101 north about 0.5 mile out of town. Exit onto Washington Street and head west 3 miles until the road curves north, becoming Radio Road. Follow this another 1 mile until it dead-ends at a large gravel parking lot beside the former Coast Guard station. Contact: Tolowa Dunes State Park, Crescent City; (707) 464-6101 ext. 5112. *DeLorme: Northern California Atlas & Gazetteer:* Page 22, B2.

B Boy Scout Trail

An easy 7.4-mile out-and-back trail through old-growth redwoods and boggy skunk cabbage patches to the trail's namesake Boy Scout Tree, a double-trunked giant, and a little farther to a picturesque waterfall. From Crescent City, head east 1 mile on Elk River Road, turning right onto Howland Hill Road and continuing 2.7 miles to the Boy Scout Tree trailhead. At 2.8 miles up the trail, a spur trail heads right a few yards to the Boy Scout Tree. The main trail continues another 0.4 mile to the waterfall and turnaround point. Contact: Jedediah Smith Redwoods State Park, Crescent City; (707) 464–3779. *DeLorme: Northern California Atlas & Gazetteer:* Page 22, B2, B3.

Northern
Humboldt

Moving south down the Redwood Coast from Del Norte, travelers arrive in Humboldt County—a parcel of land with enough hiking opportunities that I've split it into two sections for the purposes of this book. Like its neighbor to the north, Northern Humboldt's economy was largely timber-based for much of its history but has begun to diversify in recent years. Thanks in part to the influence of Arcata's Humboldt State University, the area also has a large countercultural contingent to offset the conservatism of longtime residents. The result is a lively community, with each town showing a distinct personality, and a public-events schedule that includes everything from rodeos and stock car races to art shows and an All-Species' parade.

Like most of the Redwood Coast, Northern Humboldt's topography is a crumpled mass of low coastal mountain ranges interrupted only by the deep cuts of its many river valleys. Along this particular stretch of coast, that recipe includes the wide, shallow basin of Humboldt Bay, whose seaports once encouraged the growth of the county's main municipalities.

The best hiking lies primarily in the north, where the flagship redwood parks stretch down as an extension of Del Norte's parkland patchwork. The default starting point for most of these hikes is the tiny village of Orick. Located firmly in the center of this natural bounty, this former logging boomtown still seems to be holding a grudge against nearby Redwood National Park—whose creation they fought tooth and nail, believing it would destroy their livelihood. Orick's only visible concession to the tourist industry has been a proliferation of chainsaw-sculpture shops that line the highway as it passes through town.

Just east of Orick sits Redwood National Park's largest unit, which protects large portions of the lower and middle Redwood Creek watershed, as well as the official World's Tallest Tree. Nearby is Prairie Creek Redwoods State Park, one of the state park system's best examples of old-growth redwood forest.

Farther south, large portions of the coastal mountain land remain in the hands of giant timber corporations. As a result, recreation opportunities are limited to small, isolated parks, located mainly on the coast. Although not as vast or showy as the big parks to the north, these areas still have a lot to offer, and they are usually much less crowded. The tiny fishing village of Trinidad is the jumping-off point for several of these hikes.

For the hikes surrounding Humboldt Bay, home base will be the small blue-collar city of Eureka, with its nice Victorian old-town, or Eureka's unruly sister city, the outspoken liberal college town of Arcata, located around the bay to the north. Both are worth a visit, hiking aside.

The hills above Arcata are crisscrossed with hiking/biking trails and provide a good example of sustainable multiuse forest planning. South of Eureka, hikers can check out the beaches and wetlands of the Table Bluff area or head inland to the newly protected Headwaters Forest.

7 James Irvine/Miner's Ridge Loop

An extended jaunt through one of the best remaining old-growth redwood forests. Beginning at the Prairie Creek visitor center, the trail follows burbling Godwood Creek through the prehistoric forest carpeted with lush ferns and skunk cabbage, then shows visitors a drier side of the redwoods as it climbs a ridge and returns via the Clintonia and Miner's Ridge Trails.

Start: At the kiosk in front of the visitor center.
Distance: 6.2-mile loop.
Approximate hiking time: 2½ to 3 hours.
Difficulty: Easy to moderate, due to length and elevation gain.
Trail surface: Dirt path, wooden boardwalk.
Lay of the land: Old-growth redwood forest, both riparian and ridgetop, as well as some second-growth.
Other trail users: Hikers only.

Canine compatibility: No dogs allowed.
Land status: State park.
Nearest town: Orick.
Fees and permits: $2.00 day-use fee.
Schedule: Open year-round.
Map: USGS map: Fern Canyon, CA.
Trail contact: Prairie Creek Redwoods State Park, Orick; (707) 464-6101 ext. 5301; www.parks.ca.gov, www.nps.gov/redw/.

Finding the trailhead: From Eureka, take U.S. Highway 101 north 47 miles and exit at Newton B. Drury Scenic Parkway. Turn left at the stop sign, pass under the highway, and head north another mile along the parkway to the Prairie Creek State Park entrance, on the left. The trail starts at the large trail sign opposite the parking lot. *DeLorme: Northern California Atlas & Gazetteer:* Page 32, A3.

The Hike

The James Irvine Trail begins near the Prairie Creek Redwoods State Park visitor center and immediately delves into some of the most impressive old-growth redwood forest in California—or the world, for that matter. This park and its neighboring state-owned redwood parks are considered by many to be the crown jewels of California's state park system. Their prestige is one of the main reasons the parks have not been incorporated into the surrounding national park, as was the plan for many years.

When Redwood National Park was created in 1968, the founders stipulated that the Prairie Creek, Del Norte Coast, and Jedediah Smith State Parks would eventually become part of a larger, consolidated national park, encompassing some 45 percent of the old-growth redwood forest still left. There was a good deal of resistance to the plan, though—in particular from the state park employees, who were loath to lose control of their beloved groves. By the early 1990s, public pressure to consolidate had become intense, and all parties sat down at the table to hammer out an agreement. The result of this bargaining was a kind of loose confederation of parks:

Heavily burled old-growth redwood

In what is now known officially as Redwood National and State Parks, the state parks remain autonomous but share a management plan with the National Park System.

Politics aside, however, it is probably unimportant who manages the park, so long as the resource is protected. And it is an impressive resource. Prairie Creek alone has 14,000 acres, much of it ancient forest, and an extensive network of trails to access it all. As the name suggests, the park is centered around a meandering waterway flowing through a broad, shallow valley. The namesake prairie is at the heart of the park and seems a little out of place at first, given the huge accumulation of biomass in the surrounding forest. The deep, rich soils of the alluvial floodplain provide optimal conditions for growing the biggest redwoods, and the short grass prairie is quite a contrast to the towering giants next door. Not surprisingly, there is more at play here than just the whims of Mother Nature. Long before the white men arrived, native Yurok people kept the prairie open by occasionally setting fire to the grass. This had the dual effect of pushing back the encroaching forest and encouraging tender new growth on the prairie. This attracted large game, such as deer and elk, which were easy to hunt out in the open. The Yurok had a village nearby, close to

James Irvine/Miner's Ridge Loop

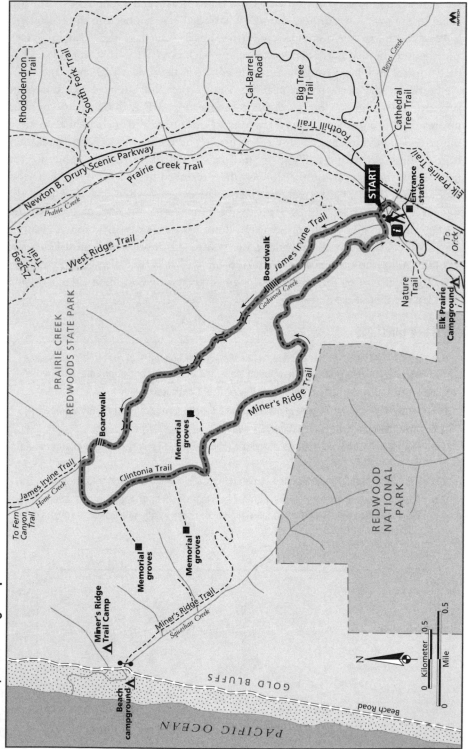

where Davidson Road comes out on Gold Bluffs Beach, and a trail led over the low ridge to the prairie. From here the path continued east, connecting the coastal village to the main Yurok population on the lower stretch of the Klamath River. Another trail headed north and west, heading back out to the coast and villages farther north. This follows roughly the same course as the modern James Irvine Trail.

From the edge of the prairie near the visitor center, the trail heads north into the ancient redwood groves, immediately crossing a loop of Prairie Creek and heading upstream along a smaller tributary. This soggy bottomland adds a riparian element to the redwood environment, with big-leaf maple and the exotic-looking skunk cabbage fleshing out the normally sparse understory. The grade remains gentle for the first half of the hike, as the trail follows the streambed up the increasingly narrow valley. At the head of the creek, the hike changes gears when you turn onto the steeper Clintonia Trail, climbing up to the much drier microclimate of Miner's Ridge. Here the hike heads inland again, along yet another historic route. This one is the Miner's Ridge Trail, remnant of a wagon road that once brought supplies and workers out to the gold mines at Fern Canyon and Gold Bluffs Beach. The trail follows this southeast to the trailhead, along a straight redwood-lined ridge that puts wooded avenues of old Europe to shame.

Miles and Directions

0.0   Start at the visitor center trailhead. (This is the large wooden sign next to a display case with elk antlers.) Go down the wooden steps and across the bridge on James Irvine Trail.

0.05 Prairie Creek Trail heads right toward Zigzag Trail. Continue straight.

0.1   Nature Trail goes left toward Miner's Ridge Trail. Keep going straight on James Irvine Trail.

0.2   West Ridge Trail heads right. Continue straight.

1.0   The trail crosses a wet spot via a wooden walkway. (FYI: Skunk cabbage, a relative of the lily, grows all around.)

2.0   The trail descends some wooden steps and crosses a small creek on a footbridge.

2.5   After descending via some steps, the trail crosses a lush, narrow gully and heads up the opposite side. (FYI: You're now in the drainage of Home Creek, which flows through Fern Canyon downstream.)

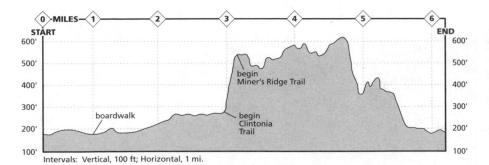

Intervals: Vertical, 100 ft; Horizontal, 1 mi.

2.8 The trail forks, with the right fork continuing to Fern Canyon. Take the left fork, following the Clintonia Trail up toward the junction with Miner's Ridge Trail.

3.1 The trail tops out on the ridge and passes three memorial redwood groves, dedicated to the philanthropists (and their loved ones) who helped preserve these groves for inclusion in the park.

3.8 Clintonia Trail dead-ends at Miner's Ridge Trail, which heads right (toward Gold Bluffs Beach), and left (toward the visitor center). Turn left onto Miner's Ridge Trail and follow it southeast along the ridge.

5.2 The trail begins to drop down off the ridge.

5.8 Cross the footbridge and continue straight.

6.0 Miner's Ridge Trail ends at the junction with Nature Trail. Turn left onto Nature Trail and head toward the visitor center.

6.1 Turn right onto James Irvine Trail and retrace the first 0.1 mile to the trailhead.

6.2 Arrive back at the trailhead.

Hike Information

Local Information

Del Norte Chamber of Commerce, Crescent City; (800) 343-8300; www.northerncalifornia.net.
Orick Chamber of Commerce, Orick; (707) 488-2885; www.orick.net.

Local Events/Attractions

Terwer Valley Fair, held in mid-July, an old-fashioned country fair, Klamath; (707) 482-3713.
Klamath Salmon Festival, held in mid-August, salmon barbecue, Native American arts, crafts, dance, and games, Klamath; (707) 444-0433.

Annual Orick Rodeo, held in mid-July, rodeo and wild horse race; (707) 488-2885; orick@orick.net.

Lodging

Hostelling International–Redwood National Park, Klamath; (707) 482-8265; www.norcalhostels.org.
State park campsite reservations: (800) 444-7275.

Restaurants

Rolf's Park Cafe, open April to October, Corner US 101 and Davidson Road, Orick; (707) 488-3841.

8 Fern Canyon Loop

A very short hike, made more challenging by the long, bumpy approach, but every bit worth the effort to find. The trail follows the bed of Home Creek up through a magical canyon, formed by hydraulic mining during the gold rush. Nature has outdone itself in healing these scars, with a lush carpet of ferns and moss hung like an emerald tapestry from the canyon's 40-foot walls. The return loop passes by the site of a gold-rush ghost town.

Start: Fern Canyon trailhead.
Distance: 1-mile loop.
Approximate hiking time: 1 hour.
Difficulty: Easy to moderate, due to little elevation gain, but several small stream crossings.
Trail surface: Dirt path, gravel streambed.
Lay of the land: Coastal bluffs, narrow fern canyon, and mixed-conifer forest.
Other trail users: None.

Canine compatibility: No dogs allowed.
Land status: State park.
Nearest town: Orick.
Fees and permits: $2.00 day-use fee.
Schedule: Open year-round.
Map: USGS map: Fern Canyon, CA.
Trail contact: Prairie Creek Redwoods State Park, Orick; (707) 464-6101 ext. 5301, www.parks.ca.gov, www.nps.gov/redw/.

Finding the trailhead: From Eureka, head north 42 miles on U.S. Highway 101 to the town of Orick, then continue another 2 miles north before turning left onto Davidson Road. Follow this rough gravel road 4 miles to Gold Bluffs Beach and the entrance station (day-use fee collected) and continue another 4 miles north to the end of the road at Fern Canyon trailhead. *DeLorme: Northern California Atlas & Gazetteer:* Page 32, A3.

The Hike

As you enter the mouth of Fern Canyon, you will no doubt notice the strange shape of the watershed, with its narrow, near-vertical walls and flat bottom. From the trailhead the hike follows the streambed up through the canyon, where vegetation carpets the walls clear to the rim, far above. Greenery aside, friends of the American Southwest might find here more topographic similarity with the slickrock slot canyons of Southern Utah than with the typical V-shaped Redwood Country creek. The unusual shape comes courtesy of the intense mining activity that took place here in the late 1800s, when the hunger for gold led people to do some very strange things, indeed.

Following the famous discovery at Sutter's mill in 1848, "Gold Fever" took hold of California, prompting prospectors to search every nook and cranny of the state

Mouth of Fern Canyon ▶

Fern Canyon Loop

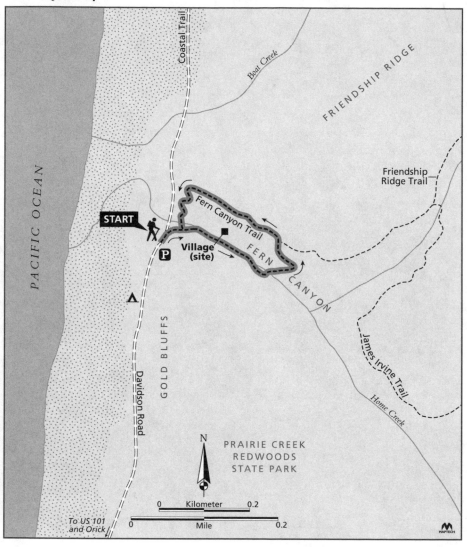

for the next mother lode. With so many out looking for the yellow stuff, it was only a matter of time before somebody noticed the telltale glint in the sand at the base of the Gold Bluffs, and beach mining soon commenced near Fern Canyon. But mining gold from the beach was difficult, backbreaking work, and it provided meager returns at best.

The beach was originally much narrower than it is today, and the waves crashed right up against the base of the bluffs. The constant pounding from the waves forced parts of the bluffs to break off, and opportunistic miners would quickly load any promising dirt onto pack mules and haul it to a spot above the bluffs that was safe from the tides. The gold was found in the form of a fine dust that was bonded to the sand and sediment. To reclaim the precious metal, miners had to use a two-step process. First the sand was run through a sluice box, where the heavier, gold-bearing particles settled to the bottom. Then the gold was separated from the sand through a complicated chemical process involving mercury.

Although miners searched for gold at the Bluffs on and off until the 1950s, the area's mining industry was effectively dead by the turn of the century. The initial rush lasted from 1850 to 1852 and had a brief renaissance from 1866 to 1900. But the gold grew increasingly difficult to remove as the bluffs were pushed back out of reach of the incoming waves. All told, the mines yielded only about $1 million dollars worth of gold; not much for a gold mine.

▶ Fern Canyon footage was used as the backdrop for a late 1990s dinosaurs documentary, "Walking with Dinosaurs." Computer-generated dinos were shown battling in the canyon, which was made to appear much larger than it is.

The shape of Fern Canyon is a product of hydraulic mining, dating from this same era. Hydraulic mining is a particularly destructive surface-mining method that involves washing away topsoil with high-pressure water cannons to uncover any buried gold. In California, miners turned to hydraulic mining only after most of the "easy" nuggets had been recovered by placer mining (panning for gold). Although stripped of plant life by the mining activity, the years of inactivity have allowed the flora to recover nicely. The canyon is a gorgeous example of the lush plant life that thrives in these temperate rain forests. Every square inch of the nearly vertical canyon walls are now covered with greenery, much of which belongs to one of several species of fern. Lady fern, wood fern, five-finger fern, deer fern, leather leaf fern, and sword fern grow in the canyon and the surrounding forests, along with a host of mosses and other small plants.

Pioneer Edson Adams acquired the land around Fern Canyon soon after gold was discovered there in the early 1850s, and he promptly rented it out to a larger gold-mining operation. Before long a tiny community of half a dozen buildings had been established on the north rim of the canyon at Lincoln Prairie. After reaching the upper end of the canyon, the trail climbs a series of steps to the rim, and begins the return loop. The trail passes the "Prairie"—actually just a small meadow—shortly before it reaches the mouth of the canyon, although nothing remains but ghosts and memories of the short-lived town that briefly thrived here.

Miles and Directions

0.0 Start at the kiosk on the north side of the parking lot. Follow the faint path across the gravel flats to the mouth of the canyon and head upstream.

0.1 The canyon walls are covered with a thick carpet of vegetation.

0.2 An old-growth trunk is down across the canyon. The trail passes under on the right.

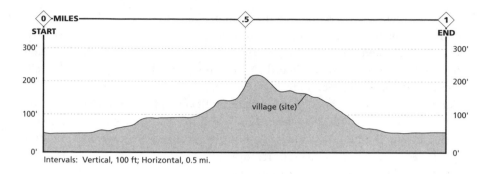

Intervals: Vertical, 100 ft; Horizontal, 0.5 mi.

0.5 Follow the steps up to the rim of Fern Canyon.

0.7 The James Irvine Trail heads right through the park to the visitor center. Turn left and follow the Fern Canyon Trail west along the rim.

0.9 The meadow on the left is called Lincoln Prairie; it was once a mining camp.

1.0 Descend steps to the mouth of Fern Canyon. Cross the gravel flats and return to the trailhead.

Hike Information

Local Information

Del Norte Chamber of Commerce, Crescent City: (800) 343-8300; www.northerncalifornia.net.

Orick Chamber of Commerce, Orick; (707) 488-2885; www.orick.net.

Local Events/Attractions

Terwer Valley Fair, held in mid-July, old-fashioned country fair, Klamath; (707) 482-3713.

Klamath Salmon Festival, held in mid-August, salmon barbecue, Native American arts, crafts, dance, and games, Klamath; (707) 444-0433.

Annual Orick Rodeo, held in mid-July, rodeo and wild horse race; (707) 488-2885; orick@orick.net.

Lodging

State park campsite reservations: (800) 444-7275.

Restaurants

Rolf's Park Cafe, open April to October, Corner US 101 and Davidson Road; (707) 488-3841.

9 Trillium Falls Trail

One of the newest trails in the park, Trillium Falls Trail was finished in 2002 and opens up a whole new stretch of old-growth forest to exploration by eager hikers. Beginning at the Elk Meadows Day Use Area—recently restored from its longtime use as a lumber mill log deck—the trail also skirts the edges of the aptly named Elk Meadow, where dozens of Roosevelt elk can regularly be observed grazing on the soggy grass along the meandering Prairie Creek.

Start: Elk Meadow Day Use Area.
Distance: 2.6-mile loop.
Approximate hiking time: 1.5 hours.
Difficulty: Easy to moderate, due to some elevation.
Trail surface: Asphalt path, gravel road, and dirt path.
Lay of the land: Open meadow, old-growth redwood forest.
Other trail users: Bird- and elk-watchers.

Canine compatibility: No dogs allowed.
Land status: National park.
Nearest town: Orick.
Fees and permits: None.
Schedule: Open year-round.
Map: USGS map: Orick, CA.
Trail contact: Redwood National and State Parks, Crescent City; (707) 464-6101; www.nps.gov/redw/.

Finding the trailhead: From Eureka, take U.S. Highway 101 north 42 miles to Orick, then continue another 2 miles and turn left onto Davidson Road. Follow this for 0.4 mile, across Elk Meadow and over the bridge, then turn left into the Elk Meadow Day Use Area parking lot. The trailhead is at the sign near the rest rooms. *DeLorme: Northern California Atlas & Gazetteer:* Page 32, B3.

The Hike

As with so much of California's modern history, the story of this hike begins with gold. In the late 1850s, white miners were scouring every last inch of the state for the precious metal, spurred on by the rich claims struck in the Sierra foothills. It was only a matter of time before someone stumbled across the gold-laden sands at the base of nearby Gold Bluffs Beach. Hosts of eager men showed up to work the mines there, but few struck it rich. One of those men, a young emigrant named Arthur Davidson, soon realized that a better living could be made in the dairy business. By 1890 Davidson was working his own ninety-acre dairy ranch centered around the present-day Elk Meadow Day Use Area. Four generations of the Davidson family continued to work much of this land until 1991, when it was sold to Redwood National Park.

The bucolic landscape you see today looked very different only a few years ago. Beginning in 1909 plans were laid to build a railroad through the valley, connecting

Trillium Falls Trail

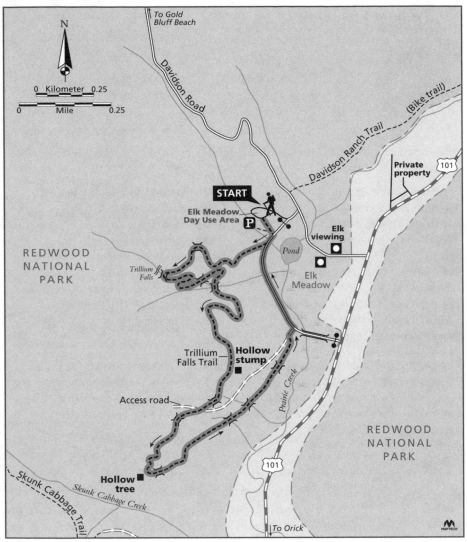

the distant cities of San Francisco and Grants Pass, Oregon. Although the railroad scheme was never realized, a right-of-way was purchased from the Davidsons, passing through several hands as the years progressed. By World War II, the property was owned by the Arcata Redwood Company, and construction was under way on a new sawmill and accompanying log deck, where huge redwood logs were stacked high while they awaited the buzz saws of Mill B. In all, eight acres of forest, meadow, and streambed were knocked flat and paved with asphalt to make the deck. Scores of ancient trees were converted to board feet here over the next few decades, as logging reached a fever pitch. By the time Redwood National Park was created in

1968, the logging industry was already in decline, since there was little old growth left to cut. The mill was closed in 1970, and the log deck languished for a quarter century.

All that changed in 1996 when the national park acquired the mill site. Together with the old Davidson property, they now had a significant chunk of land along the creek, but there was a lot of work to do. Bulldozers went to work undoing the damage that bulldozers had originally caused. Between 1996 and 1999, crews restored the natural contours of the land, using buried tree stumps as a guide. The eight acres of asphalt were ripped up and used to create the base fill of the new day-use area. As a final touch, trail crews constructed the 2.6-mile-long Trillium Falls Trail through adjacent redwood groves.

The hike starts at the new day-use area parking lot, heading down a short asphalt path to the pond, already thick with recovering vegetation, and a favorite with the local population of Roosevelt elk. From here the trail follows a gravel road a short distance south to the edge of the forest, where the singletrack Trillium Falls Trail heads up into the redwoods. Just less than half a mile up is the trail's namesake water fall, a 10-foot cascade in a deep ravine, enlivened somewhat by the bright green foliage of a big-leaf maple. From here the trail contours around the hill, leading hikers on a tour through classic redwood forests. Eventually, the trail pops out on the gravel road and leads back to the creek. A side trail leads out across a long footbridge—an excellent vantage point for watching elk. The final leg follows the gravel road north along the edge of the wetlands to the trailhead.

Miles and Directions

0.0 Start at Davidson parking lot, Elk Meadow trailhead. Follow the asphalt path down toward the pond. Turn left at the first junction, then immediately right, following the path south along the pond.

0.1 About halfway past the pond, turn right onto the Trillium Falls Trail, and follow the dirt path up into the forest. As the trail enters the trees, an old skid road is visible, heading up to the right. Continue straight.

0.2 A very large log has been used as cribbing to hold the trail in place. The trail switchbacks to the right, then straightens out and passes the Redwood Volunteers Grove on the right.

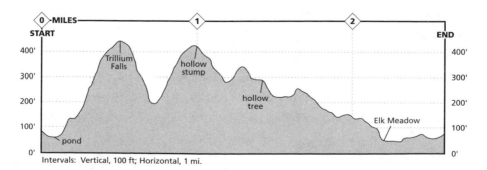

Intervals: Vertical, 100 ft; Horizontal, 1 mi.

0.4   The trail crosses a 12-foot bridge, after which the trail switchbacks briefly down.

0.5   Cross the creek on a long fiberglass/plastic bridge. To the right is Trillium Falls.

0.7   An old skid road crosses the trail. Continue straight.

0.8   The trail begins to switchback up.

1.0   Another old skid road heads up to the right. Continue straight. To the left, a hollow stump is large enough to climb inside.

1.1   The trail crosses a section of causeway and a short bridge. Skunk cabbage grows to the right.

1.3   The trail crosses a gravel road and continues on the other side. Go straight.

1.4   Start switchback descent.

1.6   A memorial bench is next to the trail on the left. Across the trail from the bench is a big hollow tree, burned hollow all the way to the top, but still alive.

1.7   The trail crosses a wet area via a nice section of causeway and a short bridge.

1.8   Cross two more bridges.

2.0   Cross a bridge. Notice the vegetation changing.

2.1   The trail dumps out onto a gravel road. Turn right on the road, heading downhill.

2.2   To the right, Davidson Trail heads over a long wooden bridge spanning Elk Meadow. Check out the bridge, then head north (straight) along the gravel road.

2.4   The trail leaves the forest and crosses a culvert, returning to the pond.

2.5   End of the loop. Continue straight, retracing the first leg of the trail to the parking lot.

2.6   Trailhead.

CALIFORNIA INDIANS
The mild climate and natural abundance of California has always been attractive to people, and the first humans began arriving here at least 10,000 years ago. Over the eons, successive waves of migration from the north, east, and south created a layered population of different cultures and languages. At the time of European contact, there were nearly forty distinct tribes (each consisting of several smaller groups) living in Northern California alone, speaking hundreds of dialects and languages from six major language families. An abundance of food, including salmon, acorns, deer, elk, kelp, and marine animals, allowed a surprisingly high population density—especially along the Redwood Coast. It has been estimated that the California Indian population prior to European contact was greater than that of Native American populations in all other states combined. Unfortunately, contact soon changed that, decimating the Native population with new diseases, destruction of lands used for gathering and hunting, and outright slaughter. From the estimated 300,000 California Indians living here in 1769, only 16,000 were left by the 1900 census. Today the population has risen again to around 320,000, putting one of every six U.S. Native Americans in California.

Hike Information

Local Information

Orick Chamber of Commerce, Orick; (707) 488-2885; www.orick.net.
Klamath Chamber of Commerce, Klamath; (707) 482-7165; info@klamathcc.org.
Del Norte Chamber of Commerce, Crescent City: (800) 343-8300; www.northerncalifornia.net.

Local Events/Attractions

Terwer Valley Fair, held in mid-July, old-fashioned country fair, Klamath; (707) 482-3713.
Klamath Salmon Festival, held in mid-August, salmon barbecue, Native American arts, crafts, dance, and games, Klamath; (707) 444-0433.
Annual Orick Rodeo, held in mid-July, rodeo and wild horse race; (707) 488-2885; orick@orick.net.

Lodging

State park campsite reservations: (800) 444-7275.

Restaurants

Rolf's Park Cafe, open April to October, Corner US 101 and Davidson Road, Orick; (707) 488-3841.

10 Ladybird Johnson Grove Trail

This is a very short excursion through some very tall trees. Ladybird Johnson Grove was the location chosen for the dedication of Redwood National Park in 1969. The grove is named for Pres. Lyndon B. Johnson's wife, a woman known for her pioneering conservation work, aimed at keeping America beautiful.

Start: Ladybird Johnson Grove trailhead.
Distance: 1.5-mile loop.
Approximate hiking time: ½ to 1 hour.
Difficulty: Easy, due to good trail and little elevation gain.
Trail surface: Packed gravel path.
Lay of the land: Old-growth redwood forest.
Other trail users: None.
Canine compatibility: No dogs allowed.

Land status: National park.
Nearest town: Orick.
Fees and permits: None.
Schedule: Open year-round.
Map: USGS map: Orick, CA.
Trail contact: Redwood National and State Parks, Crescent City; (707) 464-6101; www.nps.gov/redw/.

Finding the trailhead: From Eureka, drive north on U.S. Highway 101 42 miles to Orick, then continue another 1.3 miles before turning right onto Bald Hills Road. Head up the hill (not suitable for large mobile homes or cars with weak brakes) for 2.5 miles, and turn right into the Ladybird Johnson Grove parking area. The trail starts at the kiosk at the west end of the parking lot. *DeLorme: Northern California Atlas & Gazetteer:* Page 32, B3.

The Hike

Although most hikes offer a pretty good workout for the hiker, the Ladybird Johnson Grove Trail gets most of its climbing done before you even get out of the car. From US 101 the Bald Hills Road switchbacks up the ridge for 2.5 miles, gaining what seems like nearly that much in elevation before finally reaching the trailhead. The actual hike then begins with a flourish—crossing over the road via a gracefully arching wooden footbridge.

Once across the road, the trail quickly leaves the sound of struggling autos behind, as it plunges deep into prime old-growth redwood groves. Since you are now on top of the ridge, there is little climbing to do, and the trail has been "paved" with packed gravel, making the hike nearly wheelchair accessible. The gravel may seem like overkill to the hardened hiker, but it does more than just provide a smooth surface for visitors. The trees are visited by so many people each year that the constant trampling can compact the soil around the base of the giants, damaging their shallow root system and shortening their life spans. In a sense, the redwoods can be "loved to death." Gravel tread helps diffuse the pressure and prevent compacted soil.

The Ladybird Johnson Grove Trail describes a neat loop around the knoll at the western end of Bald Hills Ridge. The trail thus lassos one of the showcase groves

Ladybird Johnson Grove Trail

Ladybird Johnson Grove Trail

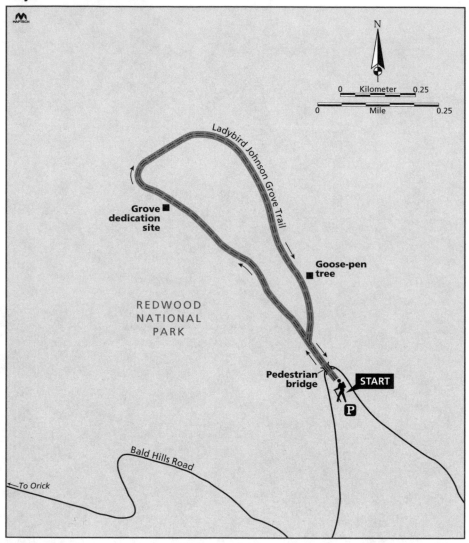

within Redwood National Park, and it was for this reason that the grove was chosen as the dedication site for the fledgling park in 1969. The story of Redwood National Park goes back as far as the turn of the twentieth century. At the time, increasingly efficient logging methods and equipment were beginning to make a serious dent in the world's stock of ancient redwoods. Once thought to be virtually inexhaustible, by the 1920s fully a third of the great forest had been converted to lumber. Members of the Save-the-Redwoods League tried repeatedly to convince Congress of the need for a national park, but the pleas fell on deaf ears. Between 1911 and 1947, no fewer than six attempts at legislation had been tried and had failed. It wasn't until 1964 that the idea took serious hold in Washington, and it was another four years before the deal was done. At long last the country had a national park protecting some of the remaining ancient redwood forest. Unfortunately, for many the park is a case of too little, too late—today only 3 percent of the original old-growth redwoods survive.

The legislation authorizing the park was signed into law by Pres. Lyndon B. Johnson in 1968. It wasn't until the following year, however, that the park was dedicated, by which time Richard Nixon had assumed office as the new president.

A little less than halfway around the loop, the Ladybird Johnson Grove Trail comes to the little clearing—surrounded by stately redwood trunks—where the park dedication ceremony was held. As well as inaugurating the new park, Nixon dedicated the founding grove to his predecessor's first lady, Claudia Taylor Johnson—known to the world as Ladybird. Known for her work as one of America's most prominent conservationists, Ladybird was a good choice as a namesake for the grove. While her husband was in office, she created a First Lady's Committee for a More Beautiful Capitol, soon expanding the program to include the whole country. In 1982 she founded the National Wildflower Research Center in Austin, Texas.

From the dedication site, the trail curves through old-growth giants around the remainder of the loop, before returning to the trailhead.

Miles and Directions

0.0 Start at the trailhead at the west end of the parking lot. The hike starts by crossing the footbridge over Bald Hills Road.

0.1 A small box on the right holds interpretive trail guides. A few yards later, the trail comes to a bench and kiosk, just across from a tree that has been hollowed by fire.

0.2 The trail forks, beginning the loop. Take the left fork.

0.6 The clearing is the dedication site for the national park, and Ladybird Johnson Grove. A bronze plaque tells more.

0.7 The trail reaches the end of the ridge and curves around to the right.

1.2 The trail arrives at a large goose-pen—or burned-out—tree, probably 12 feet in diameter.

1.3 End of the loop. Turn left and return the way you came in.

1.5 Reach the trailhead.

Hike Information

Local Information

Orick Chamber of Commerce, Orick; (707) 488-2885; www.orick.net.
Klamath Chamber of Commerce, Klamath; (707) 482-7165; info@klamathcc.org.
Del Norte Chamber of Commerce, Crescent City: (800) 343-8300; www.northerncalifornia.net.

Local Events/Attractions

Terwer Valley Fair, held in mid-July, old-fashioned country fair, Klamath; (707) 482-3713.
Klamath Salmon Festival, held in mid-August, salmon barbecue, Native American arts, crafts, dance, and games, Klamath; (707) 444-0433.

Annual Orick Rodeo, held in mid-July, rodeo and wild horse race; (707) 488-2885; orick@orick.net.

Lodging

State park campsite reservations: (800) 444-7275.

Restaurants

Rolf's Park Cafe, open April to October, Corner US 101 and Davidson Road; (707) 488-3841.

11 Tall Trees Grove Trail

A short but impressive walk through the world's tallest trees. Besides redwoods, there are also rhododendrons, giant ferns, and moss-hung maple trees, as well as access to wild Redwood Creek. The drive to preserve this grove led to the establishment of Redwood National Park. A permit is required to visit the Tall Trees Grove and is available free of charge from the visitor center just south of Orick. There they will give you the code for the combination lock on the gate (changed on a regular basis) and answer any questions you might have.

Start: From the Tall Trees Grove Trail trailhead.
Distance: 4.2 miles, partial loop.
Approximate hiking time: 2 hours.
Difficulty: Moderate, due to steep return trip.
Trail surface: Dirth path.
Lay of the land: Dirt path through second- and old-growth forests and alluvial flats.
Other trail users: Hikers only.
Canine compatibility: No dogs allowed.
Land status: National park.
Nearest town: Orick.

Fees and permits: A free permit is required to access the trail, obtainable at the Redwood National Park Visitor Center, just south of Orick on U.S. Highway 101. With the permit, you'll receive the combination for the gate.
Schedule: Open year-round.
Maps: USGS maps: Bald Hills, CA; Rodgers Peak, CA.
Trail contact: Redwood National and State Parks, Crescent City; (707) 464-6101; www.nps.gov/redw.

Finding the trailhead: From Eureka, drive north 42 miles on US 101 to the town of Orick. Stop at the visitor center (open 9:00 A.M. to 5:00 P.M.) at the south end of town, and pick up a free permit. Just north of Orick, turn right onto Bald Hills Road and drive east 6.4 miles, then turn right onto the gravel Tall Trees Grove Access Road. Unlock the gate using the combination you were given with your permit and, after closing the gate behind you, continue another 5.6 miles to the trailhead. The trail begins next to the small pavilion. *DeLorme: North California Atlas & Gazetteer: Page 33, C4.*

The Hike

A living relic from the days of the dinosaur, the giant redwood is truly an awe-inspiring sight. One of three surviving species of redwood, the coast redwood *(Sequoia sempervirens)* is the tallest tree on earth, often growing well beyond 300 feet tall. The closely related giant sequoia *(Sequoiadendron giganteum)* grows only in the south-central Sierra Nevada range in and around Sequoia–Kings Canyon National Park. The giant sequoia is the largest living thing on earth, in terms of sheer mass, but with an average height of 225 feet, it falls far short of the coast redwood in height. The third relative is a distant cousin of the other two: The dawn redwood is a much smaller, unremarkable tree found in China, and sometimes grown in the United States as an ornamental.

The coast redwood grows only on the Pacific coast of Northern California, where the mild climate and heavy fog provide ideal growth conditions for these silent giants. Of the estimated two million acres of old-growth redwoods existing here at the time of European arrival, only about 3 percent survive today. The rest have fallen to the ax and, more recently, the chainsaw. Of the remaining groves, more than half are protected on public land. The logging of old-growth forests, a source of very heated debate in the area, is seen as a vital source of jobs and revenue by some, and as wasteful destruction of irreplaceable habitat by others. As forests were depleted and public outcry became louder, stronger environmental laws were enacted to protect species endangered by the loss of habitat. This further reduced timber jobs—the result being that the timber industry supporters increasingly blamed environmentalists for their loss of prosperity. Both fronts have become increasingly embittered, and as outside pressures grow to end the logging of old growth, loggers become ever more militantly anti-environment. The low point of the conflict saw local schools banning a Dr. Seuss children's book (The Lorax), which depicted the tragic depletion of an imaginary forest for short term gain.

Created in 1968, Redwood National Park is tiny as national parks go, and it is split into four isolated subsections, surrounded by state parks and private land. Nonetheless, it is still possible to find something approximating backcountry in the large southern end of the park, which encompasses the lower drainage of Redwood Creek.

Although the Tall Trees Grove was within the original boundaries of the park, most of the surrounding land was not included until 1978, by which time most of it had already been clear-cut by the timber company. Twenty years of recovery have stabilized the topsoil and allowed a primary red alder forest to grow up, mixed with young second-growth redwoods and other species, but it will be another thousand years until a true old-growth forest stands here again, if ever.

Fortunately, you can still experience the real thing in the surviving ancient redwoods of Tall Trees Grove. The sheltered, fog-drenched location and nutrient-rich soil of the small floodplain provide ideal conditions for truly mammoth timber. Here, on the edge of Redwood Creek, stand the tallest trees on Earth. The world-record holder—a double-trunked beauty first surveyed by a National Geographic crew in 1963—stands a full 367.8 feet tall (more than 60 feet taller than the Statue of Liberty and its base combined). The second, third, and sixth tallest trees in the world are also in this grove.

You access the grove via a locked gate off of Bald Hills Road and a long, windy ex–logging road leading down through the young second growth of the upper slopes. At the end of the road is the trailhead for Tall Trees Grove, and a small pavilion with a guest book for hikers. The first leg of the hike is a steep downhill, cool

◀ Big-leaf maple

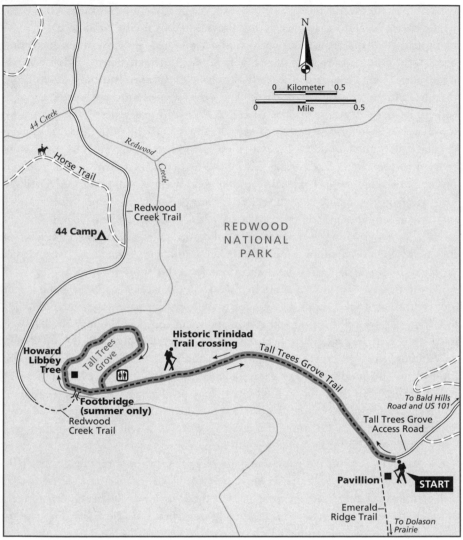

and shady beneath the dense canopy far above, with giant ferns and rhododendron thickets to both sides.

Eventually the trail reaches the floodplain and flattens out. This is where the giants are well marked along the loop with signs. At several spots along the loop, it's possible to access the rocky bar alongside Redwood Creek, which is an excellent place to break out the food and have lunch. If you keep quiet, you have a good chance of spotting some of the abundant wildlife here. The second half of the lower loop winds through a grove of primal big-leaf maples. On sunny days, light passing through the maples' leaves dapples the forest floor in a bright green color that blends well with the thick moss carpeting the trees' limbs and trunks.

An alternative to the gate and windy access road is to park at the Redwood Creek trailhead—at the foot of the Bald Hills Road—and hike up the much longer Redwood Creek Trail to the grove. This route involves crossing the creek a few times. There are temporary bridges installed in the summer, but if you're planning to go in winter or spring, it's best to avoid this route. The creek is generally high during the rainy season and can become a raging torrent with spring snowmelt or heavy rainstorms.

Miles and Directions

0.0 Start next to the pavilion. Trail guides are located in a box at the trailhead, with descriptions corresponding to numbered posts along the path. Follow the trail as it heads downhill into the forest.

0.1 The Emerald Ridge Trail to Dolason Prairie heads left. Continue straight on Tall Trees Grove Trail.

0.3 A section of old-growth log has been removed to make way for the trail. (FYI: This is a good opportunity to count the rings of an old-growth tree if you have some time.)

0.4 A spring wells up from under the stump on the right side of the trail.

1.1 (FYI: At this spot the historic Trinidad Trail used to head east and west. It has all but disappeared now.)

1.5 The trail passes an outhouse on the right, and enters Tall Trees Grove.

1.6 The trail forks, marking the start of the loop portion of the trail. Take the left fork. Shortly past the junction, Redwood Creek Trail heads left. Keep going straight.

1.7 (FYI: The official world's tallest tree is on the right, a magnificent double-trunked redwood known as the Howard Libby Tree.)

1.8 The trail enters a grove of big-leaf maple, thriving in the riparian zone along Redwood Creek.

1.9 (FYI: As you pass under several large bay laurels, aka pepperwood trees, the pungent smell of the leaves is discernable from the trail.)

2.6 The loop ends back at the fork in the trail. Turn left and return the way you came.

4.2 Arrive back at the trailhead.

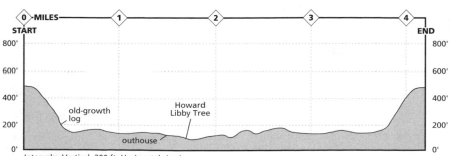

Intervals: Vertical, 200 ft; Horizontal, 1 mi.

Hike Information

Local Information

Humboldt County Convention and Visitors Bureau, Eureka; (800) 346-3482; (707) 443-5097; www.redwoodvisitor.org.

Local Events/Attractions

Annual Banana Slug Derby, held in August, Prairie Creek Redwoods State Park; (707) 464-6101, ext. 5300.

Discovery Ride, held in October, Redwood National and State Parks; (707) 464-6101, ext. 5300.

Lodging

National and State park campsite reservations: (800) 444-7275.
Car camping is allowed free of charge on the Freshwater Lagoon spit south of Orick.

NOT FOR THE SQUEAMISH: A CLOSE-UP LOOK AT THE BANANA SLUG

If there is a single animal most suited to life in a shady, rainy forest piled high with vegetation and organic matter, it is probably the banana slug. If its proportions are any indication, the climate certainly seems to have agreed immensely with it—slugs reaching 10 inches or more are not unheard of. Although often a drab and mottled green, it is the bright yellow coloration—as well as the size—of some banana slugs that has earned them the name. Such a bright color would at first appear to be counterproductive for a nonpoisonous and slow-moving creature but, in fact, they blend in very well with the old yellow leaves of bay laurels and other deciduous trees that litter the forest floor under the redwood canopy.

Hatching from a litter of approximately thirty eggs, the banana slug begins life as a colorless sluglet just ¾-inch long. They soon grow and gain color as they feed on small plants, mushrooms, dead animals, lichen, droppings, and even poison oak, all the while avoiding being eaten themselves. Small mammals, salamanders, insects, and snakes are all known to partake of the occasional banana slug, and even humans have sometimes eaten them, although this is generally done for sport or out of dire need rather than for the sheer pleasure of it. A word to the overly adventurous: Before attempting to eat a banana slug, take it home and feed it on cornmeal for about two weeks. This cleans out the digestive tract, which may contain substances that are toxic to humans. (Once while working on a trail crew, we started wondering aloud whether banana slugs would be good eating. Our foreman's face puckered up and he groaned a negative response, but we never got him to tell us how he knew.)

Another barrier to human enjoyment of banana slugs—be it culinary or tactile—is the slime that they cover themselves with. Unlike snakes, slugs really are slimy, producing a thick mucus from all parts of their bodies. A special gland produces a sticky slime, which the slug slides upon when it moves. This, combined with its suction cup–shaped foot, allows it to climb almost any surface. From heights it can then lower itself to the ground via a transparent slime cord. Slime is also one of the slug's better defenses, and if you ever get any on your hands, you will know why. It is unpleasant and nearly impossible to remove.

Fascinating as all this is, it is the sex life of the slug that is truly amazing. For one thing, they are hermaphrodites, each slug possessing both male and female sex organs. When they mate, which they may do at any time of the year, the slugs circle each other, licking, nudging, and biting the partner's right side, sometimes violently. The right side is where the reproductive organs are located—hidden under the mantle just in front of the breathing hole. When they are ready, the mates then curl into a yin-yang position and exchange sperm. Both animals are fertilized simultaneously, as they remain in the mating position for up to several hours.

Once mating is over, the slugs attempt to go their separate ways, but this is often not as simple as it sounds. Banana slugs have—throughout the eons—developed particularly large penises, and they regularly become stuck and are unable to separate, despite even more desperate hours spent trying to get unstuck. In the end the offending organ is simply gnawed off by the participants. In scientific terms, this is known as apophallation. As disturbing as all this may sound, there is still hope for the mutilated slug. Although scientists don't yet know for sure, the lost organ may regenerate.

So the next time you see a banana slug making its way slowly across your path, don't eat it, don't pick it up, and don't poke too much fun at it. After all, it's had a hard life.

12 Dolason Prairie Trail

The Dolason Prairie Trail is far from the tourist crowds that plague redwood groves along U.S. Highway 101. Beginning high in the Bald Hills, the trail explores prairies that local Native American populations once maintained with fire, then descends through thick forests to the old-growth redwood groves along Emerald Creek. Brooding fog often envelopes the valley, but on clear days the prairies offer excellent views.

Start: Dolason Prairie trailhead.
Distance: 9.6 miles out and back.
Approximate hiking time: 4 to 5 hours.
Difficulty: Moderate, due to length and elevation gain.
Trail surface: Dirt path, gravel road.
Lay of the land: Grass-covered hillsides, second-growth and old-growth redwood forest.
Other trail users: None.
Canine compatibility: No dogs allowed.

Land status: National park.
Nearest town: Orick.
Fees and permits: No fees or permits necessary.
Schedule: Open year-round.
Maps: USGS maps: Rodgers Peak, CA; Bald Hills, CA.
Trail contact: Redwood National and State Parks, Crescent City; (707) 464-6101; www.nps.gov/redw.

Finding the trailhead: From Orick, head north 1.3 miles on US 101, then turn right onto Bald Hills Road. Drive up the hill 9.5 miles, to a fork in the road below a wildland fire station. Take the right (lower) fork, following the road another 1.3 miles to the Dolason Prairie trailhead parking lot, located in a clump of trees on the right. Turn right into the lot and park. The trailhead is located at the southeast corner of the parking lot, next to the kiosk. *DeLorme: Northern California Atlas & Gazetteer:* Page 33, C4-5.

The Hike

Giant redwoods are clearly the unmitigated stars of parklands in Northern Humboldt and Del Norte Counties, but ancient forests are not the only environment protected within the park's boundaries. The Dolason Prairie Trail begins in one of these places—the open grasslands of Redwood National Park's Bald Hills area.

▶ The author helped build the 50-foot Emerald Creek Bridge as a trail crew volunteer in the park during 1990–1991.

Sprawled across the ridgetop on the southwest side of Bald Hills Road, Dolason Prairie is part of a large patchwork of similar grasslands that dot the surrounding highlands. The prairies provide habitat for myriad plant and animal species. Thousand-pound Roosevelt elk bulls graze in the open space alongside brush rabbits and dusky-footed wood mice. Predators such as bobcat, coyote, and the occasional mountain lion prowl the slopes, undeterred by the 5,000-odd insect species that also live here.

Emerald Creek Bridge

From the trailhead the hike follows a faint singletrack path down through the prairie, passing through a small clump of forest before emerging back out into the open on a gravel access road below. The road is closed to public automobile traffic but makes an excellent vantage point from which to survey the surrounding prairie. The open terrain also affords good vistas of the Redwood Creek drainage far below, providing the fog has not rolled in and obscured the view.

Following the road across the prairie, the trail veers off to the left just before the road reenters the forest, descending several switchbacks before popping out again onto prairie farther down. The historic Lyons barn stands lonely and forgotten in the center of the meadow here. Built around 1914 by sheep-rancher Sherman Lyons, the barn served as a feeding station and shelter for his large flocks. This meadow, along with Dolason Prairie, belonged to the pioneering Lyons family from the 1860s until the 1960s, when it was sold to timber interests for logging. The Park Service acquired the land in 1978, as an expansion of the newly created Redwood National Park.

Far from being a totally natural phenomenon, the prairies are actually relics from a time when human beings had a far more symbiotic relationship with the local

Dolason Prairie Trail

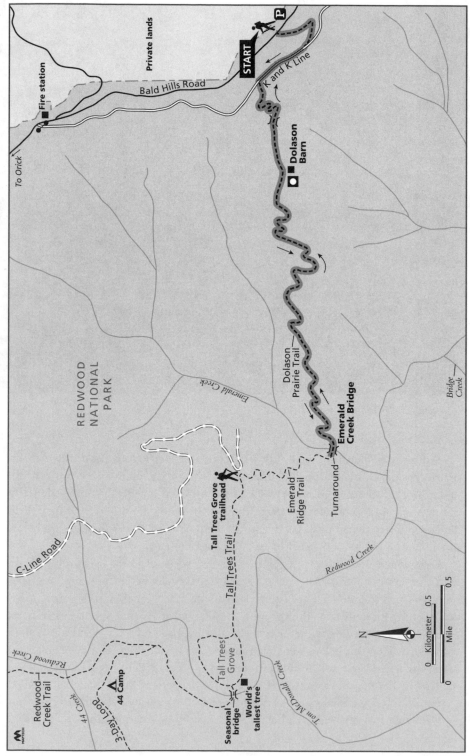

Fire station

To Orick

Private lands

Bald Hills Road

START

P

K and K Line

Dolason Barn

REDWOOD NATIONAL PARK

Emerald Creek

Dolason Prairie Trail

C-Line Road

Emerald Creek Bridge

Tall Trees Grove trailhead

Emerald Ridge Trail

Turnaround

Redwood Creek

Bridge Creek

Redwood Creek Trail

44 Creek

3-Day Loop

44 Camp

Tall Trees Trail

Tall Trees Grove

Seasonal bridge

World's tallest tree

Tom McDonald Creek

N

0   Kilometer   0.5

0   Mile   0.5

landscape, giving as much as they took. The Chilula people, who inhabited this area before the incursion of white settlers, used fire to maintain the meadows in a way that benefited both the people and the land. The fire helped keep the grassland from disappearing as the surrounding forest encroached. Young trees succumbed to the flames, but grasses soon returned, thicker than ever, as well as berries, hazelnuts, and other food plants. The fresh spring grass attracted elk and deer into the open, where they were easier to hunt. Fire also helped maintain groves of oak trees, favored by the Chilula for their acorns, which were a staple of the local diet. A small grass fire did not harm the large trees, but it removed the brush surrounding them and helped control pests that bred in the rotten acorns on the ground. Today the Park Service still uses controlled-burn techniques to mimic this traditional use of fire.

From the barn the trail descends rapidly, soon leaving the prairies behind and entering redwood forest. By the time the trail reaches the turnaround point at Emerald Creek Bridge, the second growth has merged into old growth, giving the steep-sloped watershed of Emerald Creek a primeval atmosphere. Giant trunks have fallen across the ravine, spanning the gap almost as well as the park's pedestrian bridge—an impressive 50-foot span, perched equally high above the waterway.

Unless you want to extend your hike by continuing to Tall Trees Grove, return to the trailhead the way you came.

Miles and Directions

0.0 Start at the trailhead next to the kiosk in the southeast corner of the parking lot. The trail heads down to the left, toward a clump of trees.

0.1 The trail drops down onto an unused old road. Head right, following the trail.

0.2 The old roadbed curves left. Follow the footpath as it continues straight, out into open grass.

0.3 The trail drops down onto a gravel road. Turn right and continue on the road.

0.6 Just as the road is about to enter the forest, turn left onto a singletrack footpath, heading downhill.

0.7 The trail descends several switchbacks.

0.8 Cross a small bridge.

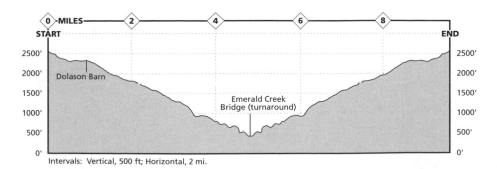

Intervals: Vertical, 500 ft; Horizontal, 2 mi.

1.1 Dolason Barn. On clear days the meadow offers great views of the watershed below. Continue across the meadow.

1.2 The trail enters brushy forest and begins a switchback descent.

1.7 Trail pops out into prairie briefly. Good views here on clear days.

2.1 A defunct trail heads back to the left. Turn right, continuing on the main trail.

2.4 Forest vegetation changes to redwoods.

2.9 On the left at a bend in the trail, an ancient redwood has tipped over, exposing an impressive root wad.

3.8 Forest now has more old-growth redwoods.

4.6 The trail passes a huge redwood with candelabra branches.

4.8 Emerald Creek Bridge. Turnaround point. Return the way you came. **Option:** Continue straight to the Tall Trees Trail. (FYI: Be very careful, the ramp on the east end is extremely slippery when moist.)

9.6 Trailhead.

Hike Information

Local Information
Orick Chamber of Commerce, Orick; (707) 488-2885; www.orick.net.
Klamath Chamber of Commerce, Klamath; (707) 482-7165; info@klamathcc.org.
Del Norte Chamber of Commerce, Crescent City: (800) 343-8300; www.northerncalifornia.net.

Local Events/Attractions
Terwer Valley Fair, held in mid-July, old-fashioned country fair, Klamath; (707) 482-3713.
Klamath Salmon Festival, held in mid-August, salmon barbecue, Native American arts, crafts, dance, and games; Klamath; (707) 444-0433.

Annual Orick Rodeo, held in mid-July, rodeo and wild horse race; (707) 488-2885; orick@orick.net.

Lodging
There are several state park campgrounds in the Prairie Creek area north of Orick.
State park reservations: (800) 444-7275. Camping is also allowed on the Freshwater Lagoon spit south of town (for a small fee). Contact Redwood National and State Parks, Crescent City; (707) 464-6101; www.nps.gov/redw.

13 Skunk Cabbage Trail

This trail is a veritable cornucopia of habitats that leads through massive spruce and melancholy alder stands, into deep green canyons, and along pristine coastal bluffs. Along the way, hikers have a chance to see abundant wildflowers and the very plant that gives the trail its name, the skunk cabbage. Very quiet, observant nature-watchers might even be lucky enough to catch a glimpse of elk through the trees.

Start: Skunk Cabbage Trail trailhead.
Distance: 10.5 miles out and back.
Approximate hiking time: 5 to 6 hours.
Difficulty: Moderate, due to length and some steep sections.
Trail surface: Dirt path.
Lay of the land: Temperate swamp and second-growth forests with some old growth, as well as coastal bluffs and beaches.
Other trail users: Hikers only.

Canine compatibility: Dogs not permitted.
Land status: National park.
Nearest town: Orick.
Fees and permits: No fees or permits required.
Schedule: Open year-round.
Maps: USGS map: Orick, CA.
Trail contact: Redwood National and State Parks, Crescent City; (707) 464-6101; www.nps.gov/redw.

Finding the trailhead: From Eureka, drive north 42 miles to the town of Orick. Just north of town, turn left at the sign for Skunk Cabbage Trail trailhead and continue another 0.6 mile to the trailhead. The trail begins where the road ends. *DeLorme: Northern California Atlas & Gazetteer:* Page 32, B3.

The Hike

There is no one thing that makes this hike so special. Rather, it's the combination of a unique array of habitats and the trail's mood of isolation that earns it a place on the list of top regional hikes. The first section of the trail follows the path of an old logging road that cuts through a forest ravaged long ago—not surprising, given its proximity to the logging town of Orick. Nevertheless, there are still a number of remnant old-growth giants scattered throughout the area. Some of these redwoods were left as seed trees or were deemed unsuitable for the mill because they were twisted or hollow. Others were only broken stumps at the time the area was logged and remain in nearly the same condition, thanks to redwood's natural rot resistance.

The second-growth forest that has replaced the ancient redwoods is comprised mainly of spruce and alder, trees that create a somber, isolated mood. The addition of a swamp along the floor of the drainage further darkens the area's atmosphere. This wetland is filled with exotic-looking skunk cabbage, unflatteringly named for the strong odor of the leaf that surrounds its flower spike. A relative of the calla lily, the skunk cabbage blooms in spring and summer. A single burst of tiny blossoms is partially covered by a bright yellow hood, an arrangement that complements the

Gold Bluffs Beach and driftwood

plant's large, waxy leaves. The root and young leaf are edible—after sufficient cooking to remove the unpleasant calcium oxalate present in the plant—and were used as a food source by some Native Americans and early miners. (Another relative of skunk cabbage—called *taro*—was a traditional staple in the diets of many Polynesians.)

After crossing the swamp, the trail heads up a fern-lined ravine and eventually reaches the crest of the coastal bluffs at the junction with the now-defunct South Beach Access Trail. The bluffs are steep and brushy here, so the trail ducks back inland to follow the ridge north through the forest. This part of the forest has that lived-in look that's achieved only where large mammals regularly visit. In this case, the large mammals aren't humans—they're Roosevelt elk. Game trails crisscross the ridges and hollows, and there are many open, flat spaces under the canopy where elk like to bed down. While elk are commonly seen in the meadows along U.S. Highway 101 north of Orick and in Prairie Creek Redwoods State Park, it's fairly unusual to see them in the forest. But you have a good chance of glimpsing one of the beasts in this area. In any setting, keep a healthy distance from the elk, which are unpredictable.

Skunk Cabbage Trail

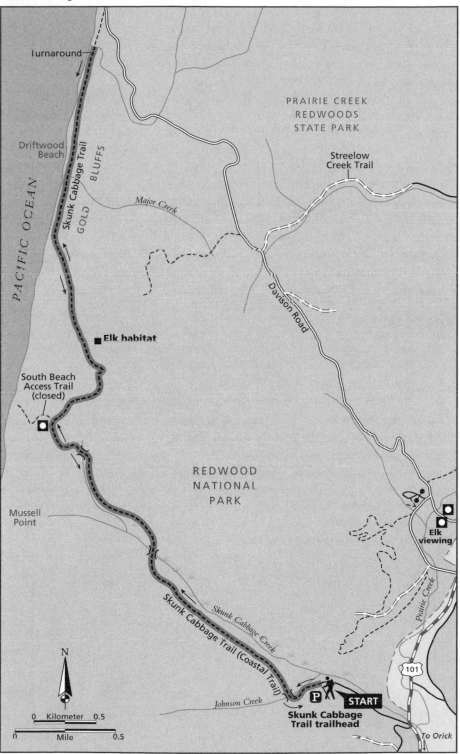

Turnaround

PRAIRIE CREEK
REDWOODS
STATE PARK

Driftwood
Beach

Streelow
Creek Trail

Skunk Cabbage Trail

GOLD BLUFFS

Major Creek

PACIFIC OCEAN

Davison Road

■ Elk habitat

South Beach
Access Trail
(closed)

REDWOOD
NATIONAL
PARK

Mussell
Point

Elk
viewing

Prairie Creek

Skunk Cabbage Creek

Skunk Cabbage Trail (Coastal Trail)

N

Johnson Creek

Skunk Cabbage
Trail trailhead

P START

101

0   Kilometer   0.5

0   Mile   0.5

To Orick

The trail soon pops onto the bluffs again and quickly drops down to follow the beach northward. There are fields of driftwood on the beaches here, and some of the pieces are quite large. It's not uncommon for floods to wash old stumps and logs out to sea, where waves bring many of them back onto nearby beaches. In fact, some areas here seem to attract the stuff like a magnet.

The hike ends at the creek crossing where Davison Road leaves the woods and heads north along Gold Bluffs Beach. The bluffs are pushed back here and drop off vertically from the ridge, leaving ochre cliffs of exposed dirt and rock perched above low, grassy dunes. If the scene looks a little unnatural, that's because it is. These "Gold Bluffs" were created by hydraulic mining operations, which reached their peak in the late 1800s. Mining had been occurring here since the 1850s, when gold was discovered on the bluffs, but it wasn't until prospectors cleaned out the "free" deposits of gold with placer-mining techniques that miners switched to the rougher hydraulic system. Gold seekers aimed water cannons at the bluffs to wash away their soil and soft rock, a process that left the heavier gold behind. Eventually, this method also proved unprofitable, and mining in the area stopped by the 1920s.

Return the way you came.

Miles and Directions

0.0 Start at the Skunk Cabbage Trail trailhead. Follow the Skunk Cabbage Trail (aka the Skunk Cabbage Section of the Coastal Trail) west into the forest.

0.4 The trail crosses a small wooden bridge.

0.5 (FYI: The swamp below to the right is full of the trail's namesake skunk cabbage.)

1.2 The trail does an S curve and crosses a wooden bridge over the swamp.

1.8 Cross another bridge and follow the trail as it heads up the canyon.

1.9 The trail begins to switchback up.

2.2 (FYI: The white-barked stand of trees across the ravine are red alder.)

2.4 A spur trail used to lead down to the beach on the left, but it has been closed due to trail deterioration. There is a good view of the ocean from here. Continue to the right, following the main trail.

3.1 The trail begins to descend to the beach.

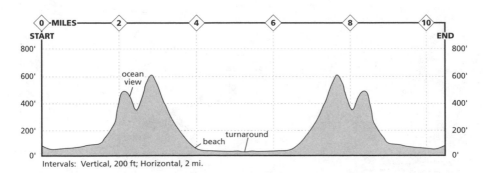

Intervals: Vertical, 200 ft; Horizontal, 2 mi.

3.3 The trees open up briefly to offer another view of the ocean.

3.5 (FYI: This area is heavily trafficked by elk. There are game trails and bedding areas everywhere around the trail.) Continue straight.

3.9 The trail exits the forest and switchbacks down the bluffs to the beach. At the bottom, turn right and head north along the narrow beach. There is no visible trail from here until the turnaround point.

4.4 The trail crosses a small creek. On the right is a large field of driftwood.

5.3 The trail reaches a wide creek. Davison Road is visible as the trail exits the forest on the left and heads north along the dunes. This is the turnaround point for the hike. Return the way you came.

10.5 Arrive back at the trailhead.

Hike Information

Local Information

Humboldt County Convention and Visitors Bureau, Eureka; (800) 346-3482; (707) 443-5097; www.redwoodvisitor.org.

Local Events/Attractions

Annual Banana Slug Derby, held in August, Prairie Creek Redwoods State Park; (707) 464-6101, ext. 5300.

Discovery Ride, held in October, Redwood National and State Parks; (707) 464-6101, ext. 5300.

Lodging

National and state park campsite reservations: (800) 444-7275.

Car camping is allowed free of charge on the Freshwater Lagoon spit south of Orick. Contact Redwood National and State Parks, Crescent City; (707) 464-6101; www.nps.gov/redw.

14 Rim Trail Loop

If you enjoy scenic vistas of rocky Pacific Ocean coastline, then this is the trail for you. The hike circumnavigates Patrick's Point State Park—a lesser-known tourist attraction but a favorite with the locals. From the Rim Trail, numerous side trails lead to postcard-perfect views, which also offer excellent whale-watching opportunities. A bit of culture is thrown in for good measure, with the reconstructed traditional Yurok Indian village near the end of the hike.

Start: Agate Beach parking lot.
Distance: 3.6-mile loop, with shorter variations possible.
Approximate hiking time: 2 to 3 hours.
Difficulty: Easy, due to good trails and little elevation gain (moderate if taking spur trails).
Trail surface: Dirt path.
Lay of the land: Coastal forest, second-growth redwood forest, and rocky cliffs.
Other trail users: None.

Canine compatibility: No dogs allowed.
Land status: State park.
Nearest town: Trinidad.
Fees and permits: $2.00 day-use fee.
Schedule: Open year-round. Call for day-use hours.
Map: USGS map: Trinidad, CA.
Trail contact: Patrick's Point State Park, 4150 Patrick's Point Drive, Trinidad; (707) 677-3570; www.parks.ca.gov.

Finding the trailhead: From Trinidad, head north on U.S. Highway 101 for 5 miles, and take the second "Patrick's Point Drive" exit. Turn left, passing under US 101 and following Patrick's Point Road around to the left. Turn right into the park entrance 0.5 mile later. Follow the park road past the entrance station and continue another 0.9 mile, following the signs for Agate Beach. Park at the Agate Beach parking lot. The trail begins at the south end of the lot, on the ocean side. *DeLorme: Northern California Atlas & Gazetteer:* Page 32, C2.

The Hike

Patrick's Point State Park is often overlooked by visitors, who tend to flock to the nearby parks that boast large groves of old-growth redwoods. There are few large redwoods at Patrick's Point, mainly because of its proximity to the salty ocean breezes, but there are still plenty of reasons to explore this little coastal gem.

The bulk of the park sits atop a raised marine terrace, perched about 200 feet above sea level. This position allows for breathtaking views from the many coastal overlooks scattered along the park's rocky cliffs. Beginning at the Agate Beach parking lot, the Rim Trail follows along the top of the marine terrace for much of the park's convoluted coastline. From it, several spur trails lead to rocky promontories that overlook the crashing waves below. Chief among these is Wedding Rock, a large knob jutting out into the Pacific, connected to the mainland only by a narrow wedge of land. Located about 0.75 mile from the trailhead, the rock can be reached via a 0.2-mile spur trail, which leads across the narrow land bridge and climbs a

Mushroom heaven

series of steps to reach the overlook. From here hikers can see the forbidding cliffs to their best advantage, and the thick fog that often rolls over the park only heightens the drama. Looking left down the coast from here will give you a view of the park's namesake, Patrick's Point.

As the wind and waves carve away the soft rock of the coastline, these rocky knobs will someday become isolated sea stacks, standing alone out in the pounding surf. That is how nearby Lookout Rock was formed millions of years ago. The fact that it now stands 500 feet above sea level, safely up on the marine terrace, can be chalked up to plate tectonics. This area has been uplifted over the eons, raising the formation well out of reach of the waves that formed it. Another spur trail leads to the top of the small peak. The views are good from the summit, but only on fog-free days.

From Lookout Rock the trail circumnavigates the park on a scenic, if largely uneventful course. This changes when the trail passes the visitor center on the inland portion of the loop, arriving at Sumeg Village, a reconstructed traditional Yurok settlement. This is a cluster of houses built of split redwood planks over sunken square

Rim Trail Loop

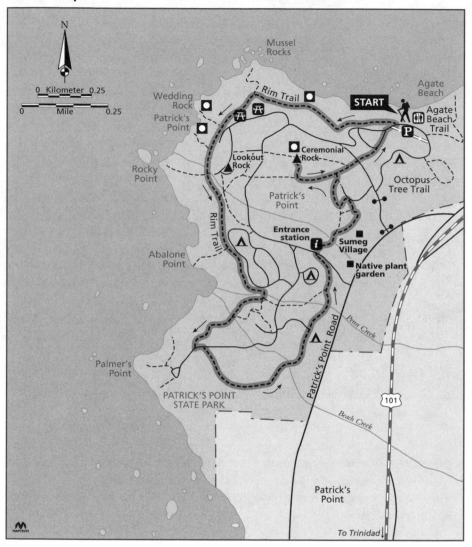

pits. Also included in the village are a sweat house and a ceremonial dance pit. A nearby traditional dugout canoe demonstrates the most important mode of precontact transportation.

Prior to the invasion of European–Americans that disrupted their way of life, the Yuroks used this area as a seasonal camp, from which seals and sea lions were hunted on the coast and offshore rocks. Although they had no permanent village here, the area figured prominently in Yurok beliefs. According to their oral history, the supernatural beings who walked the earth in early times came to live in this spot when the world changed, and they became the porpoise people. In the Yurok language,

Patrick's Point and the surrounding area was known as Sumeg, hence the name for the reconstructed village. Far from being just an interpretive display for tourists, the village was constructed by surviving Yurok tribal members, and it is used by them for annual ceremonies. A nearby native plant garden is used by the tribe as a source of plant material for basket weaving and other traditional uses.

After exploring the village, the trail makes a short detour to Ceremonial Rock— another landlocked sea stack, similar to Lookout Rock—before heading back across a meadow and campground to the trailhead.

Miles and Directions

0.0 Start at the Rim Trail trailhead at the south end of the Agate Beach parking lot.

0.1 An overlook is on the right side of the trail. A spur trail heads left toward the entrance road. Continue straight.

0.2 The trail forks, with the right fork leading a few yards to an overlook. Continue on the left fork, crossing a footbridge soon thereafter.

0.4 A spur trail heads right to Mussel Rock (0.2 mile). Another heads left to a parking lot. Continue straight along the Rim Trail.

0.5 The trail passes a large rock outcrop on the left. Just past the rock, there is a picnic area on the left. Keep going straight.

0.6 Another picnic area is on the left, with a parking lot beyond. Take the right fork. Shortly thereafter, you come to the junction with Wedding Rock. A spur trail heads right, down to the rock (0.2 mile). Continue straight.

0.7 A spur trail heads right to Patrick's Point (0.1 mile). (FYI: Patrick's Point, like Wedding Rock, is a great place to spot whales.) Go straight.

0.75 At the fork in the trail, the left branch heads up to the top of Lookout Rock (0.1 mile). Take the right branch.

0.8 At the junction, a spur trail to Rocky Point heads right (0.15 mile), while the Rim Trail continues to the left (straight). Go straight.

0.9 A spur trail heads left to the park entrance. Continue straight.

1.1 A spur trail goes left to Abalone Campground. Go straight. Several yards later, the trail forks. To the right, a spur trail heads down to Abalone Point. Take the left fork.

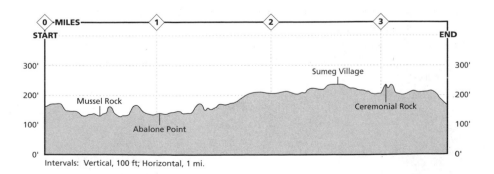

Intervals: Vertical, 100 ft; Horizontal, 1 mi.

1.4 The campground is visible through the trees to the left.

1.5 At the junction, a spur heads left to the campground. Turn right, cross the footbridge, and turn right again on the other side, heading toward Palmer's Point.

1.6 The trail arrives at the other end of the Campfire Center Cutoff. Continue to the right on the Rim Trail, immediately crossing a small bridge.

1.9 The trail pops out onto the access road for Palmer's Point. Turn left, heading north on the road for several yards, then turn right again onto Rim Trail, where it reenters the woods on the other side of the road.

2.3 Beach Creek Group Camp. At the parking lot, head straight across the pavement and continue north on the other side, at the sign leading to Penn Creek.

2.4 At the junction the trail to the left heads west to the Rim Trail, but go right instead.

2.5 Cross the short section of causeway and head left on the other side, following the faint trail up along the stream. A few yards later, the trail crosses back over the drainage and becomes more obvious.

2.6 The trail takes a sharp left and crosses an 8-foot bridge.

2.7 At the four-way junction, head straight. A few yards later the trail reaches the entrance road near the entrance station. Cross the road and head toward the visitor center on the other side.

2.8 The trail continues in the upper right-hand corner of the visitor center parking lot. Just past the kiosk and the replica dugout canoe, the trail forks. Take the right fork to Sumeg Village. A few yards after that, a spur trail heads right to the native plant garden. Continue straight.

2.9 Sumeg Village. Continue straight between the reconstructed houses to the parking lot.

3.0 At the parking lot, head left to the end of the lot, then left again to a second lot near the Red Alder Group Picnic Area. On the other side of the village is a picnic area, and after that a parking lot.

3.1 At the midpoint of the second parking lot, turn left onto a connector trail leading into the woods. A few yards later, turn right at the junction. A few yards after that, turn left toward Ceremonial Rock.

3.2 At the T junction turn left. Almost immediately, there is another T junction. Turn left again, toward Ceremonial Rock.

3.3 A spur trail heads right up to the top of Ceremonial Rock (0.1 mile). This is the turn-around point. Head back to the last junction.

3.4 At the junction, head straight toward Agate Beach Campground.

3.5 The trail pops out into a meadow, then crosses the paved access road. Continue straight along the trail on the other side.

3.55 The trail arrives in Agate Campground. Head straight down the paved road. At the junction with the access road, turn right and follow the road back to the Agate Beach parking lot.

3.6 Trailhead.

Hike Information

Local Information

Trinidad Chamber of Commerce, Trinidad; (707) 677-1610.

Humboldt County Convention and Visitors Bureau, Eureka; (800) 346-3482; (707) 443-5097; www.redwoodvisitor.org.

Local Events/Attractions

Clam Beach Run & Walk, 5-mile run/walk and 3-mile or 8.75-mile challenges from Trinidad to McKinleyville; (707) 677-1610; www.trinidadtoclambeach.com.

Cher-Ae-Heights Casino, Trinidad; (707) 677-3611; (800) 684-2464; www.cheraeheightscasino.com.

Trinidad Bay Charters, ocean-fishing charters, Trinidad; (707) 839-4743; (800) 839-4744 (CA only).

Trinidad Art & Fish Festival, held in June, tasty barbecue—deep-fried white fish and salmon dinners with coleslaw, beans, and bread—arts and crafts, entertainment, children's entertainment, plant sale, tours, Trinidad; (707) 677-1610.

Lodging

State park campsite reservations: (800) 444-7275.

Hotels and rental cabins in nearby Trinidad.

Restaurants

Moonstone Grill, fine seafood dining (pricey, but very good), Westhaven; (707) 677-1616.

Other Resources

Indian Lore of the North California Coast, by Austen D. Warburton and Joseph F. Endert. Covers the beliefs and history of the Yurok people.

15 Trinidad Head Loop

This is a short but dramatic loop around Trinidad Head, a rocky promontory jutting out into the Pacific Ocean near the rustic fishing village of Trinidad. The hike offers either spectacular views of the ocean and a very scenic little fishing harbor or an eerie stroll through soupy fog, as the weather allows. Foghorns and lighthouses complete the scene.

Start: Sandy Beach parking lot.
Distance: 1.4-mile loop.
Approximate hiking time: 1 hour.
Difficulty: Easy to moderate, due to good trail, but some elevation gain.
Trail surface: Dirt path, gravel road, and paved road.
Lay of the land: Dome-shaped rocky Pacific headland.
Other trail users: None.

Canine compatibility: Dogs not allowed.
Land status: U.S. Coast Guard reservation.
Nearest town: Trinidad.
Fees and permits: None.
Schedule: Open year-round from dawn to dusk.
Map: USGS map: Trinidad, CA.
Trail contact: Trinidad Chamber of Commerce, Trinidad; (707) 677–1610.

Finding the trailhead: From U.S. Highway 101, exit at the main Trinidad exit and head into town on Main Street. About 0.2 mile into town, Main Street curves sharply left, becoming Stagecoach Road. Follow Stagecoach Road 0.1 mile to the end, then turn right onto Edwards Street. Continue another 0.3 mile down to the large gravel Sandy Beach parking lot. The trailhead is on the southeast corner of the parking lot, where steps head up the hill. *DeLorme: Northern California Atlas & Gazetteer:* Page 32, D2.

The Hike

Looming large from the Sandy Beach parking lot on the edge of town, Trinidad Head just begs to be explored. The shaggy dome of rock, with its covering of thick coastal scrub vegetation, juts out into the pounding waves of the sea like a balled fist, shielding the fishing boats in tiny Trinidad Harbor from the worst the misnamed Pacific Ocean has to offer. It is also a darned good place for a lighthouse, which is why they built one there in 1871. The historic building is still used by the Coast Guard today, although it has been automated since 1974. The structure is fairly short and squat for a lighthouse, gaining any needed elevation from its position high on the head.

There is a road leading to the lighthouse, but unfortunately, it's closed to public traffic. The first portion *is* open to foot traffic, however. And it is up this steep road that the hike leads, after having climbed a series of steps from the Sandy Beach parking lot. The road makes a switchback before long, and the hike continues around a

Little Head, with Trinidad in the background

Trinidad Head Loop

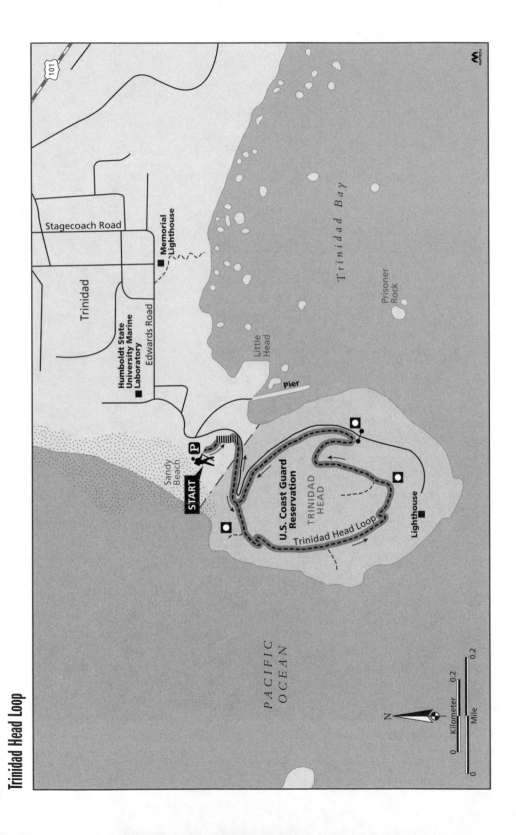

more level singletrack path. Several benches are strung out along the western side of the loop, allowing hikers to stop and enjoy the view on days when there is one. Fog is an equally likely proposition, but the eerie mood created by hiking in such conditions makes up for the loss of scenery.

When the trail reaches its southern apex, the lighthouse's squat tower can be seen far below to the right of the trail. A small viewing platform has been built to improve the view of the structure, but it can still be disappointing. For those who want to get a better idea of what it looks like close up, check out the duplicate lighthouse built by the town in 1948. It is located on the cliff along Edwards Road, right in town, and houses the lighthouse's original fourth-order Fresnel lens and fog bell.

Just above the viewing platform is a stone cross, set here by a local women's club in 1913. The monument marks the spot where Spanish explorers landed on Trinity Sunday back in 1775. The spot was named Trinidad for the holy day, and the land was formally claimed for Spain prior to the Spaniards' departure. The local Yurok population, which occupied a small village called Tsurai just below and to the east of the memorial lighthouse, might have had other ideas. Fortunately for them, it would be at least fifty years before another white man showed up, and nearly seventy-five before the inevitable ugliness of white settlement rolled in.

From the monument the trail heads up the grassy clearing to a gravel road, which leads down to the paved lighthouse access road. The access road is gated just above where the trail comes out, and a wide turnaround across the road offers some excellent views of the quaint little harbor. To the right a large offshore rock can be seen guarding the entrance to the bay. Known as Prisoner Rock, it was once used as a handy spot to deposit rowdy drunks for the night. To the left is Trinidad's fishing pier, flanked by a smaller dome of rock known as Little Head. For fans of aquatic mammals, the pier is a good spot to view harbor seals. A family of river otters has also made the harbor its home, and the playful critters can often be seen dining on scraps cast into the water by returning fishermen. The pier can be accessed from the trailhead by following the road down to the right.

From the overlook the trail follows the paved access road down past the loop junction to the wooden stairs, and from there to the trailhead.

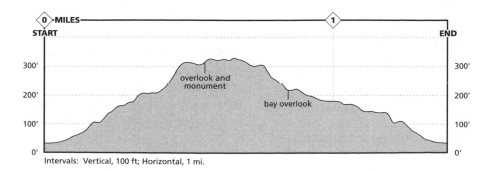

Intervals: Vertical, 100 ft; Horizontal, 1 mi.

Miles and Directions

0.0 Start at the bottom of the steps in the southeast corner of the parking lot. Climb the stairs, then head right on the paved road.

0.2 At the bend in the road, continue straight on the singletrack path. An overlook and a couple of benches are on the right, shortly after the junction.

0.25 A spur trail heads right to another vista point. Follow the main trail to the left.

0.3 The trail climbs a couple of switchbacks.

0.4 An overlook with more benches is alongside the trail.

0.5 A spur trail heads right up and out to a point. Continue straight on the main trail. Some benches are on the left.

0.6 The trail leaves the cliff and switches back inland a little.

0.7 The trail tops out at a clearing with a large stone cross monument. Below to the right is a small wooden platform, from which the old lighthouse and a wooden water tank can be seen far below. The trail turns left at the cross, heading uphill. When you reach the gravel road, turn right and head down the road.

0.9 The gravel road dead-ends onto a paved road. To the right is the gated entrance to the Coast Guard area. Straight ahead is a viewpoint overlooking Trinidad Bay. Turn left and head down the paved road.

1.2 The road meets the dirt path, which began the loop. Continue down the paved road to the stairs and trailhead.

1.4 Trailhead.

Hike Information

Local Information

Trinidad Chamber of Commerce, Trinidad; (707) 677-1610.
Humboldt County Convention and Visitors Bureau, Eureka; (800) 346-3482; (707) 443-5097; www.redwoodvisitor.org.

Local Events/Attractions

Clam Beach Run & Walk, 5-mile run/walk, and 3-mile or 8.75-mile challenges from Trinidad to McKinleyville; (707) 677-1610; www.trinidadtoclambeach.com.
Cher-Ae-Heights Casino, Trinidad; (707) 677-3611; (800) 684-2464; www.cheraeheightscasino.com.
Trinidad Bay Charters, ocean-fishing charters, Trinidad; (707) 839-4743; (800) 839-4744 (CA only).
Trinidad Art & Fish Festival, held in June, tasty barbecue—deep-fried white fish and salmon dinners with coleslaw, beans, and bread—arts and crafts, entertainment, children's entertainment, plant sale, tours, Trinidad; (707) 677-1610.

Lodging

There is a campground at the nearby Patrick's Point State Park, 4150 Patrick's Point Drive, Trinidad; (707) 677-3570. Several hotels and rental cabins are also nearby.

Restaurants

Moonstone Grill, fine seafood dining (pricey, but very good), Westhaven; (707) 677-1616.

Other Resources

The Four Ages of Tsurai, by Robert F. Heizer and John E. Mills. A documentary book covering the history of the Yurok Indian village at Trinidad.

16 Arcata Community Forest Loop

A leisurely jaunt through second-growth redwood forest along gravel and dirt tracks, just a stone's throw from the quirky college town of Arcata. Plenty of clearings and small meadows provide contrast to the deep shadows of the forest, and numerous connecting trails are available to customize the hike.

Start: At #3 trailhead.
Distance: 4-mile lollipop.
Approximate hiking time: 1.5 to 2 hours.
Difficulty: Easy to moderate, due to some steep sections.
Trail surface: Gravel road, dirt road, and dirt path.
Lay of the land: Steep, rolling hills with second-growth redwoods and small meadows.
Other trail users: Mountain bikers and equestrians (only on portions of the trail), Frisbee golfers.
Canine compatibility: Dogs permitted.
Land status: City-owned forest.

Nearest town: Arcata.
Fees and permits: No fees or permits required.
Schedule: Open year-round.
Maps: USGS maps: Arcata South, CA; Arcata North, CA.
Trail contact: Department of Environmental Services, Arcata; (707) 822-8184; www.arcatacityhall.org.
  The Arcata Community Forest hosts volunteer work days to do trail work, plant trees, and remove invasive species. Call for more information.

Finding the trailhead: From downtown Arcata, take G Street north and turn right on 14th Street. Cross the bridge over U.S. Highway 10 and continue east on 14th Street until it enters the Arcata Community Forest. When the road makes a sharp bend to the right, park at the gravel turnout on the side of the road. The trailhead is at the bulletin board on the east side of the road, just at the bend. *DeLorme: Northern California Atlas & Gazetteer:* Page 42, A-B 3.

The Hike

Tucked up against the progressive little college town of Arcata is a jumble of densely forested hills that represent an ongoing experiment in modern silviculture. Dedicated in 1955, the Arcata Community Forest was originally acquired by the city as a source of drinking water, which was collected by building small reservoirs on the creeks flowing through the forest. This function became obsolete when Arcata began drawing water from the nearby Mad River in 1964, but the community forest has continued to serve the city as a source of education, wildlife habitat, sustainably harvested timber revenue, and numerous recreational opportunities.

When you consider the town as a whole, it is little wonder that Arcata came up with such a creative use of its neighboring forests. Aside from the resident academia of Humboldt State University, Arcata is home to a thriving community of artists, aging hippies, and eclectic small businesses that give the town its particular flavor and

Fern on an old-growth redwood

shape its left-of-center politics. Beneath the bohemian surface, however, lies an older
cultural layer of rural conservatism that is represented by the descendants of the original white settlers, who first came to this area in the 1850s. These are the logging and
ranching folk, who look skeptically on the doings of most modern Arcatans and—
unlike most of "that bunch"—can brag of being born here.

Whatever the old-timers might think, it has been the successive waves of former
students and free spirits that have made Arcata what it is today. Aside from the community forest, the town's most visible evidence of its forward thinking is the Arcata
Marsh and Wildlife Sanctuary. The 154-acre marsh is a combination park/wastewater
treatment plant/wildlife refuge that was created in the early 1980s on land that had
formerly housed a sawmill and landfill. As the first project of its kind, the marsh uses
a series of plant-filled ponds in conjunction with a small sewage treatment plant to
filter the city's wastewater prior to being released into Humboldt Bay. Along the way
it has changed the landscape from an urban wasteland populated mainly by feral cats
and seagulls to a wildlife sanctuary that is home to more than 200 resident and seasonal bird species.

Although there are several walking trails in the marsh, it is the 600-plus acres of
the community forest that provide the main local attraction for hikers. Thanks to a

Arcata Community Forest Loop

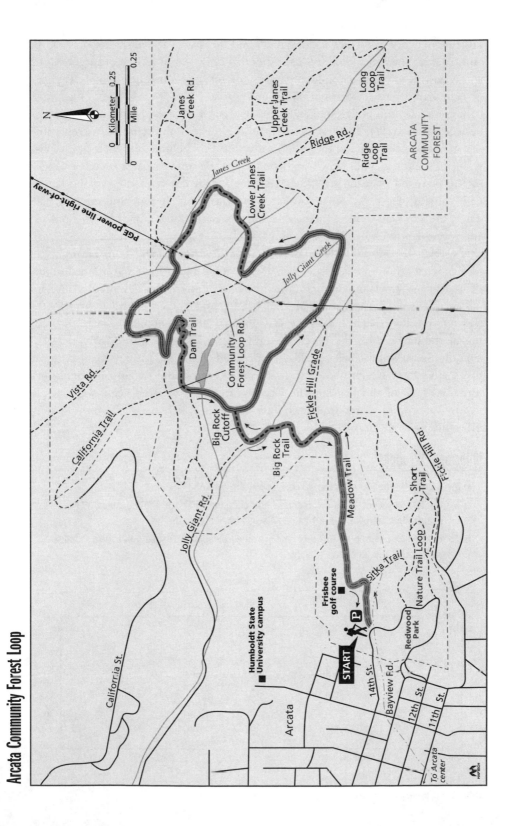

10-mile network of former logging roads and dirt paths, a variety of routes can be constructed. The route chosen for this book is only one of several possibilities, and it was chosen to create a good sampling of the forest in a medium-length day hike.

The trail begins at a turnout on the access road to Redwood Park, a large grassy park complete with playground and picnic tables, which provides the main interface between city dwellers and the forest. From the turnout, the trail heads steeply into the woods, quickly leaving the sounds of civilization behind and entering the lush realm of mature second-growth redwood forest. Because this area has been logged in the past, and occasionally still is, the forest does not have the pristine feel of national and state parks. Roads are closed to the public but are still used by staff. There are also signs of recent harvesting activity, in the form of fairly fresh log decks and forest debris left behind by logging.

Nevertheless, there is plenty of natural beauty around, and the visitor gets an idea of what an alternative to the usual "either thrash it or lock it away" dichotomy of land management might be. With the Arcata option, the community forest is managed equally for recreation, natural habitat, and timber. In order to make the first two possible, timber harvesting (last done in 2000) is done sustainably, according to the standards of the Forest Stewardship Council—and thus earns the eco-friendly SmartWood label. In addition, proceeds from the timber sales go into a forest trust fund, which is used to maintain the forest and to purchase additional forest land. As of this writing, the city was in the process of acquiring acres of nearby forest from a large timber company. With any luck, there will soon be even more hiking to do in Arcata.

Miles and Directions

0.0 Start at the trailhead for the #3 Trail. Follow the dirt road steeply uphill.

0.1 The trail levels out at a small meadow and becomes dirt path. The #2 Trail heads straight, but we follow the #3 Trail as it switchbacks up to the left.

0.15 The trail tops out on a ridge and enters a small clearing. A Frisbee golf course is below and around you. Continue straight.

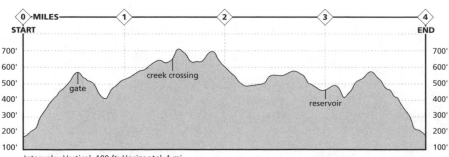

Intervals: Vertical, 100 ft; Horizontal, 1 mi.

0.3 An unmarked trail heads down to the right. Continue on #3 as it curves to the right.

0.35 Another unmarked trail heads off to the left. Continue straight, passing through an open log deck/clearing.

0.4 An unmarked trail forks off to the left. Continue along the right fork.

0.5 At the gate, turn left onto the gravel road (#9 Trail) and continue to the first curve, then turn left again onto the dirt path #4 Trail.

0.65 At the short signpost turn right, following #4 Trail.

0.7 An unmarked trail heads right. Continue left as the trail switchbacks and heads down a few steps. Cross the creek via a small footbridge.

0.75 Turn right onto #16 Trail, heading uphill.

0.85 #16 Trail dead-ends onto a gravel road (#8 Trail). Turn right onto #8.

1.2 The trail tops out, and an unmarked trail heads left. Continue straight.

1.25 Take the left fork.

1.3 The #9 Trail heads downhill to the right, but we continue to the left on #8 Trail. The trail then passes beneath a high-voltage power line.

1.5 The trail crosses the upper reaches of Jolly Giant Creek

1.65 The #12 Trail heads off to the right. Continue straight on #8.

1.75 Turn right onto #6 Trail (dirt path), heading down several steps.

1.85 Cross a stream via a small bridge.

2.0 The trail jogs left into the path of an old trail, crosses a sagging culvert, then jogs right again, heading up some steps.

2.1 The trail begins to follow a creek.

2.35 At the clearing (under the power line again), turn left onto the gravel #11 Trail.

2.55 The #10 Trail heads off to the right. Take the left fork, following the #11 Trail.

2.65 The #8 Trail heads right. Continue to the left on the #11 Trail, heading uphill.

2.7 Turn right onto the #15 Trail (dirt path), heading up a couple of steps to the ridge, then down the other side.

2.9 A large snag (dead tree) is on the left. The trail makes a sharp left, then another right at the edge of a cliff.

3.0 An old reservoir is on the left. At the junction, turn left onto the #8 Trail, crossing the earthwork dam.

3.1 Turn right onto the #16 Trail, retracing your route to the trailhead.

4.0 Trailhead.

Hike Information

Local Information

Arcata Chamber of Commerce, Arcata; (707) 822-3619; fax: (707) 822-3515; chamber@ arcatachamber.com.
Humboldt County Convention and Visitors Bureau, Eureka; (800) 346-3482; (707) 443-5097; www.redwoodvisitor.org.

Local Events/Attractions

Arcata Marsh and Wildlife Sanctuary, guided tours most Saturdays, excellent bird-watching, several walking trails, and great views of Humboldt Bay, Marsh Interpretive Center, Arcata; (707) 826-2359.

Godwit Days, held in April, annual bird-watching conference, with docent-led tours, speakers, workshops, and more, Arcata; (707) 822-4500.

Humboldt International Film Festival, held in April, in the historic Minor Theater, downtown Arcata; (707) 826-4113.

Kinetic Sculpture Race, held Memorial Day weekend, a three-day race with wacky people-powered vehicles, beginning on the Arcata Plaza at noon and following a course over roads, dunes, open water, and mud slopes to the finish line 38 miles away in historic Ferndale; (707) 786-9259.

Oyster Festival, held in June on the plaza, Humboldt Bay oysters prepared by local restaurants and served with live music, Arcata; (707) 822-4500.

Pastels on the Plaza, held in October, local artists paint the plaza sidewalks for charity, Arcata; (707) 822-7206.

Lodging

Hotel Arcata, a historic building directly on the plaza, Arcata; (800) 344-1221; (707) 826-0217.

Northern Redwoods Bed & Breakfast Association; (707) 443-8119.

Eureka KOA campground, Eureka; (707) 822-4243.

Mad River Rapids RV Park, Arcata; (707) 822-7275.

Restaurants

Don's Donut Bar & Deli, donuts at all hours, Arcata; (707) 822-6465.

Live From New York, great pizza, Arcata; (707) 822-6199.

Los Bagels, quick Jewish/Mexican cuisine, Arcata; (707) 822-3150.

Wildflower Cafe & Bakery, Arcata; (707) 822-0360.

17 Headwaters Forest Trail

A decent hike up through second-growth forest to the fringe of one of Northern California's newest and most politically charged parks: the Headwaters Preserve. The trail explores some history early on, passing by the site of Falk—once a flourishing logging boomtown, and now in the process of being rapidly reclaimed by the forest. Farther up, the path leads to the edge of an old-growth grove saved from clear-cutting by the efforts of environmental activists, public outcry, and political dealing. The preserve was created in the late 1990s, but there is a cloud to this silver lining....

Start: From the Headwaters Trail trailhead.
Distance: 11.2 miles out and back.
Approximate hiking time: 4 to 5 hours.
Difficulty: Moderate, due to steep hills on the second half of the hike.
Trail surface: Pavement, gravel road, and dirt road.
Lay of the land: Riparian lowland and steep, forested hills.
Other trail users: Hikers only.
Canine compatibility: Leashed dogs permitted.

Land status: Bureau of Land Management land.
Nearest town: Eureka.
Fees and permits: No fees or permits required.
Schedule: Open year-round.
Maps: USGS maps: McWhinney Creek, CA; Fields Landing, CA.
Trail contact: Bureau of Land Management, Arcata; (707) 825-2300; www.ca.blm.gov/arcata/headwaters.html.

Finding the trailhead: From Eureka, take U.S. Highway 101 to the south end of Eureka, exit left (east) onto Herrick Road, then turn right onto Elk River Road. Follow Elk River Road south 1.7 miles to a fork in the road. Take the right fork (still Elk River Road) and continue another 3.4 miles to a bend in the road with a bridge on the right. Turn right, crossing over the bridge, and continue another 0.9 mile (still on Elk River Road) until the road dead-ends at the Headwaters Forest Reserve parking area. The trail starts at the bulletin board on the left. *DeLorme: Northern California Atlas & Gazetteer:* Page 42, C3.

The Hike

There are at least two major reasons why people come to the Headwaters Forest Reserve—to see the land at the heart of the Headwaters controversy and to visit the former town of Falk. The town is referred to as the former town of Falk because it is, for all practical purposes, no longer there. From roughly 1884 to 1937, Falk was a bustling little mill town where loggers scrambled to convert acres of old-growth forest into lumber to be sold in distant ports. But all that remain now are the wild-looking, overgrown remnants of once-orderly orchards and a pair of ornamental yew trees that once guarded the walkway to someone's front door.

The town gets its name from Noah Falk, a latecomer to the Gold Rush who moved west in 1854. Upon his arrival, Falk was promptly recruited as a carpenter

Northwest view of the coast and Eureka from the vista

for a new sawmill in Mendocino. He later married and in 1867 moved to Eureka with his new bride. Falk was hoping to make a career as a baker here. But once again, he got sidetracked with an offer of employment from Eureka's leading citizen, William Carson, the timber baron whose mansion still stands as the town's milestone of Victorian architecture. Falk worked for the Carson Lumber Company in Eureka for two years before venturing into the lumber business for himself, creating Falk, Chandler & Co. He ran several successful milling operations before finally beginning work in a valley just southeast of Eureka, along the Little South Fork of the Elk River. The sawmill built in that valley came to be known by the Falk name, as did the bustling town that sprung up around the mill. A spur railroad was built to carry the freshly milled lumber to Bucksport—now part of Eureka— where it was loaded onto ships for transportation south. With a forest full of trees at hand and a ready transportation system to ferry lumber to the coast, the Falk Mill was soon a hive of activity.

At its peak the town was home to around 400 people, including mill workers and their families. But the mill was closed in 1937. With no other reason for people to stay, the population quickly dwindled. By 1979 Falk was a ghost town, and landowners burned and bulldozed the last remaining structures to avoid paying liability insurance.

The Headwaters Trail starts at the newly constructed trailhead and follows the old road—now closed to all but pedestrian traffic—for about a mile, past blackberries and alders, to the old town site. A leaflet that points out some of the more obvious signs of former life here can be picked up at the trailhead. A sign marks the meadow that was once the center of Falk. From here the trail continues southeast into the heart of the preserve. Watch your step, as the path's surface soon switches from asphalt to gravel, and, eventually, to dirt.

People who continue past the Falk town site generally do so to get a glimpse of what sparked the so-called Headwaters Deal hubbub. Details of the land venture—far less quaint than the particulars of the Falk tale—involve years of heated debate and protest demonstrations that are still fresh in local residents' minds. The controversy centers on the Headwaters Grove, a nearly 3,000-acre grove of old-growth redwoods located in the hills just east of Fortuna. The grove, which lies between isolated forests in Humboldt Redwoods State Park and Redwood National Park, is an important link for the gene pools of plants and animals in those two areas. The grove provides critical habitat for the endangered marbled murrelet and shelters the headwaters that are home to the equally threatened coho salmon.

In the early 1980s, Headwaters Grove was the largest unprotected stand of old-growth redwoods in the world and belonged to the Pacific Lumber Company. Over the years, Pacific Lumber had developed a reputation as an environmentally responsible company, with practices that were a model of sustainable forestry. That was before 1985, however—the year Charles Hurwitz's MAXXAM Corporation acquired the Pacific Lumber Company in a hostile takeover. In addition to looting the company's pension fund and selling off major assets, Hurwitz stepped up logging in an effort to pay off the huge debt incurred by the takeover. Pacific Lumber's forestry practices changed. The company began using clear-cuts as the preferred cutting method and applying diesel-based herbicides to the cleared slopes. Environmentalists were horrified and began seeking ways to protect the remaining old-growth groves. With the help of sympathetic lawmakers, several attempts were made beginning in 1989 to pass legislation authorizing the purchase of the groves for public parkland. But the Headwaters forest contained prized old-growth groves, worth millions as lumber, and Pacific Lumber was in no mood to part with the trees so easily. In 1995 Pacific Lumber announced it would begin logging in the Headwaters, at which point things immediately began heating up. Activists took to the woods—while the Environmental Protection Information Center and the Sierra Club took to the courtroom—in an attempt to stop the logging. A series of court battles ensued, which delayed the logging but failed to win lasting protection for the Headwaters.

Finally, in late 1996 MAXXAM and government officials reached a complex agreement. It involved money—lots of it—and included a Habitat Conservation

Headwaters Forest Trail

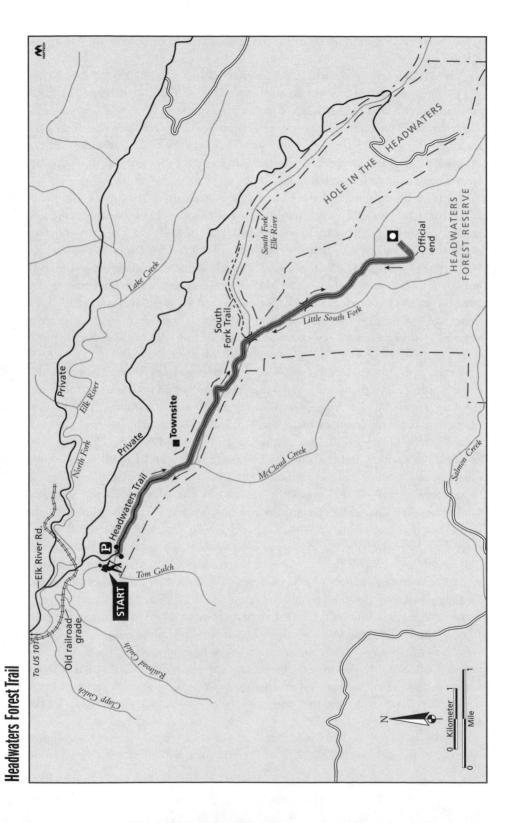

MAPTECH

HOLE IN THE HEADWATERS

South Fork Elk River

South Fork Trail

Little South Fork

Official end

HEADWATERS FOREST RESERVE

Salmon Creek

McCloud Creek

Townsite

Private

Elk River

North Fork

Lake Creek

Private

Headwaters Trail

Tom Gulch

P

START

Elk River Rd.

To US 101

Old railroad grade

Railroad Gulch

Clapp Gulch

N

0   Kilometer   1

0   Mile   1

Plan and Sustained Yield Plan that would cover Pacific Lumber's remaining forest-land. It took three years to hammer out the agreement, and the deal was finally sealed in the spring of 1999. State and federal governments purchased the Headwaters Grove, along with 5,000 acres of second growth and a smaller old-growth grove, for $380 million. Ironically, the final plan was bitterly opposed by many environmentalists because it left out several small groves of old-growth forest and gave Pacific Lumber permission to "take" (or carry out operations that may result in the death of) endangered species on its remaining land. Perhaps the biggest environmental sticking point with the deal, however, was the so-called Hole in the Headwaters area—a 1,000-acre parcel of land within the Headwaters Forest Reserve that may still be logged by Pacific Lumber. Inclusion of the hole has prompted many environmentalists to continue fighting the Headwaters deal.

The trail leads past Falk into second-growth forest, climbing a series of steep slopes into the heart of the preserve and ending on the northern fringe of the Headwaters Grove. The turnaround point is a vista point—an old logging deck—which offers a view over Eureka to the northwest and Hole in the Headwaters to the north. Return the way you came.

Miles and Directions

0.0 Start at the Bulletin Board. Follow the paved Headwaters Trail east through an alder forest.

0.1 (FYI: Cherry trees can be seen on the left side of the trail. These trees once grew in the gardens of Falk residents. The houses are gone, but the trees remain.)

0.3 (FYI: The pair of yews on the right once flanked the entrance to someone's front yard. A cement paving stone can be seen between the yews.)

0.6 The trail surface changes from pavement to gravel.

1.0 (FYI: The town of Falk once occupied the clearing to the left and the surrounding lands. The forest is encroaching rapidly on the town site, and almost nothing remains of the buildings.)

2.8 (FYI: An old truck has found a resting place in the underbrush on the right. During the protests that led to Headwaters Grove being saved from logging, protestors pushed this vehicle into the road to block logging equipment.)

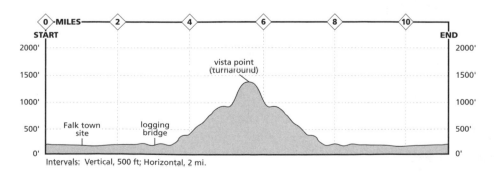

Intervals: Vertical, 500 ft; Horizontal, 2 mi.

THE KINETIC SCULPTURE RACE

Way back in 1969, Ferndale artist Hobart Brown converted his son's tricycle into a mobile sculpture. Intrigued, a metal-sculpting friend built his own contraption and challenged Brown to a race. One thing led to another, and by the time race day rolled around, twelve contestants found themselves locomoting down Main Street in a variety of human-powered monstrosities, to the cheers and laughter of the assembled townsfolk. The Kinetic Sculpture Race was born!

The race was a resounding success, and it became a yearly event in Ferndale, until the crowds drawn by the spectacle began to outgrow the tiny dairy hamlet. The start of the event moved from Ferndale to Eureka, finally settling on college town Arcata, while the length of the course grew from its original 3-block street run to the present 3-day, 38-mile Tour-de-Farce. Entries must now be land-, sea-, and sand-worthy, in addition to being totally people-powered— as they are required to traverse streets and dunes and to make three water crossings, including a stretch of Humboldt Bay with more than a mile of open water! Over the past thirty years, the Kinetic Sculpture Race has spawned similar events in other cities, and even in countries as far away as Australia.

The race takes place over the three days of Memorial Day weekend, beginning on the Plaza in Arcata, making two mandatory evening stops, and ending the third day where it all began, in downtown Ferndale. Entries have become very sophisticated, with decorated multiperson human-powered sculpture/vehicles of breathtaking design racing alongside last-minute garage contraptions made of leftover bicycle parts. The only limits to creativity are the laws of street and nautical legality, as presided over by the local police and coast guard. Volunteer Kinetic Kops ensure the race's often bizarre and zany rules are obeyed, although bribery is not only permitted but also encouraged—as attested by the awarding of the Best Bribe prize at race's end. Other awards include Best Performance, Best Costume, the Outrageous Award, and Worst Honorable Mention.

For more information on the Kinetic Sculpture Race, call (707) 786-9259 or visit www.humguide.com/kinetic.

3.0 South Fork Trail goes left along the narrow strip that hems in the Hole in the Headwaters. Continue to the right on the main trail, which changes from gravel to dirt.

3.1 Cross the steel logging bridge over the South Fork Elk River. The trail heads steeply uphill from here, and the going can be slippery and muddy after heavy rains.

3.8 Cross another logging bridge, continuing uphill.

5.0 The old bridge that used to span this creek has been removed. Follow the narrow footpath down to the right. Cross the creek and follow the footpath back up the other bank until it rejoins the road. Continue uphill on the road.

5.4 An old log deck is visible on the right. (FYI: In the logging days, this was used as a place to stack logs, prior to loading them onto trucks for transport to the sawmills.)

5.5 This is the official end of the trail. You can catch a glimpse of the old-growth Headwaters Grove straight ahead. Follow the road as it curves left to the vista point.

5.6 Reach the vista point. This is another old logging deck, next to a recovering clear-cut. Due to the lack of trees, to the left there is a good view of the ocean and the south end of Eureka. Straight ahead, on the other side of the ridge, is the "Hole in the Headwaters." This spot is the turnaround point for the hike. Return the way you came.

11.2 Arrive back at the trailhead.

Hike Information

Local Information
Eureka Chamber of Commerce, Eureka; (800) 356-6381; (707) 442-3738; www.eurekachamber.com.
Humboldt County Convention and Visitors Bureau, Eureka; (800) 346-3482; (707) 443-5097.

Local Events/Attractions
Redwood Acres Fair, held in late June, rodeo, stock-car racing, carnival rides, and live music, Eureka; (707) 443-3037.
Blues by the Bay, held in mid-July, two-day blues festival, Eureka; (707) 445-3378.

Restaurant
Roy's Club, Eureka; (707) 442-4574.

Hike Tours
Bureau of Land Management, Arcata; (707) 825-2300. Rangers guide hikers to Falk and to the edge of Headwaters Grove from the south.

Organizations
North Coast Earth First, Arcata; (707) 825-66598; www.treesfoundation.org/affiliates—Bay Area Coalition for Headwaters (BACH).

18 Hookton Slough Trail

This short hike is an excursion into a landscape loved by wildlife but rarely visited by humans: the coastal wetland. Birders especially will find plenty to marvel at along this trail, which follows a historic dike out through the marsh along Hookton Slough, itself a branch of Humboldt Bay.

Start: Hookton Slough trailhead.
Distance: 3 miles out and back.
Approximate hiking time: 1.5 to 2 hours.
Difficulty: Easy, due to wide trail and no elevation gain.
Trail surface: Gravel road.
Lay of the land: Marshy saltwater and freshwater wetlands bordering the bay.
Other trail users: Bird-watchers.
Canine compatibility: No dogs allowed.

Land status: National wildlife refuge.
Nearest town: Eureka.
Fees and permits: None.
Schedule: Open year-round during daylight hours.
Map: USGS map: Fields Landing, CA.
Trail contact: Humboldt Bay National Wildlife Refuge, Loleta; (707) 733-5406; pacific.fws.gov/humboldtbay.

Finding the trailhead: From Eureka, take U.S. Highway 101 south 7 miles to the Hookton Road exit. Leave the highway, and at the stop sign continue straight on Hookton Road for another mile. Turn right onto the gravel Hookton Slough access road and follow it 0.1 mile to the parking area. *DeLorme: Northern California Atlas & Gazetteer:* Page 42, C2.

The Hike

On the surface, the Hookton Slough Trail isn't much to look at. A layperson could be forgiven for thinking there was nothing much there but a bunch of soggy meadows and a few levees. Sure, the view is pleasant enough along the winding course of the trail's namesake waterway, and Humboldt Bay offers a nice panorama at trail's end. But the landscape tucked in between the rolling pastureland of Table Bluff and the backwaters of the bay would hardly be described as spectacular. Still, appearances can be deceiving.

For one thing, there are the birds. Friends of the finely feathered will be happy to rattle off lists of shorebirds, waterfowl, seabirds, and other flying critters that can regularly be seen in the refuge. In all, well more than 200 species of bird, including 4 endangered species, make their home in the refuge for at least part of the year. Migratory birds such as the black brant and marbled godwit are attracted to the extensive eelgrass beds and rich mudflats of Humboldt Bay, while raptors such as the peregrine falcon simply like to chase the other birds. The eelgrass habitat here is some of the best south of Alaska, making the bay a prime stopover along the Pacific Flyway migration route. Fittingly, the bird-*watchers* are also migratory, with hundreds flocking to the area every year for the annual Godwit Days, when

Black-tailed deer along a side ditch

walking and boating tours of Hookton Slough are a perennial favorite for festival participants.

In considering the hike's aesthetic value, it should also be mentioned that—unlike in a park, where conservation is given equal priority with human recreation—the land managers of a wildlife refuge are concerned first and foremost with the well-being of the resource. After all, a bird doesn't care what a place looks like, as long as there is plenty to eat and a safe place to perch. Mother Nature, being an accomplished exterior decorator, can usually make landscapes both pretty *and* useful, but humans often have a harder time of it.

Humboldt Bay National Wildlife Refuge is comprised of multiple units scattered around the bay, totaling some 3,500 acres of protected habitat. The Salmon Creek and Hookton Slough units that together make up the southernmost portion of the refuge encompass more than 1,200 acres of wetland.

Prior to being included in the wildlife refuge system, the land was converted from the original salt marsh to agricultural land in the 1880s. Many of the dikes and ditches date from this period, as the marsh was drained and turned into grasslands

Hookton Slough Trail

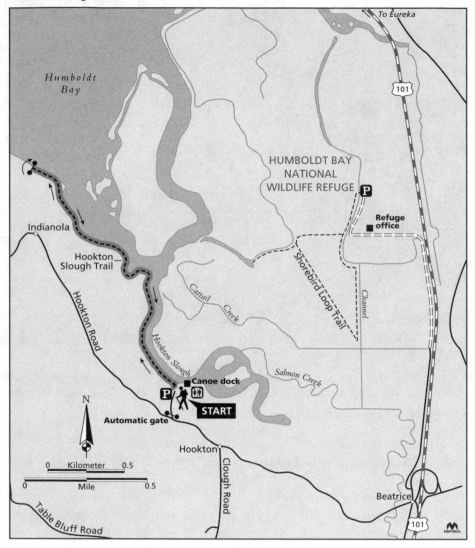

for grazing cattle. When the feds took over, they set about restoring the land to create a variety of habitats. Mostly, this meant working with the natural drainage patterns to create seasonally flooded marshes, permanent ponds, and tidal zones. Surprisingly, it also meant regularly mowing some areas in imitation of cattle grazing, since short-grass areas appeal to some species, including Aleutian geese. Today the refuge is home to many species of animal besides the birds, ranging from porcupine and mink to harbor seal and leopard shark. Take a closer look as you walk the Hookton Slough Trail, and you will probably see abundant signs of this diverse fauna.

From the trailhead the hike heads due west along the dike bordering Hookton Slough. The dike is topped by a gravel road used occasionally by refuge staff but closed to the public. As you work your way slowly out to the point, several interpretive signs appear periodically, going into greater depth about some of the natural cycles and wild residents of the refuge. The trail's turnaround point is a locked gate at the point where the dike rejoins dry land, near where Hookton Slough meets Humboldt Bay. Return the way you came to the trailhead.

Miles and Directions

0.0 Start at the kiosk on the west side of the parking lot. Head west along the dike.

0.4 (FYI: The posts on the water's edge have graduated markings to show the depth of the tides. An interpretive sign alongside the trail tells more about the tides in the slough.)

0.7 The trail arrives at a point of land. The slough splits here, flowing around the large island ahead and to the left. Another interpretive sign marks the spot.

0.8 The trail heads inland around a small cove.

1.3 At the interpretive sign about black brants, the slough opens up into Humboldt Bay. The trail veers left.

1.5 The locked gate is the turnaround point. Return the way you came. (FYI: The view straight ahead is of the bay's south spit, a long tongue of beach and dunes dividing the bay from the ocean. To the north the town of King Salmon and some of the bay's larger islands can be seen.)

3.0 Trailhead.

Hike Information

Local Information
Eureka Chamber of Commerce, Eureka; (800) 356-6381; (707) 442-3738; www.eurekachamber.com.
Humboldt County Convention and Visitors Bureau, Eureka; (800) 346-3482; (707) 443-5097.

Local Events/Attractions
Kinetic Sculpture Race, held Memorial Day weekend, from Arcata to Ferndale; (707) 786-9259; www.humguide.com/kinetic.

Redwood Acres Fair, held in late June, rodeo, stock-car racing, carnival rides, and live music, Eureka; (707) 443-3037.
Blues by the Bay, held in mid-July, two-day blues festival, Eureka; (707) 445-3378.

Hike Tours
Redwood Region Audubon Society, Eureka; (707) 826-7031; www.rras.org.

Honorable Mentions

Northern Humboldt

C Zig Zag Trail

Prairie Creek Redwoods State Park offers some of the easiest access to what are arguably the most impressive forests on the planet. This 3.9-mile loop is an excellent sampler of riparian (streamside) and drier ridgetop redwood habitats. The hike follows parts of the Prairie Creek Trail and the West Ridge Trail, connected by the aptly named Zig Zag No. 1 and Zig Zag No. 2 Trails. From Eureka, head north 47 miles on U.S. Highway 101. Exit onto Newton B. Drury Scenic Parkway and continue another 3.7 miles to the Rhododendron Trail Turnout and trailhead. Cross the road and head west into the forest on the marked trail. For more information contact Prairie Creek Redwoods State Park, Orick; (707) 464–6101, ext. 5301. *DeLorme: Northern California Atlas & Gazetteer:* Page 32, A3.

D Stone Lagoon Trail

A 3.4-mile out-and-back trail along the semipermanent sandbar separating Stone Lagoon from the ocean. The natural sand bridge makes for dramatic scenery, and hikers can choose between the roaring surf on the ocean side or the still waters of the lagoon side. Turnaround point for the hike is Sharp Point, an aptly named spike of rock that juts out into the waves, cutting off farther progress south along the beach. From Eureka, head north 38 miles on U.S. Highway 101. Between Stone Lagoon and Freshwater Lagoon, turn left onto the inconspicuous Stone Lagoon access road. Head down the hill 0.3 mile to the beach, and park in the sandy lot. For more information contact Humboldt Lagoons State Park, Trinidad; (707) 488–2041. *DeLorme: Northern California Atlas & Gazetteer:* Page 32, B3.

Southern Humboldt/ Mendocino

In the rough and tumble lands of Mendocino and Southern Humboldt Counties, the knot of coastal mountains lining the coast are divided in two by the broad Eel River Valley. The cut stretches in a nearly north-south direction from a point just south of Humboldt Bay down to central Mendocino County, at which point the south-flowing Russian River continues down along almost the same line. This "parting of the mountains" does more than just provide a convenient route for U.S. Highway 101. It also results in the creation of distinct microclimates within a relatively small geographic area. Directly on the coast, heavy fog and cool temperatures prevail. But the valley, which lies in the rain shadow of the intervening mountains, can be much drier and much hotter than on the coast. At higher elevations it is not uncommon to see snow in the area's thick forests during winter.

The vast, seemingly empty forests that make up large portions of this region have earned it the nickname "Redwood Curtain," behind which the small towns and isolated hamlets of Mendocino, Humboldt, and Del Norte Counties hide from the big-city atmosphere of the San Francisco Bay Area. These huge swaths of dark forest are tucked into steep valleys and ravines with unstable slopes and flood-prone rivers, all things that have considerably slowed the march of progress, if not the loggers' chain-saws—most of the land has been logged at least once, and much of it remains in the hands of private timber companies.

Still, there are enough exceptions to this rule that hikers will find plenty in the region to satisfy their wanderlust. In Southern Humboldt, centered around the twin towns of Garberville and Redway, several possibilities await. To the north Humboldt Redwoods State Park offers access to fully one-fifth of all remaining old-growth redwoods (a sobering thought). And to the west a veritable "land that time forgot" lies snoozing on the remote and rugged tract of land known as the Lost Coast. Here, row upon row of steep-sloped ridges march right up to the Pacific, creating a landscape as inhospitable to development as it is beautiful to behold. What's bad for the condo is good for the hiker, and several fine trails explore this lush and rugged landscape. Farther south along the same stretch of coast is Sinkyone Wilderness State Park. This hard-to-reach park is more than worth the effort involved to get there; it offers a narrow strip of meadows and elk-haunted forests, long-since-abandoned homesteads, and great hiking trails.

Mendocino County marks the beginning of a transition to a warmer, drier climate. Here the temperate rain-forest habitat that dominated up north begins to retreat, maintaining strongholds in the deep, shaded valleys and leaving more and more of the highlands to the golden grasslands and spare oak groves that are California's trademark. Travelers in this area follow two major routes: the inland river valley corridor of US 101; or the long, snaking ribbon of California Highway 1, which departs from US 101 near the Mendocino-Humboldt border, and traces the curves of the coastal bluffs as it makes its way south. The coastline here is a rugged and rocky shelf, riddled with natural bridges, sea caves, blowholes, and rock-studded coves. Numerous small state parks dot the bluffs, especially around Fort Bragg and the picturesque little town of Mendocino. The latter, perched out on a rocky headland, is partially surrounded by a park and offers a rare example of peacefully coexisting urban and natural landscapes.

19 Bull Creek Flats Loop

This trail takes hikers on a classic stroll through the Rockefeller Forest, one of the largest tracts of contiguous uncut coastal redwoods in the world. The path wanders among the majestic trees, many of which are individually named for peculiar traits—such as the Flatiron Tree, known for its distinctive cross section. Beneath the canopy, plant lovers will find a variety of floral gems, including giant horsetail, iris, blue blossom, and sweet-scented bedstraw.

Start: Big Tree parking area.
Distance: 9.2-mile loop.
Approximate hiking time: 4.5 hours.
Difficulty: Easy to moderate, due to long, flat trail.
Trail surface: Dirt path, packed gravel, and a tiny section of paved road.
Lay of the land: Old-growth and second-growth redwood forests and meadows.
Other trail users: Equestrians.

Canine compatibility: Dogs not permitted.
Land status: State park.
Nearest town: Fortuna.
Fees and permits: None.
Schedule: Open year-round. Footbridges over Bull Creek are removed for the winter season.
Maps: USGS maps: Weott, CA; Bull Creek, CA
Trail contact: Humboldt Redwoods State Park, Weott; (707) 946-2409; www.humboldt redwoods.org.

Finding the trailhead: From Eureka, head south 47 miles on U.S. Highway 101 to Humboldt Redwoods State Park. Exit at Mattole Road and turn right. Follow Mattole Road west 4.6 miles, and turn left at the sign for Rockefeller Forest: Tall Tree, Flatiron Tree, and Giant Tree. Follow this road 200 feet to the parking area. The trail begins at the bulletin board. *DeLorme: Northern California Atlas & Gazetteer:* Page 52, B4.

The Hike

This trail showcases some of the park's most spectacular plant life. The path begins at the Big Tree parking area and immediately crosses the creek to visit some of the forest's so-called celebrity trees. These "famous" redwoods are well-known for characteristics that make them special—even among the already unique trees. Among these stars are the Flatiron Tree, so named for its unusual cross section, and the Giant Tree, noted for its size. The Giant Tree was not the tallest redwood on record, but it was considered by some to be the world's champion redwood by virtue of its combined height, circumference, and crown size. Unfortunately, both of these trees have recently fallen.

Leaving these celebrity redwoods behind, the trail heads east through the heart of the Rockefeller Forest. Officially termed a temperate rain forest, this park has been shown to possess more than seven times the biomass of tropical rain forests. Biomass is the recorded sum of all living and dead organic material in a given place. And there is an estimated 1,800 tons of it per acre in the old-growth

Natural bridge over Bull Creek

stands of the park. From the dense mats of moss and ferns underfoot to the thick canopy suspended by the redwoods up to 350 feet overhead, almost everything you see here is—or was once—alive.

But the boundary between life and death in redwoods is difficult to pin down. Walking through the musty forest, you'll frequently see adult trees growing out of old trunks that are half-decayed and have long since fallen. Most of these are sprouts from the original tree and are genetically identical to it. Even when a log is rotten and completely dead, it is a host for a complex multitude of life—including an estimated 700 species of plants, lichen, mosses, and fungi; 3,228 different invertebrates; and a slew of various birds and mammals. Dead trees that remain upright, known as snags, provide vital habitat for 100-plus species of birds and mammals, including the famous spotted owl and the marbled murrelet.

Intermingled with the mammoth trees are a host of more abundant—if less impressive—plants, including redbud, Oregon grape, and maidenhair ferns. In moist, low-lying spots, you can find the unique giant horsetail. This plant looks like a relic of the dinosaur age. And as a matter of fact, it is. Horsetails have such high

Bull Creek Flats Loop

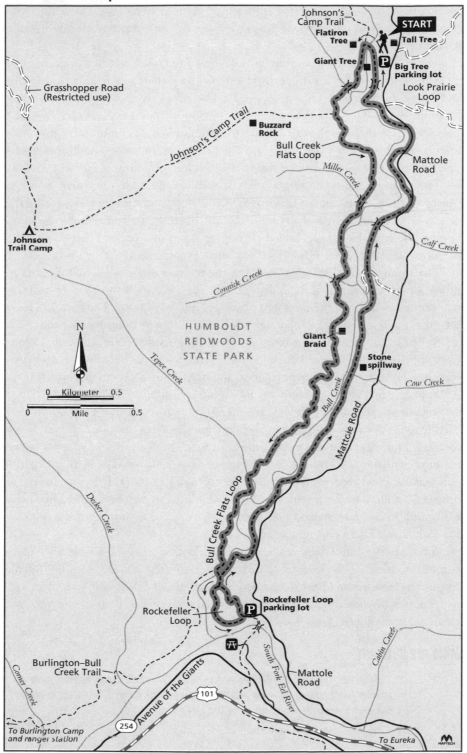

Johnson's Camp Trail
Flatiron Tree
START
Tall Tree
Giant Tree
Big Tree parking lot
Look Prairie Loop

Grasshopper Road (Restricted use)

Buzzard Rock

Johnson's Camp Trail

Bull Creek Flats Loop

Miller Creek

Mattole Road

Johnson Trail Camp

Calf Creek

Connick Creek

N

HUMBOLDT REDWOODS STATE PARK

Tepee Creek

Giant Braid

Stone spillway

Cow Creek

0   Kilometer   0.5
0   Mile   0.5

Bull Creek

Mattole Road

Bull Creek Flats Loop

Decker Creek

Rockefeller Loop parking lot

Rockefeller Loop

Cabin Creek

Burlington–Bull Creek Trail

Corner Creek

Avenue of the Giants

South Fork Eel River

Mattole Road

101

254

To Burlington Camp and ranger station

To Eureka

MAPTECH

silica content that early European settlers used them to scrub pots. Those same settlers found copious quantities of miner's lettuce, a plant named, obviously, because it's edible.

About 150 years ago—not long in the life of a redwood, which can grow to be 2,000 years old—the first European-Americans made their way to this remote area and found the Sinkyone-Lolangkok people. The tribe's name was taken from their location: Sin-ke-kok was the word for the South Fork of the Eel River, and Lolangkok, for Bull Creek—the later term distinguished this group from its southern cousins, the Shelter Cove Sinkiyone. The Lolangkok and other local tribes developed cultures that took full advantage of their region's abundant plant- and wildlife, without damaging those resources. The tribes subsisted largely on acorns from the nearby oak groves and salmon that spawn in area rivers and streams. Before using the acorns, the Lolangkok repeatedly ground and soaked the nuts to remove the bitter tannin. The end product was boiled as soup or baked into bread. These foods were supplemented with other plants, fish, and the occasional deer.

The Lolangkok also made good use of the region's native trees, finding ways to utilize almost every part of the redwood tree. They hollowed out the logs to form dugout canoes and split the trees into planks for building houses. The bark and roots served as cordage and basket-making material, as did many other native plants.

Sadly, the Lolangkoks suffered the same fate as most other California tribes. Confronted by land-hungry—and often violent—settlers, and the new diseases and alcohol they brought, the native population dwindled. Probably numbering close to 2,000 people in 1850, the population fell to just a handful by 1920.

Initially, the trees didn't fare much better. In the early part of the twentieth century, logging threatened to destroy the remaining ancient redwood groves. Some forward-thinking conservationists formed the Save-the-Redwoods League to combat the destruction. The group's goal was to purchase lands and turn them into parks. After taking a tour through the area, business tycoon J. D. Rockefeller was moved to donate $2 million to the league. The funds were used to purchase the 10,000 acres along Bull Creek, now named the Rockefeller Forest. It is through this forest that the Bull Creek Flats Loop wanders.

After crossing Bull Creek again, a side trail leads around the Rockefeller Loop before returning up the other side of the creek to the trailhead. This side of the stream has more second growth and several small glades laced with giant horsetail, sweet-scented bedstraw, and the ubiquitous redwood sorrel. Return the way you came, along the south bank of Bull Creek.

Miles and Directions

0.0 Start at the bulletin board in the Big Tree parking area. Cross Bull Creek, either via the temporary summer bridge or by wading in the off-season (be careful), and then follow Bull Creek Flats Loop as it heads left along the creek.

0.05 A spur trail to the right leads a few yards to the Flatiron Tree. Continue straight on Bull Creek Flats Loop.

0.2 Cross over a small creek on a wooden bridge.

0.3 Johnson's Camp Trail heads uphill to the right. Continue straight, keeping parallel to Bull Creek.

1.0 (FYI: The trail passes some good examples of hollow redwood logs, some of them big enough to walk through.)

1.4 Cross a small meadow, continuing straight.

1.7 The trail crosses a small bridge.

1.9 (FYI: Keep an eye out for the Giant Braid, standing alongside the trail. This living curiosity consists of three redwood trunks that have grown twisted together.)

3.3 The trail skirts the base of an enormous log, making what seems like a U-turn. Follow it anyway, because it eventually doubles back again

3.4 The trail begins to climb the only incline of the trail.

4.4 As the trail levels out, you can see the little floodplain (flat) of Bull Creek below to your left.

4.5 Burlington–Bull Creek Trail continues straight. Turn left and follow the Bull Creek Flats Loop down to the flat.

4.6 Cross Bull Creek. There is a large log conveniently down alongside the trail, spanning the creek in a natural bridge. Cross on the log or wade the creek. Once on the other side, Bull Creek Flats Loop heads left back up the other side of Bull Creek. Continue straight to explore the short Rockefeller Loop, which will return you to this junction shortly.

4.7 Rockefeller Loop begins here. Turn right and follow the trail through a prime redwood grove.

5.0 A log hanging over the trail has had an arch cut out of it, to allow easier passage for hikers.

5.1 To the right is the parking lot for the Rockefeller Loop. Continue straight on the trail.

5.4 Reach the end of Rockefeller Loop. Turn right and return to the junction with Bull Creek Flats Loop. At the junction, turn right and head upstream on Bull Creek Flats Loop.

6.6 (FYI: Passing close to the creek, the trail crosses a nice example of a stone spillway.)

7.2 The trail crosses a small bridge over a side stream.

8.2 The trail joins Mattole Road briefly. Continue straight on the road shoulder a few yards until the trail resumes, heading down to the left.

8.4 An unmarked trail veers off to the left. Continue along the right fork.

8.5 The trail joins Mattole Road again briefly. Continue straight along the road shoulder.

8.7 A picnic area has been set up in a turnout to the left of the road. Cross this open area and continue on Bull Creek Flats Loop as it enters the forest on the other side of the clearing. The trail enters the woods near the creek.

9.0 Cross a small wooden bridge.

9.2 Arrive back at the Big Tree parking area and trailhead.

Hike Information

Local Information

Humboldt County Convention and Visitors Bureau, Eureka; (800) 346–3482; (707) 443-5097.

Local Event/Attraction

Avenue of the Giants Marathon, held in May, near Humboldt Redwoods State Park, sponsored by the Six Rivers Running Club; (707) 766-3655.

Lodging

Humboldt Redwoods State Park, Weott; (800) 444-7275. There are three campgrounds within the park, with a combined total of 249 campsites, available on a first-come, first-served basis. Reservations are recommended during the peak season.

Hike Tour

Humboldt Redwoods State Park, Weott; (707) 946–2263. Ranger-guided walks are scheduled from time to time. Check with the visitor center for more information.

Other Resources

Humboldt Redwoods State Park: The Complete Guide, by Jerry and Gisela Rohde. Illustrations by Larry Eifert.

20 Mattole Beach Trail

This hike is a beach bum's paradise. The trail begins at the Mattole River Estuary and offers 3 miles of beautiful black sand beaches, dunes, and tide pools that lead to an abandoned lighthouse. Along the way, there is plenty of secluded beach to comb. Hiking beneath the cliffs at Punta Gorda can be dangerous at high tide, so be sure to consult a tide calendar and plan your hike during low tide. This information usually is posted at the trailhead.

Start: From the Mattole Estuary Campground and day-use area.
Distance: 6.2 mile out and back.
Approximate hiking time: 4 to 5 hours.
Difficulty: Easy to moderate, due to soft sand and stream crossings
Trail surface: Dirt, sand path.
Lay of the land: Grassy dunes, black sand beaches.
Other trail users: Equestrians and beach-combers.

Canine compatibility: Dogs permitted; however, the black sand beaches can be hard on paws.
Land status: Bureau of Land Management land.
Nearest town: Petrolia.
Fees and permits: $1.00 day-use fee; $5.00 camping fee.
Schedule: Open year-round.
Map: USGS map: Petrolia, CA.
Trail contact: Arcata Resource Area, Bureau of Land Management, Arcata; (707) 825-2300.

Finding the trailhead: From Eureka, head south 11 miles on U.S. Highway 101, leaving the highway at the Fernbridge/Ferndale exit. Turn right onto California Highway 211 and continue 4 miles through downtown Ferndale. Turn right onto Centerville Road, drive west 1 block, then turn left onto Mattole Road. Follow this windy road 28 miles south through forest and cattle range to the tiny town of Petrolia. Continue through town and across the Mattole River before turning right onto Lighthouse Road. Head west 5 miles to the campground and day-use area at the Mattole Estuary. The trail starts at the information board. *DeLorme: Northern California Atlas & Gazetteer:* Page 52, B1.

The Hike

Down at the end of Lighthouse Road near the tiny hamlet of Petrolia is a sandy little car-campground nestled in the dunes near the mouth of the Mattole River. A walk along the broad beach here reveals copious amounts of driftwood—some of it old stumps the size of an automobile. Many bird species frequent the estuary, and harbor seals often lounge about on nearby sandbars. From here, there are great views of the cliffs north toward Cape Mendocino.

At the southern end of the campground/parking lot is a bulletin board where fees are deposited and information gathered. From here the Mattole Beach Trail leads south past an archeological site and along the dunes before dropping hikers firmly onto the black sand beach that will serve as the trail for the remainder of the hike.

Site of the old village

Unlike many black sand beaches that have volcanic origins, this one, along with the hills above it, is made of crumbly sandstone called graywacke. Though actually dark gray, the sand appears black when wet, providing a stark contrast to the white foam of the surf that washes up onto the beach. The result is beautiful, but be warned: The graywacke is coarser than the quartz sand of other beaches, so people hiking barefoot should expect abrasions and sore feet. Even dogs are not immune and are likely to suffer tender paws if they are not used to the scratchy surface. Some hikers advise using canine booties if the dog is not accustomed to the rough turf or if you plan a longer walk along the coast.

Most of the hike is accessible at all times, but the area surrounding Punta Gorda can be hazardous at high tide, when the waves crash up against the cliffs. The ocean here is known for having treacherous riptides and undertows, and sneaker waves can suddenly sweep the unwary out to sea. So it's strongly advised that you pay attention to tide charts and plan your hike around them. The Arcata Bureau of Land Management office should be able to help you determine when it's safe to traverse the point, as well.

Mattole Beach Trail

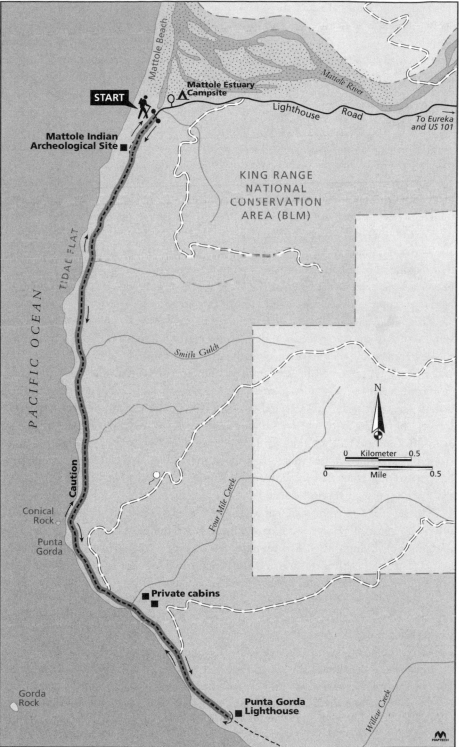

Aside from personal safety, there is another advantage to hiking at low tide—the chance to explore world-class tide pools in the exposed rocks below the beach.

▶ The first oil well in California was drilled in Petrolia in 1865, giving the town its first export— and its namesake—petroleum.

Convoluted crags and crevices create an ideal habitat for numerous mussels, urchins, and anemones, all easily observed in astounding numbers when the tide is out. Low tide also unveils a multitude of marine life, so plentiful that tidepoolers must be very careful not to step on anything that might object. High or low tide, hikers should watch their step when moving around on the slippery rocks and always keep an eye on incoming waves.

These rock habitats can be divided into five different zones based on the amount of time they're under water or exposed to air. The highest level is the *splash zone,* which is rarely under water but is kept wet by the splashing of the waves. This is mostly the domain of such shorebirds as the marbled godwit, black-bellied plover, and western sandpiper. A small crustacean called the rock louse also manages to live here as long as its gills are kept moist by the waves. Below the splash zone is the *high intertidal zone,* which is covered at high tide but exposed for long periods. Limpets, barnacles, and periwinkles can be found in this area.

The *middle intertidal zone* gets limited exposure to the air and has the strongest wave action of the five zones. Limpets, goose barnacles, mussels, and ochre sea stars thrive here because they have developed a means of hanging on to the rocks. Plants and animals that need to be wet most of the time inhabit the *low intertidal zone.* While these creatures require a lot of water, they can't be fully submerged in still waters. The intertidal creatures need waves to bring them food in the form of plankton, or they need to be close to sunlight. Some types of seaweed grow here, and anemones and urchins are present in large numbers. The urchins hollow out cup-shaped depressions in the rocks to protect themselves from the waves and have become so numerous that some of the rocks appear to have been honeycombed by the prickly, purple plankton eaters.

The *subtidal zone* is the area that is never exposed to air, even at the lowest of low tides. The constant water source makes the subtidal zone a safe haven for creatures in danger of drying out, which migrate down to this area during low tide. Nudibranchs, marine relatives of slugs and snails that can have wild shapes and colors, are some of the most interesting subtidal zone inhabitants.

Between Punta Gorda and the lighthouse lies Four Mile Creek. The trail traverses a wide but shallow crossing that may require hikers to take off their shoes and wade through the water—at least in winter. Don't stray from the path here, as the cabins on the north bank of the creek are private, and trespassing is not appreciated.

Up ahead is the Punta Gorda Lighthouse, a structure originally built in 1910 following the tragic wreck just offshore of the passenger ship *Columbia,* in which eighty-seven people died. When the lighthouse was constructed, a small village of lighthouse keepers and their families sprung up nearby. But the town of Punta Gorda disappeared in 1951 once modern navigation equipment forced the then-obsolete lighthouse to close. Though it has been out of service for some fifty years, the building and squat tower are well kept, and hikers can climb the tower and admire the view—provided they can squeeze through the narrow opening at the top of the staircase.

Be sure to give yourself plenty of time to return past Punta Gorda before high tide.

Miles and Directions

0.0 Start at the information board. Head south through the locked gate and along the dunes.

0.2 The trail comes to a fenced archeological area. Turn right following along the fence to the Interpretive exhibit. After seeing the exhibit, continue south along the fence and the dunes

0.5 The trail crosses a small creek, which sometimes disappears into the sand before reaching the sea.

0.7 (FYI: Deep gullies have been carved into the dunes by the creek.)

0.9 Head down a steep bank and across the creek, continuing south between the bluffs and the ocean.

1.5 The bluffs are closer to the water here, forcing the trail onto the beach. (Note: The trail can be dangerous at high tide, since so-called sneaker waves can catch hikers by surprise. Be careful.)

2.1 The trail rounds Punta Gorda. (Note: This is the most dangerous point on the trail during high tide, since the beach is particularly narrow here. Around the corner the beach becomes much wider (and safer) again. Avoid the point during high tide.)

2.8 A couple of private cabins huddle beneath the bluffs on the left. Wade across Four Mile Creek and continue south along the beach on the other side. There is no bridge over Four Mile Creek, but it is generally fordable even in winter.

3.0 Cross a small creek. The lighthouse is now visible ahead to the left.

3.1 Reach Punta Gorda Lighthouse. This is the turnaround point for the hike. Return the way you came, making sure to time your return to avoid high tide around Punta Gorda.

6.2 Arrive back at the trailhead.

Hike Information

Local Information
Humboldt County Convention and Visitors Bureau, Eureka; (800) 346-3482; (707) 443-5097.

Lodging
Mattole Estuary Campground, at the trailhead, $5.00 per vehicle.

In Addition

Know Your Pinnipeds

Seals, Sea Lions; What's the Difference?

"Pinniped"—meaning wing or flipper-footed—is the scientific term for the class of marine mammals that includes seals, sea lions, and walruses. If you spend a little time on the seashore in California, you will probably have the chance to watch some of these fascinating animals at home in their element. More often than not, they will also be watching *you*, as they are very curious and playful creatures. Several species of pinnipeds are found along the Redwood Coast. Telling them apart can be difficult at times, and even the common names are less than helpful. Of the animals found in California waters, two are called sea lions and three more are called seals. But only some of the latter are true seals, and the others are actually members of the sea lion family. Confused? Maybe this will help:

There are three families of pinniped, all of which belong to the order Carnivora, which includes bears, dogs, raccoons, and weasels. These three families are Odobenids, Phocids, and Otariids.

Odobenids: The only living member of this family is the walrus, and they don't live anywhere near California. Enough said.

Phocids: Also known as true seals or hair seals, there are two species common to California: the harbor seal and the northern elephant seal.

Otariids: Called eared seals, they have retained tiny ear flaps that can be helpful in identification. Local members of this family include the California sea lion, Steller sea lion, and, rarely, the northern fur seal.

Which One Is It?

There are a few clues that distinguish true seals from eared seals to the trained eye, most obvious being the way they move—on land, as well as in the water.

True seals' hind flippers are fused together and directed rearward like a whale's flukes. When on land, they have to inch along on their bellies like a caterpillar. In the water they propel themselves forward primarily with the hind flippers, much as a whale does, and use the front flippers to steer, if at all.

Sea lions and fur seals, on the other hand, can tuck their hind flippers under them when on land, and support their weight with the front flippers. This allows for a means of locomotion much closer to that of land-dwelling animals. In the water they "fly" with their front flippers, using the hind flippers as rudders.

Of course, if all you can see of an animal is its head poking above the water as it checks you out, all of the above will be of little help. Your best clue in this situation are the ear lobes—or lack thereof. True seals have no visible ear lobes at all, while sea lions have—admittedly small—little nubbins of ear lobes visible on the sides of their heads.

Can You Be More Specific?

If you see light gray animals with dark spots, these are likely harbor seals. They tend to stick close to shore, and they're commonly seen around docks and wharves. Males and females of this species are about the same size, averaging between 200 and 300 pounds.

At the other end of the scale is the northern elephant seal. The name stems from the sizable schnozz that males develop when they reach sexual maturity. While the females of the species are impressive enough at up to 2,000 pounds, old bulls can reach a stately 5,000 pounds and 18 feet in length. (Recent research has shown that the elephant seals are master divers, able to hold their breath for up to two hours and dive to depths of nearly a mile. Nearly hunted to extinction for their blubber, they are slowly making a comeback. Look for them at Point Reyes National Seashore, Año Nuevo State Reserve, and on the beaches north of San Simeon State Park.)

California sea lions are the most abundant representatives of the otariids. The sleek and playful characters are commonly observed up and down the coast. They can often be seen hauled out on rocks or swimming in groups, and they express themselves through loud, raucous barks.

You are less likely to see Steller sea lions. A threatened species, they have been reduced to a few scattered breeding colonies in California. They keep relatively quiet, but when a Steller sea lion does vocalize, it comes out more of a roar than a bark. They are the largest member of the otariid family, with males reaching 10 feet and 2,000 pounds. Their heads tend to be broad and bearlike, with a wide black nose.

Last but not least is the northern fur seal—aka the Alaska fur seal. Rarely seen on shore, they can sometimes be seen sleeping on their backs on the open ocean with fore flippers in the air. They have a shorter, blunter snout than other seals and sea lions, in addition to a thicker coat, and the most obvious ears of all the resident pinnipeds.

21 Lost Coast Trail

This relatively easy piece of the Lost Coast Trail follows a narrow strip of grassy meadows nestled between driftwood-strewn beaches and densely forested slopes. There are two excellent walk-in campgrounds along the trail for those who want to spend more time here. Pelicans, gray whales, and harbor seals can be seen, as well as Roosevelt elk. The complete Lost Coast Trail covers more than 25 miles of shoreline, inaccessible by other means.

Start: From the Needle Rock visitor center.
Distance: 4.4 miles out and back.
Approximate hiking time: 2 hours.
Difficulty: Easy, due to good trails and little elevation gain.
Trail surface: Dirt path.
Lay of the land: Coastal bench lands, meadows, and sparse forest.
Other trail users: Equestrians.
Canine compatibility: Dogs not permitted.

Land status: State park.
Nearest town: Shelter Cove.
Fees and permits: $3.00 day-use fee.
Schedule: Open year-round from dawn to dusk.
Map: USGS map: Bear Harbor, CA.
Trail contact: Sinkyone Wilderness State Park, Whitethorn; (707) 986-7711; www.parks.ca.gov.

Finding the trailhead: From Redway, head west 10.7 miles on Briceland Road and take the left fork (still Briceland Road), following the sign for Whitethorn and Shelter Cove. Continue another 2 miles, then take the left fork again (still Briceland Road) to Whitethorn. Drive 8.8 miles and turn left at the signed junction leading to Sinkyone Wilderness State Park. From here it's another 3.2 miles along a narrow dirt road (still Briceland Road) to the Needle Rock visitor center. The trail starts a few feet back up the road from the parking lot, on the west side of the road. *DeLorme: Northern California Atlas & Gazetteer:* Page 62, A4.

The Hike

As a crow flies, Sinkyone Wilderness State Park is scarcely 10 miles from the busy U.S. Highway 101 corridor. But down on the ground, the traveler quickly learns why the area is known as the Lost Coast. Travel in this region is difficult when conditions are optimum; during the winter rainy season, it can be nearly impossible. The result is a feeling of total isolation. And when the weather is right, the effect can be downright paradisiacal. For some, the park can be difficult to reach—the main road in is virtually a jeep trail, after all—but hikers are rewarded with gorgeous scenery and relative privacy. This hike includes the option of a short spur trail to the beach and a chance to see the park's resident herd of Roosevelt elk, which were reintroduced here in 1982.

Though relatively undeveloped now, the region bustled with inhabitants in the past. Before Europeans began emigrating and settling the West, the Northern

What's left of Needle Rock

California coastline had one of the highest population densities in North America—and the Lost Coast, home to the Sinkyone Indians, was no exception. The Athabaskan-speaking tribe represents a line of human occupation that may reach back more than 14,000 years. The Sinkyone spent the summer months on the coast, harvesting the abundant sea life, before moving inland to spend the winter in permanent villages on the banks of the South Fork Eel River. To survive, they hunted seals and sea lions; collected ocean fish, seaweed, and shellfish; and gathered a variety of roots, nuts, seeds, and berries in the area. They also foraged for acorns, a major staple of the Sinkyone diet, in the tan oak groves that thrived on the coast. The native Californians set fires in the groves to clear out the undergrowth and make it easier to collect the acorns. These burnouts had an environmentally helpful side effect: They improved the health of the groves by removing the insect-infested, rotten acorns from the forest bed.

The Sinkyone population declined rapidly during and after the Gold Rush, when settlers poured into the area to look for land. Inevitable tensions arose between the newcomers and the native Sinkyone. And as was often the case, the Native Americans were forced to cede in these situations. One of the most famous instances of

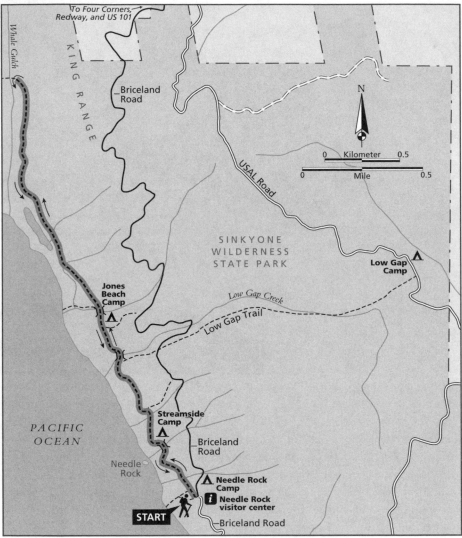

the Sinkyone-settler conflict is the story of Sally Bell. In the 1930s the elderly Sinky-one woman told white friends about her childhood on the Lost Coast in the 1860s. The episode that figured most prominently in the tale was the night Bell saw her family massacred by U.S. soldiers and how she survived by hiding in the bushes.

Bell's life story inspired an activist arrested in 1983 to give police the name Sally Bell in place of her own to call attention to logging on one of the Lost Coast's last remaining old-growth redwood groves. Eventually, more than 7,000 acres of the groves were purchased from the Georgia–Pacific lumber company. Nearly half of that land was added to the state park, doubling the park's total acreage. The remaining 3,800 acres were bought by the InterTribal Sinkyone Wilderness Council, a nonprofit consortium of Native American tribes. The council plans to manage the area as a unique park, with land-use guidelines inspired by the ancient stewardship ethics of native Californian tribes.

The hike begins at the Needle Rock visitor center, where you can see the first of many relics of the park's past habitation. The visitor center itself is housed in what once was a ranch house belonging to dairyman Calvin Cooper Stewart and his family. Both of the walk-in campsites are located on former homesteads; and if you look carefully, you can find other vestiges of the pioneer era. These artifacts range from a small dam and an abandoned railroad bed, to a rancher-planted eucalyptus grove, to the rusted skeleton of a vintage automobile.

The homesteaders left another important mark on the region: the disappearance of the tan oak groves. Settlers originally grazed livestock in the meadows and harvested tan oak bark, which was used in commercial leather tanneries. But the practice of stripping the trees of bark and leaving them to rot eventually resulted in the disappearance of the indigenous tan oak groves. In time, settlers turned their focus to logging and established a town and sawmill at Bear Harbor, where 300 workers were employed by the turn of the century. The remoteness and inaccessibility eventually took its toll, and the highways were built around—rather than through—the convoluted King Range.

The turnaround point for this hike is Whale Gulch. But hikers with more time can continue along the path as far as the Mattole River Estuary, some 35 trail miles north of here.

Miles and Directions

0.0 Start at the Needle Rock visitor center parking lot. Hike back up the road 100 yards to the Horse Camp building. Follow the narrow footpath as it veers off from the road to the left, passing just below the Horse Camp building and heading north.

0.1 The trail crosses a small creek on a tiny footbridge.

0.2 (FYI: Needle Rock is visible in the surf to the left. Due to natural erosion, the moniker is no longer quite accurate.)

0.3 Cross a wooden bridge. Follow the main trail as it switches back to the left and continues north. **Side trip:** A short spur trail after the bridge leads straight ahead to Streamside Camp.

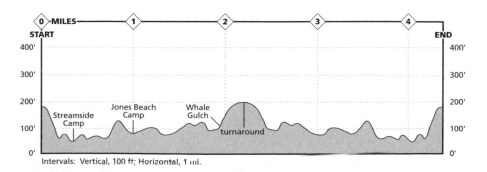

Intervals: Vertical, 100 ft; Horizontal, 1 mi.

0.6 Low Gap Trail heads to the right. Continue straight.

0.8 (FYI: After crossing a creek via a wooden bridge, an old dam is visible to the left, a remnant from the homesteaders who used to live here.)

1.0 The eucalyptus stand to the right of the trail marks Jones Beach Camp, site of a former homestead. A spur trail from the entrance road leads to the right. Continue straight and cross the creek via a footbridge. The rusted remains of a vintage automobile can be seen on the left.

1.1 Continue straight. **Side trip:** Jones Beach Trail, on the left, leads down 0.2 mile to the ocean.

1.5 The trail skirts the edge of a long narrow pond. (FYI: Herds of Roosevelt elk are often seen here.)

1.8 The trail heads inland, following Whale Gulch.

1.9 (FYI: Mats of periwinkle can be seen on both sides of the trail.)

2.2 The trail reaches the Whale Gulch stream crossing. The Lost Coast Trail continues on the other side, but this is the turnaround point for this hike. Return the way you came.

4.4 Arrive back at the trailhead.

Hike Information

Local Information

Humboldt County Convention and Visitors Bureau, Eureka; (800) 346–3482; (707) 443–5097.

Lodging

There are several campsites within the park, mostly walk-in sites.

22 Toumey Trail

Beginning at a favorite redwood-rimmed swimming hole, this trail crosses a seasonal bridge and climbs steeply up into drier oak-and-madrone woodlands overlooking the steep-walled Eel River Canyon. Panorama Point offers a great aerial view of the river valley, while the trail follows a series of old skid trails and logging roads along the ridge, ending up at Oak Flat Campground, and returning via the campground access road.

Start: At the river-access parking lot.
Distance: 2.4-mile loop.
Approximate hiking time: 2 hours.
Difficulty: Moderate to difficult, due to steep trails and confusing junctions.
Trail surface: Dirt path, gravel road, and paved road (briefly).
Lay of the land: Riverside old-growth redwood forest, drier oak forest.
Other trail users: Automobiles (briefly).
Canine compatibility: No dogs allowed.

Land status: State park.
Nearest town: Benbow.
Fees and permits: $2.00 day-use fee.
Schedule: Open year-round. Seasonal bridges are in place from approximately mid June through mid-September, depending on water level. Call park to make sure.
Map: USGS map: Garberville, CA.
Trail contact: Richardson Grove State Park, Garberville; (707) 946-1812; www.humboldtredwoods.org.

Finding the trailhead: From Garberville, head south 7 miles on U.S. Highway 101 to Richardson Grove State Park. Turn right into the park's main entrance. Continue straight past the entrance station 0.2 mile to the T junction. Turn left, passing under US 101, and continue another 0.1 mile to a small parking lot overlooking the Eel River. *DeLorme: Northern California Atlas & Gazetteer:* Page 53, D5.

The Hike

There are several trailheads in this book that can only be found at the end of long, twisting roads, with the help of detailed directions and a good map. This isn't one of them.

In fact, the main artery of the region, US 101, plows right through the middle of "the Grove's" prime old-growth redwood stands. Ironically, it was the highway plans that spurred the Save-the-Redwoods League to push for park status back in 1922. While they couldn't prevent the highway from coming through (along the path of an older wagon road), they and others have managed to keep it from being substantially widened over the years. So if the highway seems surprisingly narrow here, and the giant trees a little too close for comfort, remember: They were here first.

The park, happily, *has* been expanded over the years, from its original 120 acres to around 2,000 today. This hike explores some of those added acres, traversing a high ridge east of the park's headquarters. From the river-access parking lot near the

Swimming hole on the South Fork Eel River

visitor center, the trail heads down to the banks of the lazy South Fork Eel River, crossing the stream via a seasonal footbridge. Continuing across the rocky flats, the trail enters a small grove of redwoods before heading up the hill. The climb is steep at first, but eventually mellows somewhat, contouring around the steep slopes of the ridge. The effort of the ascent is rewarded about three-quarters of a mile up, where a short spur trail leads up to Panorama Point, overlooking the South Fork Eel River Valley far below.

Named for the slim, slippery fish that traditionally swarmed up the river annually, the Eel River has its headwaters in the coastal mountains of Mendocino County. From those remote and largely untouched slopes, the various forks and tributaries run in a more or less northerly direction before finally running into the sea 150 miles north, just south of Humboldt Bay. For Southern Humboldt and Northern Mendocino Counties, the river system has traditionally been the lifeblood of the local economy. The original Native American inhabitants, and later white settlers, took advantage of the river's rich harvest each year, as anadromous (migratory) fish moved upstream in huge numbers to spawn. In later years the river valleys served as transportation corridors for roads and railways. The railway has since ceased operating, following a series of winter storms that blew out portions of track in the late 1990s. Upstream water diversions have also taken their toll on fish populations, as much-needed summer water has been rerouted to feed thirsty cities and farmland farther south. Nevertheless, the mighty Eel continues to be the focal point of the local community, especially in summer, when the swimming holes are at their best.

▶ **Humboldt County's main cash crop is illegally grown marijuana.**

From Panorama Point the trail continues along the side slope of the ridge, alternately following singletrack paths and dirt roads. The roads are part of a network of old skid roads left behind by logging crews years ago. The scars of that activity are slowly healing, but it will be a long time (if ever) before ancient redwoods grace these hills again. For the time being, shady oak groves mixed with conifers fill the space nicely, providing a pleasing backdrop for the hike.

Eventually the trail turns and begins heading downhill via increasingly steep switchbacks. At the bottom of the slope, the aptly named Oak Flat Campground spreads out along an alluvial plain at a bend in the river. From here it is simply a matter of following the road down through the campground and across a seasonal auto bridge back to the trailhead.

Miles and Directions

0.0 Start at the river-access parking lot directly east of the US 101 underpass. Head north between the riverbank and the picnic area.

0.1 The trail descends to the river and crosses a seasonal summer bridge. Continue straight across the gravel flats into the forest.

Toumey Trail

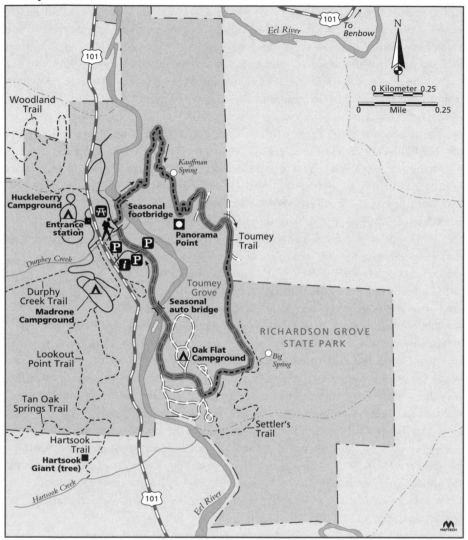

0.2 The trail passes through some old-growth redwoods, then begins to climb steeply.

0.4 The grade becomes less steep. A game trail heads left. Turn right and follow the main trail.

0.5 The trail heads up into a narrow gully, then crosses and contours around the hill.

0.8 At a switchback in the trail, a spur heads right a few yards to Panorama Point. Excellent view of the river far below. Follow the main trail up to the left.

0.9 The trail passes through a small grove of residual redwood.

1.0 The singletrack trail joins an old dirt road. Turn left and follow the road up.

1.1 The roadbed curves up to the left, but the Toumey Trail continues straight, dropping slightly.

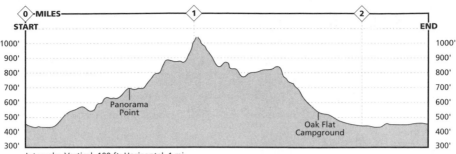

Intervals: Vertical, 100 ft; Horizontal, 1 mi.

1.3 The trail joins a wider, gravel road. Continue straight.

1.4 At a bend in the road, the trail leaves the gravel road and heads west down a steep singletrack path.

1.5 The trail crosses a hollow with a nice oak grove to the right. The trail is following an old logging roadbed.

1.6 The roadbed forks. Continue straight down the steeper grade.

1.7 The roadbed stops abruptly, but the trail continues straight down a singletrack path.

1.75 The trail drops down onto an old roadbed running north-south. Continue straight down the gully.

1.8 The trail drops down onto another roadbed. Settler's Trail heads left. Continue straight down the gully.

1.9 The trail emerges into Oak Flat Campground near a water tank. Follow the paved road straight to the main campground loop. Turn right on this and follow it to the river.

2.0 At the river, turn right and head toward the bridge.

2.2 Cross seasonal auto bridge (or bridges).

2.4 Back at the trailhead.

Hike Information

Local Information

Garberville-Redway Area Chamber of Commerce, Garberville; (707) 923-2613; www.garberville.org.

Local Events/Attractions

Shakespeare at Benbow Lake, annual summer Shakespeare festival, Garberville; (707) 923-3399, www.shakespeare@asis.com.

Garberville Rodeo Bull-O-Rama, held in mid-June, Benbow; (707) 986-7414; www.garberville.org/rodeo.

Summer Arts and Music Festival, Benbow Lake State Park, held the third weekend in June, Benbow; (707) 923-3368.

Reggae on the River Festival, held the first weekend in August, Piercy; (707) 923-4583.

Lodging

The Huckleberry and Madrone Campgrounds in the park are open year-round.

The Oak Flat Campground in the park (accessed via seasonal bridges) is open mid-June through mid-September, as water levels allow.

23 Ten Mile Beach Trail

This trail is an old logging road, now closed to motorized vehicles due to several washed-out sections. The path leads past MacKerricher Dunes, one of the coast's longest dune systems, and Inglenook Fen, a coastal wetland. The fen shelters rare plants, such as marsh pennywort and the rein orchid, and is home to several endemic insect species.

Start: From the Laguna Point parking lot.
Distance: 10.4 miles out and back.
Approximate hiking time: 4 to 5 hours.
Difficulty: Easy, due to flat terrain and partially paved trail.
Trail surface: Pavement, gravel, and sandy beach paths.
Lay of the land: Beaches, dunes, and a salt marsh.
Other trail users: Equestrians and cyclists.
Canine compatibility: Leashed dogs permitted.

Land status: State park.
Nearest town: Fort Bragg.
Fees and permits: No day-use fee, but camping costs $16.
Schedule: Open year-round, with reduced facilities from October through February.
Maps: USGS maps: Inglenook, CA; Fort Bragg, CA.
Trail contact: Russian River–Mendocino Sector, MacKerricher State Park, (707) 937-5804; www.parks.ca.gov.

Finding the trailhead: From Fort Bragg, drive north 3 miles on California Highway 1, and turn left into MacKerricher State Park. After passing the entrance station, continue 0.4 mile to the first junction, turn left, and continue 0.4 mile down to Lake Cleone. Turn right just past the lake and pass under the bridge, continuing another 0.2 mile to the Laguna Point parking lot. The trail starts near the entrance to the parking lot, on the east side of the road. *DeLorme: Northern California Atlas & Gazetteer:* Page 63, D5.

The Hike

It is easy to imagine that you're walking some postapocalyptic stretch of highway as you follow the torn and battered tarmac north along Ten Mile Beach. The bridge passing over the park entrance road is one of the better-preserved sections of the old Haul Road, which once connected area loggers to the mill in Fort Bragg. The story of this road is also the story of the park, as the histories of both are intertwined and can be traced back to the man the park was named after, Duncan MacKerricher. Canadian-born MacKerricher and his new bride, Jessica, sailed for California from New York in 1864. In those days the voyage was a long one that involved departing in precanal Panama and traveling by rail across the isthmus. The voyage continued on the Pacific side by ship to San Francisco, where the MacKerrichers boarded another vessel and headed north along the dangerous north coast. MacKerricher found work in the mill for a while, then signed on as an assistant with the local

Gray whale skeleton at the visitor center

Indian agent. At that time the Mendocino Indian Reservation occupied the land north of Fort Bragg—including the current site of the state park—and the fort existed to oversee it. The reservation eventually was relocated to the Round Valley, but MacKerricher stayed on and set up shop as a dairy farmer.

In 1915 the Union Lumber Company obtained MacKerricher's permission to build an extension of the California Pacific Railroad from Fort Bragg to the Ten Mile River. Loggers used the new route to transport wood from the river to the mill. The railroad hugged the coast, following a trail used for centuries by the Coast Yuki and neighboring Pomo Indians as they traveled up and down the coast. In 1949 the well-worn tracks were taken up and replaced with a paved logging road, allowing the logs to be moved by truck instead of train car.

But being so close to the ocean was hard on the road, which had to be repaired many times throughout the years. By 1968 the cost to maintain the road had become prohibitive and it was abandoned. At this point the land adjacent to the road had already been sold to the state in the 1950s for use as a park. The state acquired the stretch of road in 1995, and MacKerricher State Park was complete.

As the trail continues north into the park's less-visited areas, hikers will notice a break in the dunes through which a small pond is visible. This is Sandhill Lake, and

Ten Mile Beach Trail

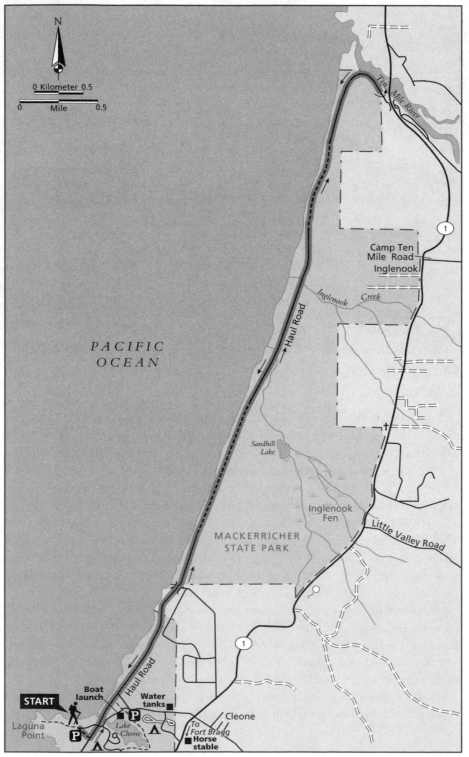

N

0 Kilometer 0.5

0 Mile 0.5

Ten Mile River

1

Camp Ten
Mile Road
Inglenook

Inglenook Creek

Haul Road

Sandhill Lake

Inglenook Fen

PACIFIC OCEAN

Little Valley Road

MACKERRICHER STATE PARK

1

Haul Road

START

Boat launch

Water tanks

Cleone

Laguna Point

P

P

Lake Cleone

To Fort Bragg

Horse stable

it forms the centerpiece of one of California's rarest landscapes. Inglenook Fen, home to dozens of rare, indigenous species, belongs to the category of wetland known as coastal fen. Floristically speaking, a fen is somewhere between a bog and a marsh. The difference lies in the soil and the plants that grow in those soils. In a marsh, grasslands are flooded or partially flooded, and the soil is mostly mineral. In a bog, the soil is mostly organic—made up of decaying plant matter that allows the formation of thick peat moss layers. A fen has aspects of both, with a mixture of mineral and organic soils that allows some formation of peat. Inglenook Fen was created about 5,000 years ago when the formation of dunes along the beach blocked the outflow of water from the fen's drainage.

If fate had been less kind, Inglenook Fen could easily have wound up as a parking lot for a shopping mall before its uniqueness was discovered. The fen's special gifts were not really uncovered until the 1960s when scientists began studying the wetlands and realized that this was more than just your run-of-the-mill damp spot. Within this small area are dozens of endemic insect species—species found nowhere else in the world—and a variety of rare plants. Some of these plants are typically found only in arctic zones, a fact that has sparked suspicions that the Inglenook plants are remnants of the last ice age. But there's more: A 1970s study discovered more than 500 arthropods living here; of those, many were previously unknown to science.

Though incredibly rare now, fens were originally commonplace. At the time of European contact, they were found interspersed all along the Northern California coast. But today Inglenook Fen is the last one existing in the state. While the trail does not go through the fen (the protected land is far too fragile an environ to withstand much human contact), it does travel through the dunes on the fen's western edge. Hikers will have plenty of opportunity to admire the fragile ecosystem from this vantage point. The state park system is working to preserve the rare habitat, so please respect the restrictions and stay on the path.

The trail continues through the northern dunes until it reaches the turnaround point at the broad mouth of the Ten Mile River. Return the way you came.

Miles and Directions

0.0 Start at the entrance to the Laguna Point parking lot. Follow the short gravel trail that heads east (away from the ocean) through the bushes. Follow this about 150 feet, then turn left onto the paved road (now closed to cars).

0.3 At the first washed-out section of the road, the trail turns to gravel, dips sharply, and climbs again to paved road. (FYI: Mats of ice plant cover the ground next to the trail.)

0.4 Horse Trail goes off to the right. Continue straight along the old road.

0.8 The trail passes several houses on the right. At this point the state park is just a thin strip of beach and dunes.

1.1 A spur trail goes down to the right, then curves left and passes through a culvert under the road to access the beach. Continue straight along the old road.

1.4 The old road is washed out here. Take the short gravel trail down to the beach and continue along the upper edge of the beach.

1.6 A creek comes out of the dunes, often vanishing into the sand before it reaches the ocean.

1.8 Keep to the left of the posts in the sand on the edge of the dunes.

2.0 The road resumes after a long absence. Climb back up onto it and continue on the old road.

2.1 The beach is very narrow at this point, and waves frequently reach the old road, causing it to wash out in places. Continue straight along the remaining pavement.

2.3 The road has been completely washed out. Continue straight, north along the beach.

2.4 The road resumes. Climb back onto it and continue north. (FYI: The ground to the right is covered with thousands of crushed seashells. These are midden heaps left from precontact Native American settlements and are protected archeological sites.)

2.7 (FYI: The marsh to the right is Inglenook Fen. A few buildings from an old cattle ranch remain on the edge of the dunes. In January you can hear hundreds of frogs chirping in the fen.)

3.5 The vegetation is now changing to include more brush and even some small trees.

5.0 The old road is half buried in spots by the surrounding dunes, which are larger here than they have been. The trail curves inland along the banks of Ten Mile River, on the left.

5.2 The trail reaches the park boundary where CA 1 bridges Ten Mile River. This is the turnaround point for the hike. Return the way you came.

10.4 Arrive back at the trailhead.

Hike Information

Local Information
Fort Bragg–Mendocino Coast Chamber of Commerce, Fort Bragg; (800) 726-2780; (707) 961-6300; www.mendocinocoast.com.

Local Events/Attractions
Skunk Train, this historic line crosses thirty bridges or trestles and two tunnels between Fort Bragg and Willits, 40 miles inland on U.S. Highway 101, Fort Bragg; (800) 77-SKUNK; Fort Bragg Depot: (707) 964-6371; Willits Depot: (707) 459-5248.

Mendocino Coast Botanical Gardens, Fort Bragg; (707) 964-4352; mcbg@gardenbythesea.org.

Mendocino Music Festival, held every July in a tent on the Mendocino headlands, Mendocino; (707) 937-2044; www.mendocinomusic.com.

Arts & Crafts Fair, July, Mendocino; (707) 937-5818; www.mendocinoartcenter.org.

Mendocino Wine & Mushroom Fest, mid-November celebration of two of Mendocino's premiere products, with dinners, cooking classes, and guided mushroom tours; (707) 961-6300.

Lodging
There is a developed campground within the park.

State park campsite reservations: (800) 444-7275.

Hike Tours
MacKerricher State Park: (707) 937-5804. There are seasonal ranger-led hikes. Call for more information.

24 Ecological Staircase Trail

This easily overlooked park packs a lot into a relatively small package, with four distinct vegetation zones ranging from wind-sculpted coastal cypress groves to a rare pygmy forest at the upper end of the reserve. The Ecological Staircase Trail is named for the natural terraces in the landscape, formed by a combination of geological uplifting and wave action.

Start: Ecological Staircase trailhead.
Distance: 4.2 miles out and back.
Approximate hiking time: 2 to 2.5 hours.
Difficulty: Easy, due to wide trails and little elevation gain.
Trail surface: Dirt path
Lay of the land: Coastal bluffs, second-growth redwood forest, riparian area, and pygmy forest.
Other trail users: None.
Canine compatibility: Dogs not allowed.

Land status: State reserve, state forest.
Nearest town: Fort Bragg.
Fees and permits: No fees or permits required.
Schedule: Open year-round; day-use hours vary.
Maps: USGS maps: Mendocino, CA; Fort Bragg, CA.
Trail contact: Mendocino Sector Headquarters, Mendocino; (707) 937-5804; www.parks.ca.gov.

Finding the trailhead: From Fort Bragg, drive south 4 miles on California Highway 1. Turn right into the parking lot for Jughandle State Reserve, located on the southern side of Jughandle Cove, just south of the Jug Handle Creek Bridge. *DeLorme: Northern California Atlas & Gazetteer:* Page 73, A–B5.

The Hike

To hike the Ecological Staircase Trail at tiny Jughandle State Reserve is a hands-on lesson in geologic change and the ways such change influences living systems. All along this hike the forces of weather, geology, and biological adaptation have conspired to create dramatically varied displays within the local flora. From the crashing waves of the Pacific to the gnarled and stunted branches of the pygmy forest, this trail can make ecology interesting even to the scientifically challenged.

The hike begins on a small grassy headland and traces a short loop around the rocky cliffs before heading back inland to where the first row of hardy conifers braves the constant off-shore winds. These trees, the same Sitka spruce and grand fir that can be seen farther inland growing to 200 feet, are sculpted by the salty winds into short, compact, twisted forms known collectively as krummholz, a German word meaning "bent wood." They form a bulwark for the taller forest behind, bearing the brunt of the oceanic weather's assault.

Passing through the krummholz, the trail ducks under the south end of the CA 1 bridge and heads down a long series of steps to the riparian zone alongside Jug

Jughandle Cove from the bluffs

Handle Creek. Here willows, alders, and other deciduous trees rule over a community of lush vegetation nourished by the creek's waters and fertile silt. A look back to the left reveals a small beach and deep cove at the mouth of the creek, framed by the surprisingly graceful arch of the bridge. After crossing the creek bed on a short boardwalk, the trail climbs again to the other side, and here begins the real meat of the hike.

At this point you are still on the first step of the trail's namesake "staircase"—a series of five distinct marine terraces that rise, each one roughly 100 feet higher than the previous step, to the coastal hills beyond. The hike explores the first three of these terraces, ending at a patch of pygmy forest that owes its existence to the same forces responsible for the staircase itself.

The story begins about half a million years ago, in the Pleistocene, as retreating glaciers caused a rise in sea level. Water lapped up onto the land, creating a smooth, shallow terrace between the new shoreline and the old. At the same time the land itself was slowly rising at a rate of about 1 inch every hundred years, thanks to the forces of plate tectonics and geologic uplifting. A new ice age settled in, and the land rose to the point that when glaciers melted and sea levels rose again 100,000 years later, the terrace was too high for the waves to reach. Instead, a new terrace was formed below the old one. The process has repeated itself fairly regularly since, with each new sea-level rise creating a new terrace, and geologic uplifting raising those terraces ever higher, so that the fifth, highest terrace is now about 650 feet above sea level. Since the terraces are each 1 to 2 miles wide, it is hard to tell exactly when you reach the next one. Fortunately, numbered signposts along the way point out these and other ecology facts in conjunction with a free brochure obtainable at the trailhead.

From the north end of the bridge, the trail climbs gently across the first terrace through mature stands of Bishop and Monterey pine. The second terrace is dominated by tall grand fir and Sitka spruce, which give way to second-growth redwood groves about halfway up. The best is saved for last, as the trail emerges from the thick forest and tops the third terrace. Due to the flatness of this terrace, an underlying layer of nonpermeable hardpan, and the resulting poor drainage, the nutrients have been leached from this soil over the past 300,000 years to the point where plants find it difficult to survive. A short boardwalk loop takes hikers on a tour of this sensitive habitat. Return along the same trail to the trailhead.

Miles and Directions

0.0 Start at the large kiosk. Head due west to the meadow.

0.1 On the bluffs turn right and follow the edge around.

0.2 The trail is now back at the krummholz forest. Turn left, following the trail along the edge of the trees.

Ecological Staircase Trail

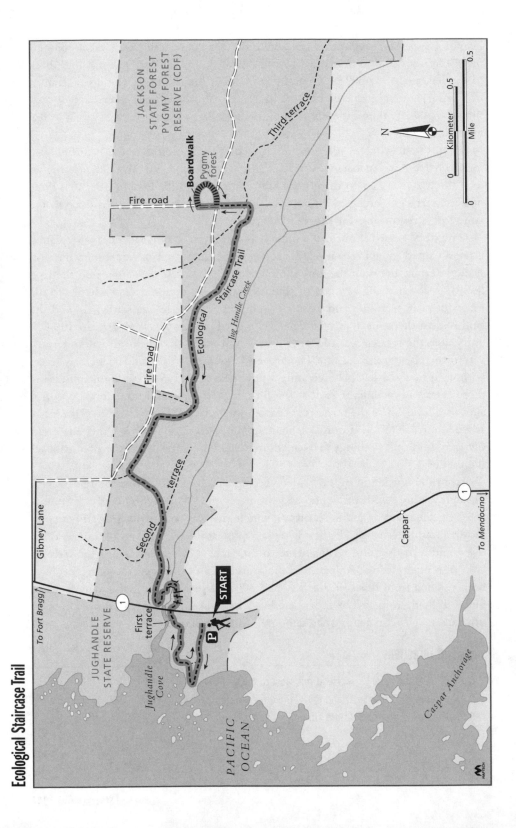

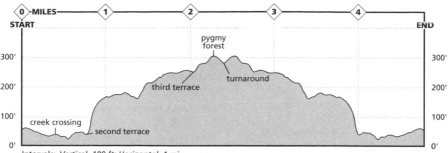

Intervals: Vertical, 100 ft; Horizontal, 1 mi.

0.25 A spur trail heads left. Take the right fork. A few yards later, a spur trail heads right to the parking lot. Continue along the main trail to the left.

0.3 A beach-access trail heads down to the left. Continue straight.

0.35 The trail ducks under the south end of the CA 1 bridge, then heads down a long series of steps to the creek.

0.4 Cross the bridge and boardwalk over the creek. Climbing stairs again on the other side.

0.5 At the north end of the bridge, turn right and follow the trail upstream.

0.8 You have now reached the second terrace.

1.0 At the junction, turn right onto the wide dirt track.

1.2 The trail curves left and crosses a marshy area.

1.5 The forest is second-growth redwood here.

1.6 The trail climbs a few steps. The creek drainage is now visible on the right.

1.9 An unofficial trail forks left. Take the right fork. A bog is visible on the left.

2.2 The trail leaves the dense forest. You are now at the third terrace.

2.25 Pass through the wooden gate and continue straight at the four-way dirt road junction.

2.3 Turn right onto the boardwalk trail. Pygmy forest is all around you.

2.4 At the end of the boardwalk, turn right onto the dirt road and continue back to the four-way junction. Turn left through the wooden gate and return the way you came.

4.2 Back at the trailhead.

Hike Information

Local Information

Redwood Coast Chamber of Commerce, Gualala; (800) 778-5252; (707) 884-1080; www.redwoodcoastchamber.com.
Fort Bragg-Mendocino Coast Chamber of Commerce, Fort Bragg; (707) 961-6300; www.mendocinocoast.com.

Local Events/Attractions

Skunk Train, this historic line crosses thirty bridges or trestles and two tunnels between Fort Bragg and Willits, 40 miles inland on U.S. Highway 101, Fort Bragg; (800) 77-SKUNK; Fort Bragg Depot: (707) 964-6371; Willits Depot: (707) 459-5248.

Mendocino Coast Botanical Gardens, Fort Bragg; (707) 964-4352; mcbg@gardenbythesea.org.

Mendocino Music Festival, held every July in a tent on the Mendocino headlands, Mendocino; (707) 937-2044; www.mendocinomusic.com.

Arts & Crafts Fair, July, Mendocino; (707) 937-5818; www.mendocinoartcenter.org.

Mendocino Wine & Mushroom Fest, mid-November celebration of two of Mendocino's premiere products, with dinners, cooking classes, and guided mushroom tours; (707) 961-6300.

Lodging

There are several state park campgrounds in the area.

State park campsite reservations: (800) 444-7275.

There are also numerous hotels, motels, B&Bs, and private campgrounds in the Mendocino/Fort Bragg area.

25 Russian Gulch Double Loop

This trail leads up through a lush coastal canyon filled with ferns, maples, berries, and second-growth redwood to a 36-foot waterfall. On the coast, hikers can awe at the Punchbowl, a 100-foot-diameter collapsed wave tunnel resembling a large crater, churning at its base with waves injected through a tunnel from the nearby shoreline.

Start: From the first gate, just before the campground.
Distance: 7-mile loop.
Approximate hiking time: 3 hours.
Difficulty: Moderate, due to some steep sections.
Trail surface: Pavement, gravel, and dirt path.
Lay of the land: Second-growth redwood forest, riparian streamside habitat.
Other trail users: Cyclists (for a short section).

Canine compatibility: Dogs not permitted.
Land status: State park.
Nearest town: Mendocino.
Fees and permits: $5.00 day-use fee. Camping is $16.
Schedule: Open year-round dawn to dusk. Campground is closed from November 1 to March 31.
Map: USGS map: Mendocino, CA.
Trail contact: Russian Gulch State Park, Mendocino; (707) 937-5804, www.parks.ca.gov.

Finding the trailhead: From Fort Bragg, drive south 6 miles on California Highway 1 to Russian Gulch State Park. Turn right at the entrance sign, then immediately left again, which brings you to the park entrance booth. Follow the entrance road 0.2 mile as it curves around and passes under the highway. Park in the lot just before the first gate, which is locked in winter. The trail starts at the gate. *DeLorme: Northern California Atlas & Gazetteer:* Page 73, B5.

The Hike

Officially called the Fern Canyon Trail, this double loop passes through a narrow valley filled to the brim with diverse plant life. The thick, moss-covered maples, alders, and willows that live along the stream give way to mature second-growth redwood forest as the path climbs the steep North Trail to the ridge. From there the trail drops back to the valley floor and begins the second loop, which brings you to the base of a 36-foot waterfall.

The ancient redwoods in this valley were among the first to be chopped down by white men. Beginning in 1852, San Francisco engineer and promoter Harry Meiggs erected a sawmill on the nearby Big River to harvest the trees. The recreation hall adjacent to the trailhead parking lot stands on the site of an old shingle mill, which was part of this milling operation. In those days the process of felling the giants was a long and labor-intensive one, but getting the lumber to market was the true challenge, due to the difficulties involved in transporting it.

Much of the demand for redwood lumber came from the southern part of the state, where the Gold Rush had turned San Francisco into a boomtown. The great

Waterfall from the trail

Victorian "painted ladies" of that era—large, ornate wooden mansions—were built from redwood, as was everything from railroad ties to shingles to grapevine pickets for California's vineyards. The tree served as a near-perfect building material. It is easy to work, easy to split, and more resistant to rot and insect damage than almost any other wood. In the years following the Gold Rush, California's population exploded, as easterners and foreigners alike flooded into the state to stake a claim. Early on, lumber barons formed plans to exploit the great forests of the north, but many of those dreams went bust under the weight of the difficult logistics and harsh realities of transporting lumber. Steep, muddy hillsides and numerous flood-prone waterways in Redwood Country effectively blocked any road-building efforts, while stormy seas and a treacherous coastline made shipping equally dangerous.

The challenges involved in harvesting the redwoods, while difficult, often sparked inventive solutions. For one thing the trees were so huge that new tools and techniques had to be developed to fell them. Because the redwoods tend to swell at the butt, chopping them down at their base was incredibly difficult. So foresters devised a system whereby notches were cut in the trunk to support a scaffolding, so the lumberjacks could make the cut 4 to 10 feet above the ground, where the trunk

Russian Gulch Double Loop

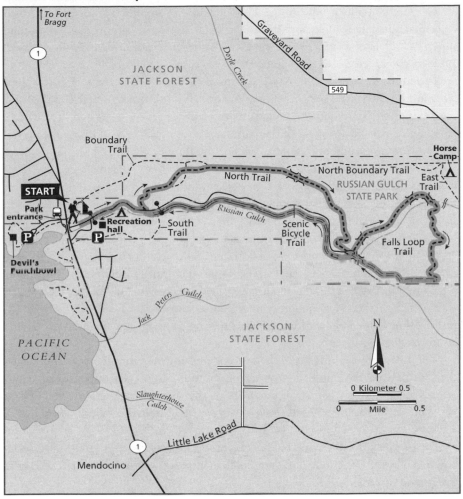

was noticeably smaller in diameter—and thus easier to cut. Special two-man cross-cut saws—sometimes more than 20 feet long—had to be made to saw through the mammoth trees. Next, foresters had to figure out a way to prevent the redwoods from shattering as they hit the ground from their great height. To solve this problem, beds of branches and forest litter were prepared to cushion the impact. There were more obstacles to overcome, such as cutting the trunks into pieces (called bucking) and getting them to the mill. Special sawmills were constructed that were capable of handling the huge logs. Even after the bucking was done, the lumber still had to be transported out of nearly impenetrable forests and steep ravines. The treacherous terrain meant overland travel was virtually impossible for many years, and that left only one option. Though dangerous, the only avenue open was to move the lumber by sea.

Getting the lumber onboard the schooners was a complicated process. The north coast of California is rocky and hazardous, with few good harbors and a punishing surf. The only ports available are small, rock-strewn coves known as "dog holes." Builders constructed elaborate chutes that were suspended by cables anchored in the rocks, and the wood was slid onto the ships as they bobbed in the surf. Many ships were lost on the jagged rocks using this method, but it proved profitable enough for the practice to continue until better modes of transport were devised. If you look closely, you can still see some of the worn and rusty iron rings adorning the jagged rocks of the headlands, once used to anchor the lumber chute cables.

Although it can not replace the unique habitat of an ancient forest, the area's mature second growth harbors an impressive amount of vegetation. It is a common sight to see full-blown trees standing atop old redwood stumps, either as new off-shoots of the original tree or as another species that found purchase on the rotten hulk and sent out roots to find the ground. Redwoods are famous for their regenerative abilities, and by producing new shoots, felled or toppled trees can continue to grow, forming new trunks and branches in a potentially limitless cycle. Another phenomenon peculiar to redwoods are the fairy rings—or Cathedral Trees—that form when a redwood stump sends up shoots all around its base. When these shoots mature, they form a circle of living pillars that are, among other things, very popular for weddings.

The hike through this landscape is a relaxing journey through a verdant wonderland. Beyond the photogenic waterfall, the trail climbs the opposite ridge and returns along another branch of the creek to the spot where the loops join. From here you return to the trailhead along an old road that hugs the valley floor as it parallels the creek.

Before you leave the park, take a few minutes to check out the Devil's Punchbowl, a collapsed wave tunnel in the middle of a meadow that demonstrates the erosive power of waves.

Miles and Directions

0.0 Start at the parking lot just before the first gate. Head past the gate, following the paved road through the campground.

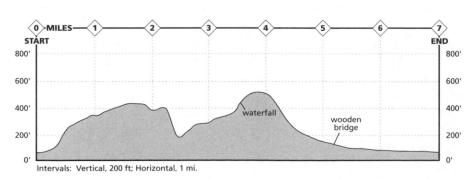

Intervals: Vertical, 200 ft; Horizontal, 1 mi.

0.2 Turn left onto the narrow dirt North Trail, and follow it up as it climbs several switchbacks.

0.6 The trail reaches the top of the ridge and levels out.

0.8 (FYI: The circle of trees on the right sprouted from an old-growth stump, long since rotted away.)

0.9 The trail crosses the Horse Trail. Continue straight.

1.4 Boundary Trail heads to the left. Continue straight.

1.9 North Boundary Trail heads left. Continue straight.

2.0 The trail crosses two small wooden bridges.

2.5 Descending with several switchbacks, the trail drops back down to the valley bottom.

2.6 North Trail connects to Falls Loop Trail. Turn left onto Falls Loop Trail, then take the left fork, as the trail splits. This is the beginning of the loop section of the trail.

3.0 The trail crosses a long footbridge.

3.1 (FYI: The regenerative power of redwoods is shown again by the trees growing out of an old stump on the left.)

3.3 Cross a bridge and follow the trail as it climbs a series of wooden steps.

3.4 An unmarked trail continues straight. Take the right fork, continuing on the main trail to the waterfall.

3.5 Cross the creek on a wooden bridge below the small but scenic waterfall and follow the trail as it heads up the other side, passing by the top of the falls before climbing steps that have been hewn into the rock.

3.6 An unmarked trail heads left. Take the right fork, following the main trail uphill.

4.0 The trail levels out on top of a low ridge.

4.7 The trail descends to a creek, then joins an old skid road. Turn right on the dirt road and continue downstream.

5.1 Cross a wooden bridge and return to the main junction, where the loop section of the trail ends. Continue straight, retracing the short section of trail to the junction with North Trail. Keep going straight, on the paved main trail back to the campground. (This section of trail is open to bicycles.)

5.6 Road turns to gravel. (FYI: Several species of ferns are growing everywhere in this moist canyon bottom, even high in the trees. Maples, willows, and alders grow along the creek, contrasting their light foliage with the dark green of the coniferous forest beyond.)

6.6 South Trail heads off to the left. Continue straight.

6.8 North Trail heads uphill to the right. Continue straight, retracing the first part of the trail to the parking lot and trailhead.

7.0 Arrive back at the trailhead.

Hike Information

Local Information

Fort Bragg–Mendocino Coast Chamber of Commerce, Fort Bragg; (800) 726-2780; (707) 961-6300; www.mendocinocoast.com.

Local Events/Attractions

Skunk Train, this historic line crosses thirty bridges or trestles and two tunnels between Fort Bragg and Willits, 40 miles inland on U.S. Highway 101, Fort Bragg; (800) 77-SKUNK;

Fort Bragg Depot: (707) 964-6371; Willits
Depot: (707) 459-5248.
Mendocino Coast Botanical Gardens,
Fort Bragg; (707) 964-4352;
mcbg@gardenbythesea.org.
Mendocino Music Festival, held every July
in a tent on the Mendocino headlands,
Mendocino; (707) 937-2044;
www.mendocinomusic.com.
Arts & Crafts Fair, July, Mendocino; (707)
937-5818; www.mendocinoartcenter.org.

Mendocino Wine & Mushroom Fest, mid-
November celebration of two of Mendocino's
premiere products, with dinners, cooking
classes, and guided mushroom tours; (707)
961-6300.

Lodging
There is a campground in the park, as well as
several in nearby parks.
State park campsite reservations: (800)
444-7275.

26 Mendocino Headlands Loop

Beginning and ending in the quaint little fishing village-cum-tourist attraction that is Mendocino, this hike follows the convoluted curves of the Mendocino Headland's picturesque sea cliffs and "doghole" ports. Sea caves and sinkholes heighten the drama of this stretch of coastline, a favorite subject of the area's many local artists. The loop is completed by a brief stroll through the heart of town.

Start: At the corner of Main Street and Heeser Drive.
Distance: 2.4-mile loop.
Approximate hiking time: 2 hours.
Difficulty: Easy, due to flat terrain and unmistakable trail.
Trail surface: Dirt path, paved road.
Lay of the land: Coastal bench grasslands, rocky bluffs.
Other trail users: Automobiles and bicycles (briefly).

Canine compatibility: No dogs on trails.
Land status: State park and municipal roads.
Nearest town: Mendocino.
Fees and permits: None.
Schedule: Open year-round. Ford House visitor center hours vary.
Map: USGS map: Mendocino, CA.
Trail contact: California State Parks, Mendocino District Office, Mendocino; (707) 937-5804, www.parks.ca.gov.

Finding the trailhead: Park anywhere on Mendocino's Main Street and walk to the western end of the busy tourist strip. The trail starts at the corner of Main Street and Heeser Drive. *DeLorme: Northern California Atlas & Gazetteer:* Page 73, B5.

The Hike

Walking along the open headlands around the picturesque little town of Mendocino, it is easy to think that the place just evolved "naturally" to its present state. The pastoral scene is so picture-perfect that Hollywood has been a fan for many years. The James Dean classic *East of Eden* was filmed here in 1955, and more recently, it served as stand-in for Detective Jessica Fletcher's hometown in the TV series *Murder, She Wrote*. Still, first impressions can be deceiving, and the town's preservation can be attributed more to visionary activism than to chance. If not for a few far-thinking artists, the headlands and the town would likely have changed significantly over the years, and probably not for the better.

> ▶ Cape Mendocino was named in 1542 in honor of Don Antonio de Mendoza, the first viceroy of "New Spain."

The town of Mendocino got its start in 1852, when one Henry Meiggs showed up, determined to build a sawmill and start harvesting the "red gold" of the towering redwood forests. He was true to his word and had a mill running within the year. (Curiously, Meiggs was not the first white man in the area. When he arrived, a man named William Kasten was already here, living in a small house he had built

Sea arches

himself. It is said that Kasten washed up on the beach in 1850, as a castaway from a shipwreck. Kasten traded part of his land to Meiggs in return for a small fee and enough lumber to build a new house. This "new" house still stands as part of the historic Heeser House.) The town boomed, reaching a population of 700 by the end of the Civil War. It soon became an important center of coastal activity.

Most of the town's historic buildings date from the mid-to-late nineteenth century. As fate would have it, they were still in pretty good shape in the 1950s, although the town's lumber industry had begun to fade, and the population was dwindling. The place was discovered by beatniks and their successors, the hippies, who liked the groovy old houses and beautiful landscape. Mendocino soon became a haven of sorts for artists, back-to-the-landers, and counterculture dropouts. The townsfolk reacted with dismay when rumors began circulating in 1968 that a big corporation was planning to build condominiums between the historic town and the coast. A strong opposition formed to protest the development. Soon the idea surfaced of creating a state park from the headlands, to protect them permanently. The park system was interested, but only if the town developed some sort of historic preservation plan.

Mendocino Headlands Loop

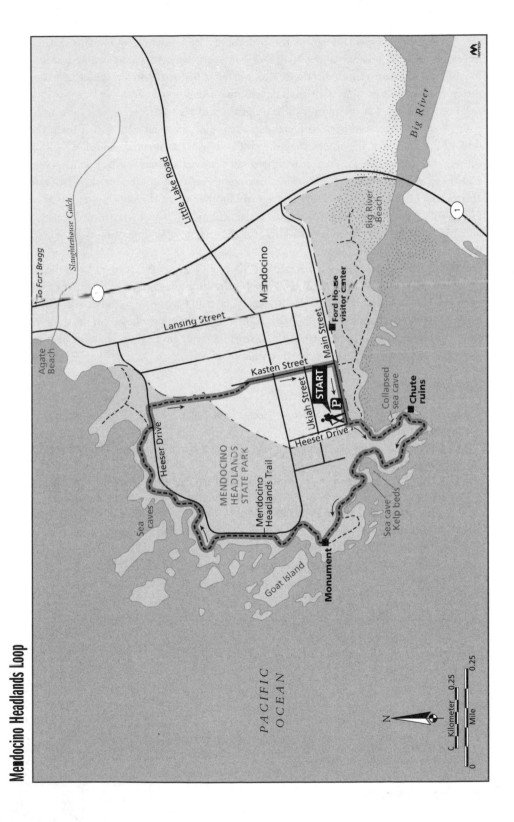

It was a fight, especially given the probusiness elements in town who favored development and free-market government, but eventually the park became a reality in 1972. At the same time, the town also created a historic district, which explains the refreshing lack of ugly strip-mall development in town today.

The hike begins at the corner of Main Street and Heeser Drive. From here a dirt path heads south toward the coast, crossing the wide, grassy tablelands that form the bulk of the state park. Upon reaching the cliffs, the trail heads right and follows along the edge of the bluffs, a course it maintains all the way around the headlands. Here and there, wooden timbers and iron moorings serve as reminders of the elaborate chutes that once stood here. During the early lumber years, the chutes were used to load lumber onto small ships, anchored a safe distance out in the harbor. Nearby, a collapsed sea cave has formed a sinkhole in the meadow, giving walkers a view of the wave-carved tunnel below.

As the trail rounds the headlands, there are plenty more sea caves and "doghole" ports—as the tiny coves are known locally. By the time the trail reaches a line of tall trees on the north side of the headlands, you will have completed a half-circle around the town. At this point you turn right, crossing the headlands on the edge of town and returning through part of the historic district along Kasten Street (named after that early castaway) to the starting point.

Miles and Directions

0.0 Start at the corner of Main Street and Heeser Drive. Follow the path southwest toward the coast.

0.1 The trail reaches the coast. Straight ahead is a sea cave in the headland. Turn right, following the cliff's edge.

0.2 (FYI: The large sinkhole in the meadow is the collapsed roof of the sea cave you saw a moment ago. Iron moorings and timbers are scattered about. These are ruins of the old chute system used to load ships in the harbor.)

0.4 The trail curves sharply inland around a deep pocket cove. (FYI: In the water below, a small kelp forest can be seen.)

0.5 Having rounded the cove, the trail now heads west again, then curves north around another cove.

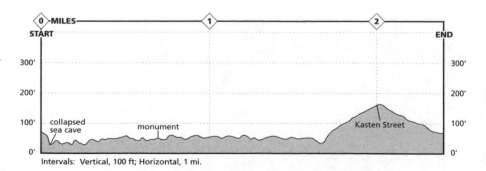

Intervals: Vertical, 100 ft; Horizontal, 1 mi.

0.6 The trail rounds the upper end of the cove, and heads northwest, cutting across the next headland.

0.7 The trail arrives at the westernmost point of the headlands. (FYI: A small monument stands here to peace and ecological protection, and the friendship between Mendocino and a sister city in Japan.) The trail heads right at the monument, heading toward the parking lot.

0.8 At the paved road, turn left. At the north end of the parking lot the trail heads left again, leaving the road.

0.9 The trail joins the road again. Turn left onto the road, and follow it north.

1.0 The trail leaves the road, heading left toward the cliff.

1.2 The trail curves inland around a small cove.

1.3 (FYI: To the left, a long island stretches out to sea, with deep sea caves visible from the coast.)

1.4 The trail reaches the north side of the headlands and begins heading due east.

1.6 The trail joins the paved road again. Continue east along the shoulder.

1.7 Just before the trail reaches a line of trees, turn right. On the other side of the road, follow the faint trail up the hill, heading due south along the fence row.

1.9 The trail arrives at a small Frisbee golf course and a soccer field. Pass by on the left, and head uphill on the gravel road.

2.0 At the top of the hill, continue straight on paved Kasten Street. Follow it down through town.

2.2 Turn right onto Main Street and follow it to the trailhead.

2.4 Trailhead.

Hike Information

Local Information
Fort Bragg–Mendocino Coast Chamber of Commerce, Fort Bragg; (800) 726-2780; www.mendocinocoast.com.

Local Events/Attractions
Ford House, museum and de facto park visitor center, located on Main Street, Mendocino; (707) 937-5397.
Mendocino Art Center, Mendocino; (707) 937-5818.
Mendocino Coast Botanical Gardens, Fort Bragg; (707) 964-4352.

Mendocino Music Festival, held in mid-July, Mendocino; (707) 937-2044; mendocinomusic.com.

Lodging
Mendocino and nearby Fort Bragg have more hotels and B&Bs than you can shake a stick at. There are also campgrounds in the larger state parks north and south of town.
State park campsite reservations: (800) 444-7275.

27 Fern Canyon/Logging Road Loop

This pleasant hike begins and ends at one of a small handful of publicly accessible pygmy forests in the state. From here it plunges down into a deep ravine clothed in mature second-growth redwoods to the headwaters of the Little River. After a stretch along the lush riparian streamside, the trail climbs steeply and returns to the trailhead via an old logging road, now closed to vehicle traffic.

Start: Pygmy Forest trailhead.
Distance: 4.2-mile loop.
Approximate hiking time: 2 to 3 hours.
Difficulty: Moderate, due to some rapid elevation gain.
Trail surface: Gravel road, dirt path, and wooden boardwalk.
Lay of the land: Second-growth redwood forest, riparian forest, and pygmy forest.
Other trail users: Wheelchairs (on pygmy forest boardwalk).

Canine compatibility: Dogs not allowed.
Land status: State park.
Nearest town: Mendocino.
Fees and permits: None, if accessed from the Pygmy Forest trailhead.
Schedule: Open year-round; day-use hours vary.
Map: USGS map: Mathison Peak, CA.
Trail contact: Mendocino Sector Headquarters, Mendocino; (707) 937-5804; www.parks.ca.gov.

Finding the trailhead: From Mendocino, drive south 2.5 miles on California Highway 1 (0.5 mile south of the main entrance to Van Damme State Park). Turn left (east) onto Little River Airport Road and continue up another 2.8 miles to the signed pygmy forest access road. Turn left onto the access road and park in the small lot at the road's dead end. *DeLorme: Northern California Atlas & Gazetteer:* Page 73, B5.

The Hike

This hike begins where Hike 24: Ecological Staircase Trail left off—in one of Mendocino's unique pygmy forests. This particular example is a few miles south of that one, in Van Damme State Park.

The park is named after Charles Van Damme, son of Flemish immigrants who settled in the region in the mid-nineteenth century. John Van Damme—Charles's father—had been a sailing man who decided to weigh anchor and put down roots in the tiny port of Little River, then a thriving frontier lumber town. John went to work in the sawmill, and at home, siring several children. As logging eventually denuded the area's supply of marketable timber, Little River declined and jobs became scarce. Charles moved to San Francisco and set up a ferry business between San Rafael and Richmond, but he never forgot his hometown, and in 1928 he moved back, buying up forty acres from the erstwhile lumber barons. He didn't enjoy it for long, however. He died in 1930, two years after his return. The land was deeded to the state, and it was used to form the core of the park that now bears his name.

Fern Canyon/Logging Road Loop

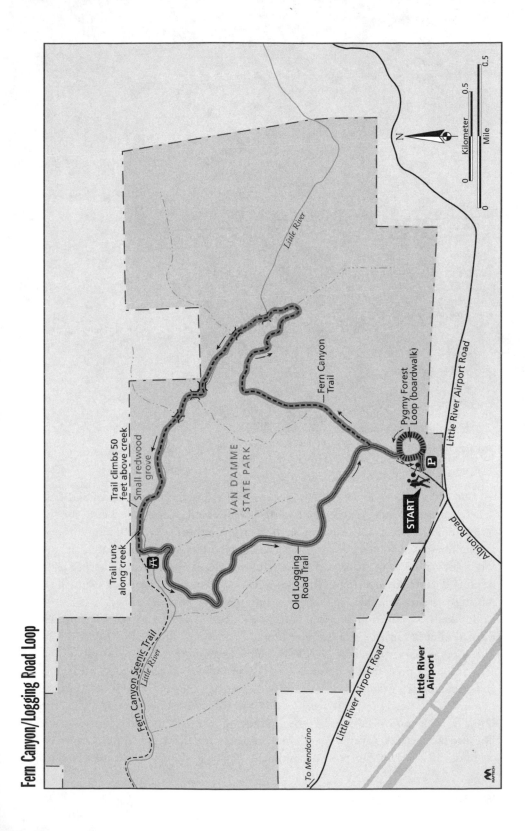

Little River

Trail runs along creek

Trail climbs 50 feet above creek

Small redwood grove

Fern Canyon Scenic Trail

Little River

VAN DAMME STATE PARK

Old Logging Road Trail

Fern Canyon Trail

Pygmy Forest Loop (boardwalk)

START

Little River

Little River Airport Road

Albion Road

To Mendocino

Little River Airport Road

Little River Airport

N

Kilometer 0 0.5

Mile 0 0.5

Boardwalk through the pygmy forest

Our hike begins about 3 miles upriver from this mill-town boom-and-bust drama, amidst the woody descendants of the great trees that once fueled it. To the left of the trailhead is a mature pine forest; to the right, a short boardwalk loop through pygmy forest, which intersects with the Old Logging Road Trail midway. If a pygmy forest doesn't jerk your chain, you can skip the boardwalk and start at the locked gate, heading directly down to Fern Canyon on the road. However, know that you will be missing a rare natural phenomenon, with an interesting story of its own.

It takes a combination of circumstances to make a pygmy forest, starting with the formation of flat marine terraces over hundreds of thousands of years (see Hike 24 for more on marine terraces). Needle-bearing evergreen trees began to grow in the area, and since these trees did not need much in the way of base minerals (calcium and potassium, for example), they did not take in many minerals. Over eons, the base minerals were slowly leached away, leaving the soil PH leaning toward the acidic side. The acidic pine needles fell to the ground and increased its acidity even further. Because the terraces were so flat, no new minerals were brought in from above by erosion, and the leaching process continued. To make things even harder for the plants that still hung on, the acidic soil combined with silica and iron precipitates to form a shallow, concretelike hardpan layer a foot below the surface. Today the third, fourth, and fifth terrace of the "staircase" all have this type of soil.

In the pygmy forest, the foot or so of soil atop the hardpan has been so completely leached of nutrients that the ground has a bleached white color. In fact, this type of soil is so poor that scientists refer to it as *podzol,* a Russian word meaning "ash." Where there is any topsoil at all here, it is less than an inch thick. In essence, it is like trying to grow plants in a shallow pot with no hole in the bottom (not coincidentally, this is exactly the technique used to create Japanese Bonsai trees). Few plants can survive these conditions, and those that do are severely stunted. Bolander pine, Pygmy cypress, and Bishop pine all somehow manage, along with several hardy shrubs, but at a price—trees that normally grow to 100 feet or more rarely reach more than 8 feet here, with diameters of 6 inches or less, even though some of them are up to 300 years old.

After this brief excursion, the hike continues down into Fern Canyon, where conditions are considerably better and second-growth redwoods are rapidly attaining great heights again. Upon reaching the headwaters of the Little River, the trail follows this meandering creek downstream through lush riparian vegetation to a small picnic area. Here it joins the Old Logging Road, which climbs quickly back to the starting elevation and follows a snaking ridge back to the trailhead.

Miles and Directions

0.0 Start at the boardwalk next to the kiosk. At the first junction, turn left.

0.1 Turn left, following the short boardwalk spur to the gravel road. At the road, turn right.

0.3 The road forks. Take the right, singletrack fork.

0.7 The trail begins descending into second-growth redwood forest.

0.9 Descend into the canyon via switchbacks.

1.1 The trail crosses a side gully.

1.2 Cross another side gully.

1.3 The trail reaches the bottom of the canyon. After crossing the stream, the trail curves left and heads downstream.

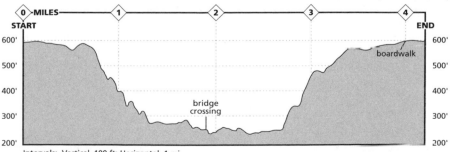

Intervals: Vertical, 100 ft; Horizontal, 1 mi.

1.5 After crossing a low ridge, the trail crosses a second stream, continuing downstream on the other side.

1.9 The trail crosses a bridge to the left side of the drainage. Shortly thereafter, the stream bends, and the trail crosses back over to the right side.

2.3 The trail enters a small redwood grove, then climbs up to the right away from the stream.

2.5 The trail drops down to creek level again.

2.6 The singletrack path ends at a junction with a small picnic area. The gravel Old Logging Road comes in from the left, and continues straight ahead. Turn left, crossing the creek via a small plank bridge, and head up the road on the other side.

2.7 The road switches back and begins to climb steeply.

3.0 The road switches back again, still climbing.

3.2 The road tops out on the ridge, and levels out.

3.8 End of the main loop. Continue straight on the Old Logging Road, returning to the Pygmy Forest Loop.

4.0 Turn left onto the boardwalk again. At the next junction, take the left fork, completing the Pygmy Forest Loop. At the final junction, head left and return to the trailhead.

4.2 Back at the trailhead.

Hike Information

Local Information

Fort Bragg–Mendocino Coast Chamber of Commerce, Fort Bragg; (800) 726-2780; (707) 961-6300; www.mendocinocoast.com.

Local Events/Attractions

Skunk Train, this historic line crosses thirty bridges or trestles and two tunnels between Fort Bragg and Willits, 40 miles inland on U.S. Highway 101, Fort Bragg; (800) 77-SKUNK; Fort Bragg Depot: (707) 964-6371; Willits Depot: (707) 459-5248.

Mendocino Coast Botanical Gardens, Fort Bragg; (707) 964-4352; mcbg@gardenbythesea.org.

Mendocino Music Festival, held every July in a tent on the Mendocino headlands,

Mendocino; (707) 937-2044; www.mendocinomusic.com.

Arts & Crafts Fair, July, Mendocino; (707) 937-5818; www.mendocinoartcenter.org.

Mendocino Wine & Mushroom Fest, mid-November celebration of two of Mendocino's premiere products, with dinners, cooking classes, and guided mushroom tours; (707) 961-6300.

Lodging

There are several state park campgrounds in the area.

State park campsite reservations: (800) 444-7275.

There are also numerous hotels, motels, B&Bs, and private campgrounds in the Mendocino/Fort Bragg area.

28 Big Hendy Long Loop

A gentle stroll through old-growth redwoods to a quiet curve of the Navarro River, then back past memorial groves and through a short stretch of oak-studded grassland to the trailhead. Numerous trails allow for longer or shorter loops.

Start: Big Hendy trailhead.
Distance: 1.6-mile loop.
Approximate hiking time: 1 to 1.5 hours.
Difficulty: Easy, due to good trails and little elevation gain.
Trail surface: Double-wide dirt path.
Lay of the land: Old-growth redwood forest, oak-studded meadows.
Other trail users: Hikers only.

Canine compatibility: Dogs not allowed.
Land status: State park.
Nearest town: Philo.
Fees and permits: $5.00 day-use fee.
Schedule: Open year-round; day-use hours vary.
Map: USGS map: Philo, CA.
Trail contact: Hendy Woods State Park, Philo; (707) 895-3141; www.parks.ca.gov.

Finding the trailhead: From Boonville, drive west 6 miles on California Highway 128. Turn left (south) onto Philo-Greenwood Road and continue another 0.6 mile to the park entrance, on the left just past the bridge. Turn left into the park and continue another 2 miles past the entrance station to the picnic area at the end of the road. *DeLorme: Northern California Atlas & Gazetteer:* Page 74, D1.

The Hike

Hendy Woods State Park lies in the little-known Anderson Valley, a burgeoning wine region. Although only about 100 miles north of San Francisco, the valley is well off the beaten track, reachable only via a narrow two-lane road. The region's vintners have earned themselves a good reputation among wine aficionados, who savor the valley's small yearly production of the noble beverage. The valley has an east-west orientation that is fairly unusual in this part of the coast, and this fact has given it a peculiar advantage over other nearby wine-producing areas. While days tend to be warm and sunny, nights are cool, with dense puffs of fog blowing in from the ocean toward morning. The combination has proven ideal for certain types of cool-season grapes.

Anderson Valley owes its name indirectly to an elk. In 1851 three members of a hunting party tracked the wounded beast into the valley, looked around, and liked what they saw. The men were the sons of Walter Anderson, who soon led the family back into the valley, setting up the first white settlement in the area near the junction of present-day California Highways 128 and 253. Wine production started a few years later, when Italian and Swiss immigrants first planted grape cuttings from their homelands in the valley's fertile soil. The resulting wine was used mainly by the

Meadow and an oak tree at a bend in the river

growers themselves, but the occasional bottle did find its way down to the miners and logging camps. By the 1890s a fledgling wine industry was eking out an existence in Anderson Valley.

The fun ended in 1920, the year Congress put Prohibition into effect. Wineries were shut down and equipment destroyed, effectively ending the wine business in the valley. With the death of the industry, farmers took to growing more acceptable produce. Apples took over as the valley's prime export, and they remained so for many years. Although Prohibition was repealed in the early 1930s, it wasn't until the 1960s that grape growing began to make a comeback. In that year Dr. Donald Emeades planted several acres of cool-season varietals—and the rest, as they say, is history. Today Anderson Valley does a brisk business in fine wine, specializing in Pinot Noir, Gewürztraminer, Chardonnay, and White Riesling varietals. Wine-tasting rooms dot the valley, providing ample distraction for fans of the fermented grape.

Big Hendy State Park is a little breath of wild air amidst all this agricultural orderliness. The green spires of its ancient redwoods provide quite the contrast to the

Big Hendy Long Loop

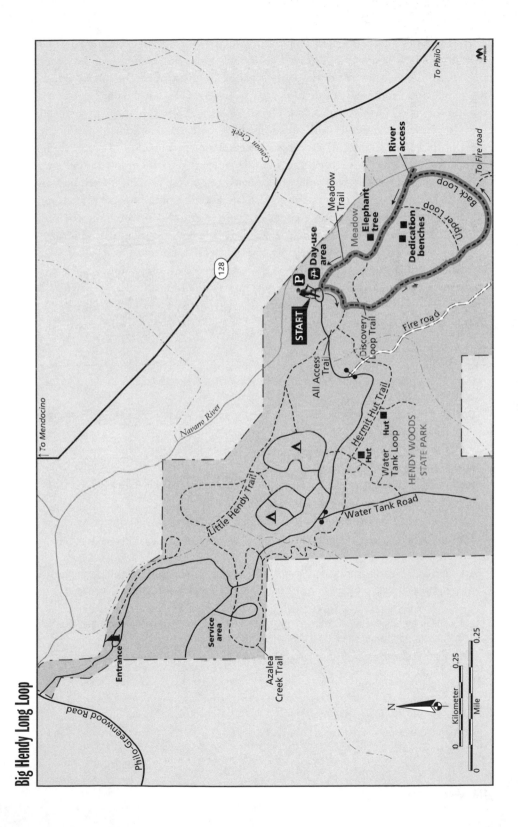

open grasslands and manicured grape arbors of the surrounding countryside. The park houses two groves of old-growth redwoods within its boundaries. The largest, Big Hendy Loop, contains about eighty acres of the giant trees. Our hike begins at the picnic area on the north side of the grove, tucked between the edge of the forest and the banks of the meandering Navarro River. The trail plunges immediately into the shade of the forest on the broad path of the All Access Trail. Here the visitor will find all of the crowd-pleasing aspects of the classic redwood forest. Living trees stand tall even with cave-size hollows burned into their trunks by long-forgotten forest fires. Massive trunks lay sprawled out on the ground, stretching hundreds of feet into the forest, while the great tangled mass of their roots spreads into the air high above hiker's heads. Dozens of "volunteer trails" surrounding the most impressive trees bear witness to the popularity of the grove among park visitors.

The hike soon leaves this living playground behind, however, as it heads south into the heart of the grove along the Discovery Loop. The remainder of the hike explores the quiet old-growth forest, describing a large loop around the parcel. The return loop offers a couple of chances for detours to the river's edge—a cool prospect on hot days.

Miles and Directions

0.0 Start at the large wooden sign with the carved trail map. Head right into the forest on the All Access Trail.

0.1 At the junction a few yards past the footbridge, turn left onto the Discovery Trail, heading deeper into the forest.

0.4 The trail arrives at a four-way junction. Head straight, on the Upper Loop.

0.5 A low ridge is visible to the right.

0.6 At the junction, the Upper Loop heads left. Continue straight on the Back Loop.

0.8 The connecting trail to the fire road heads right. Continue straight.

1.0 A spur trail heads right a few yards down to the river. Continue straight.

1.2 The Back Loop rejoins the Upper Loop at this junction. Continue straight on the Upper Loop.

1.3 A couple of benches mark dedicated redwood groves. A short spur trail heads right from the second bench, leading to a tree with a strange drooping appendage. Continue straight.

1.4 End of the Upper Loop. Continue straight on the Discovery Loop. A few yards later the trail hits another junction. Head straight toward the day-use area.

1.5 The trail exits the forest into a large grassy meadow on a bend in the river. Continue straight.

1.6 Trailhead.

Hike Information

Local Information

Anderson Valley Chamber of Commerce, Boonville; (707) 895-2379; www.andersonvalleychamber.com.

Local Events/Attractions

Anderson Valley Pinot Noir Weekend, held in mid-May, demonstrations and wine tasting, plus a barbeque and silent auction, Philo; tickets: (707) 895-WINE; www.avwines.com/pinot-wknd.

California Wine Tasting Championships, held in July, novice, amateur, and professional categories for both singles and doubles events, fine food and live music as well, Greenwood Ridge; (707) 895-2002; www.greenwoodridge.com.

Mendocino County Fair and Apple Show, held in mid-September, rodeo, sheep dog trials, parade, Boonville; (707) 895-3011.

Lodging

The park has a campground with ninety-plus sites.

State park campsite reservations: (800) 444-7275.

Honorable Mentions

Southern Humboldt/Mendocino

E King Peak Trail

A moderate-to-strenuous 5-mile out-and-back trail to the summit of King Peak—the highest point on the Lost Coast. From the trailhead the trail climbs steeply through oak and madrone forests to the peak, where spectacular views await. From U.S. Highway 101 at Redway, turn west onto Briceland Road and drive 10.7 miles before taking the left fork to Whitethorn and Shelter Cove. Continue 2 miles, take the right fork to Shelter Cove, and drive another 4.5 miles before turning right onto King Peak Road. Drive 8.5 miles, then take the left fork onto Lightning Road. Continue another 6 miles to the Lightning trailhead, on the left side of the road. For more information, contact: Arcata Resource Area, U.S. Bureau of Land Management, Arcata; (707) 825–2300. *DeLorme: Northern California Atlas & Gazetteer:* Page 52, C3.

F Big Tree Loop

This moderate 3.5-mile loop pays a visit to the Miles Standish Tree, a scarred redwood giant more than 1,000 years old. The hike begins at the Hickey Campground Campfire Center, descending the bluffs to the South Fork Eel River, and up the other side through oak and madrone forests to the lone giant redwood. The return loop offers excellent views of the river and passes the park's premier swimming hole before climbing the bluffs to the trailhead. From Garberville, head south 27 miles on U.S. Highway 101. Turn right into Standish-Hickey State Recreation Area, and follow the park entrance road around to the right, to the day-use parking lot at the end of the campground. For more information contact: Standish-Hickey State Recreation Area, Leggett; (707) 925–6482. *DeLorme: Northern California Atlas & Gazetteer:* Page 63, A5.

North Bay/ Wine Country

The mellow rolling hills and broad valleys of Sonoma County contrast starkly with the steep, wild country farther north. The Spanish certainly thought so back in the eighteenth century, when they were busy setting up California's mission system. With such hospitable landscapes here, they saw little reason to continue farther north, and the city of Santa Rosa pretty much marks the northernmost limits of their colonial expansion.

Today much of this land is given over to the production of California's famous wines, and evidence of this industry abounds along U.S. Highway 101. The gentle contours of the valleys and foothills are dominated by row upon row of grapevines, and young urban professionals cruise from one wine tasting to the next in polished SUVs. For all of the obvious money and carefully maintained quaintness on display in the lowlands, Sonoma's highlands and coastal areas still hold more than a hint of the wild. The coast especially seems to be largely forgotten by the bustling townsfolk and businesspeople farther inland. Cut off from the Russian River Valley by the ubiquitous coastal mountain range, the Sonoma Coast is totally devoid of large settlements, and the principal lodging facilities are the campgrounds at Fort Ross and Salt Point State Parks. As in Big Sur and Mendocino, the coast here consists of table-like benchlands, steep mountainsides, and rugged, rocky sea cliffs. The sea is equally rough, with undertows, riptides, and large, crashing waves that still tempt a few brave surfers out into the fray. Beaches, where they exist, tend to be narrow strips in sheltered coves, but waters are rarely safe for casual swimming. Grassy meadows run along the level tops of coastal bluffs, where trails explore the erosive power of the sea. Seals and sea lions ply the waters close to shore, and spouts of ocean spray betray the presence of migrating gray whales in deeper water. Other hikes follow narrow ravines from sheltered coves to lush, verdant forests and mossy waterfalls upstream.

But even the more civilized inland areas are dotted by numerous parks and other public lands, offering miles of good hiking for those who know where to find them (hence this book). Tucked in among the grapes are several state parks with trails enough to tempt the lug-soled crowd this way. Among other destinations, historic

Annadel State Park offers a network of hiking trails and a surprising amount of unspoiled nature, even within shouting distance of sprawling Santa Rosa.

Although closer to San Francisco, Marin County is no more tame than its northern neighbor, Sonoma. Here, the mountains pile higher again, creating a natural wall between the urban sprawl of the Bay Area and the pastoral grazing lands of the coast and Point Reyes. Much of this land falls under the jurisdiction of the Golden Gate National Recreation Area, supplemented by Muir Woods National Monument and Mount Tamalpais State Park. Perched on top of this jumble is Mount Tamalpais itself, whose peak offers amazing 360-degree views of the bay and surrounding countryside, and is flanked by miles of great trails. At its base a respectable redwood forest still hangs on in the deep valleys of Muir Woods National Monument. On the east, amid the noble homes of the well-situated, a few state parks allow the rest of us to explore surprisingly large chunks of the Bay Area's natural landscape.

West of the mountains, peaks and valleys give way to rolling dairy land, then to the oyster-raising towns on Tomales Bay. This long finger of the Pacific, actually a submerged section of the famous San Andreas Rift, neatly divides a huge triangle of land known as Point Reyes from the rest of California. Today largely protected as a national seashore, Point Reyes is host to a myriad of microclimates, habitats, and landscapes, including fog-bound shaggy forests, open grassy meadows, rocky hillsides, and miles of gorgeous beaches where elephant seals come ashore to battle and breed. One of dozens of possible routes, the Sky-Laguna Loop manages to visit several of these landscapes in a single 10-mile loop.

29 Fisk Mill to Stump Beach Trail

This hike visits a prime spot for whale watching. The trail is a short hike along steep bluffs overlooking offshore rocks, which are home to harbor seals. Deep gullies and surge channels are also interesting features found along this rugged stretch of coast.

Start: From the Fisk Mill north parking lot.
Approximate hiking time: 2.5 miles out and back.
Distance: 1.5 to 2 hours.
Difficulty: Easy to moderate, due to a couple of steep sections and a poorly maintained trail.
Trail surface: Dirt path.
Lay of the land: Pine forest, open meadows, and rocky coastline.
Other trail users: Hikers only.
Canine compatibility: Leashed dogs permitted (only in developed areas).

Land status: State park.
Nearest town: Walsh Landing.
Fees and permits: $4.00 per car for day use.
Schedule: Open all year. The visitor center is open daily from 8:00 A.M. to 4:00 P.M.
Map: USGS map: Plantation, CA. A trail map is available from the visitor center, or at Fort Ross State Park.
Trail contact: Salt Point State Park, Jenner; (707) 847-3221; www.parks.ca.gov.

Finding the trailhead: From Santa Rosa, drive 6 miles west on California Highway 12, then turn right onto California Highway 116 and follow it north and west about 28 miles to the junction with California Highway 1. Go north 20 miles on CA 1, continuing past the main entrance and the Stump Beach parking areas. Turn in to the Fisk Mill parking lot at the northernmost end of the park, and immediately turn right again for the north parking lot. On the west side of the lot is a sign for the Bluff Trail. *DeLorme: Northern California Atlas & Gazetteer:* Page 82, D2.

The Hike

The Sonoma Coast is one of California's most dramatic, in terms of scenery. Steep-walled cliffs drop off into crashing surf. Enormous waves slam against offshore rocks and explode into the air in a wall of spray. Deep coves shelter hidden beaches. And the constant attention of the ocean carves caves and natural bridges into the rock. In short, it's a fine place to take a stroll.

Salt Point State Park harbors a variety of terrain within its 6,000 acres. Gerstle Cove Marine Reserve, also within park boundaries, is one of the first underwater parks in California, protecting the diversity of marine life found here. Aside from the rocky coast, the park offers a variety of habitats that include grasslands and forests of Bishop pine. There are also stands of second-growth redwoods, and even a small pygmy forest.

In the past this area was home to several groups of southwestern Pomo Indians, also known as Kashia (or Kashaya) Pomo. Archeologists have found evidence of the villages by studying sites called middens—the garbage dumps of yesteryear. Since

Water pools near the cliff

they didn't have plastic and metals in those days, most of what went into a midden was biodegradable and has long since turned to dirt. What remains are bones, less-perishable artifacts, and—above all—shells. Shellfish was a popular item on the native menu, and it is still possible to identify old settlements up and down the coast by the profusion of broken shells in and on the ground. (Note: These sites are valuable for archeologists, so don't disturb them.)

This hike, one of several short walks within Salt Point State Park, starts at the Fisk Mill parking area at the north end of the park. The path plunges into a shady forest dominated by Bishop pine and winds around in the enchanting woods a bit before revealing the first ocean vista. In fact, most people are likely to spend the majority of their time on this hike gawking at the magical landscape around them. The trail ducks in and out of the forest and later travels over open grassland—offering a new surprise with each visit to the edge. The earth is also doing interesting things here, due in part to a series of streams that course through the region and slowly erode the natural landscape. Where water has bared the bones of the earth, you can see layers of sedimentary rock, which tend sometimes to tilt up at odd angles. The streams

Fisk Mill to Stump Beach Trail

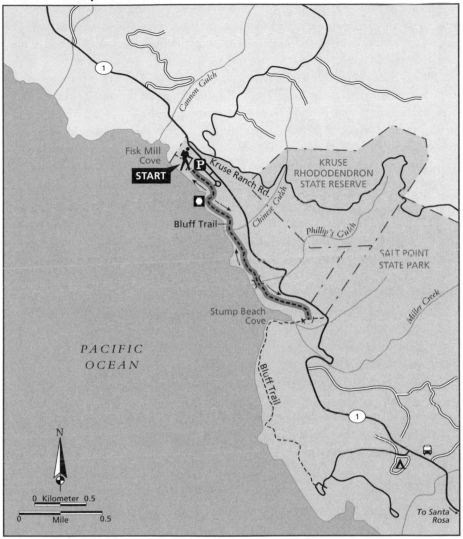

that descend from the forests form shallow pools as they encounter bedrock, shortly before taking the final plunge to the sea. Near the halfway point of the hike, a tiny creek careens over the brink of the coastal cliffs, forming a waterfall framed against a background of emerald green plant life. For aspiring postcard photographers, it doesn't get any better than this.

The trail climbs gently as it continues across broad meadows, and the trail eventually reaches the entrance to Stump Beach Cove, where it turns inland, skirting the cliffs. There are extensive kelp beds in and around the cove, and it is easy to imagine the Aleutian hunters in the early nineteenth century plying the waters in their kayaks and searching for the sea otter that once fed here in large numbers. The Aleuts were working for enterprising Russian fur traders, probing down the coast from their Alaskan settlements and seeking pelts from the increasingly rare animal. The Aleuts eventually hunted the otters nearly to extinction, but today they are protected by the Endangered Species Act and are making a slow recovery.

Heading east above Stump Beach Cove, the trail passes close to the edge of the tall, dark cliffs that rim the cove. From this vantage point, a natural bridge can be seen in the jagged rock below. The path then leads past the site of a recent forest fire as it reenters the forest. As a parting shot, the trail offers a steep scrabble down a gully before crossing the small creek and dropping down the last few feet to Stump Beach. Here you can kick off your shoes and go beachcombing. Be sure to check out the mounds of bullwhip kelp that wash up on the beach regularly.

Miles and Directions

0.0 Start from the west side of the parking lot at the sign for the Bluff Trail.

0.03 Junction. Going straight leads down to a view of the coastline. The trail continues to the left.

0.2 Nice view of the ocean to the right.

0.35 Picnic area. A spur trail heads off to the left, accessing the south parking lot. Follow the trail to the right.

0.4 Junction. Turn left.

0.7 Another junction; this time continue to the right.

1.0 Trail forks, with one branch going up and over a rock outcropping and the other continuing along the cliffs. Take either one; they meet in a couple hundred feet.

1.08 View of Stump Beach Cove; the beach to the left is your destination.

1.25 Stump Beach Cove. This is the turnaround point. Return along the same trail.

2.5 Arrive back at the trailhead.

Hike Information

Local Information
www.sonoma.com

Local Events/Attractions
Living History Day, held the last Saturday of July, craft demonstrations, period food, etc., Fort Ross State Historic Park; (707) 847-3586; (707) 847-3437.

Jazz on the River, held in early September, Guerneville; (510) 655-9471; www.jazzontheriver.com.

Russian River Blues Festival, held in late June, Guerneville; (510) 655-9471; www.jazzontheriver.com/blues.

Lodging
There are several camping areas within the park.

State park campsite reservations: (800) 444-7275. Several spots are available for cyclists and hikers on a first-come, first-served basis.

Hike Tours

Walking tours are occasionally given by park interpreters. Call (707) 847-3221 for specific information.

Public Transportation

Mendocino Transit Authority (MTA) bus route #95 runs once daily along CA 1 between Point Arena and Santa Rosa. The bus will drop you off at any safe location and you must flag the bus to be picked up. The bus runs inbound to Santa Rosa in the A.M. and outbound from Santa Rosa in the P.M. In Santa Rosa, Golden Gate Transit offers connections from San Francisco. Call (800) 696-4682 or visit www.transitinfo.org.

30 Cemetery Trail

This hike explores one of California's most fascinating historic idiosyncrasies: a Russian fur-hunting settlement on the Sonoma Coast, dating back nearly two hundred years. The fort stockade has largely been restored to its original appearance, with massive rough-hewn timber walls and log buildings filled with implements of the era. An excellent visitor center and bookstore cover the rich history admirably well. The hike leads from the fort down to Fort Ross Cove, where the Russians launched their fur-hunting expeditions, and on up the creek to the settlement's cemetery.

Start: At the visitor center parking lot.
Distance: 1.5-mile lollipop.
Approximate hiking time: 1 hour.
Difficulty: Easy, due to short length and little elevation gain.
Trail surface: dirt path, gravel road, paved road.
Lay of the land: Grassy coastal bench, riparian forest.
Other trail users: Automobiles (briefly).
Canine compatibility: No dogs allowed.

Land status: State park.
Nearest town: Jenner.
Fees and permits: $4.00 day-use fee.
Schedule: Open year-round half an hour before sunrise to half an hour after sunset. Visitor center and fort compound open daily from 10:00 A.M. to 4:30 P.M.
Map: USGS map: Fort Ross, CA.
Trail contact: Fort Ross State Historic Park, Jenner; (707) 847-3286; www.parks.ca.gov.

Finding the trailhead: From Santa Rosa, head west 6 miles on California Highway 12. In Sebastopol, turn right onto California Highway 116 and drive 28 miles to the junction with California Highway 1. Turn right (north) onto CA 1 in Jenner, and continue 12 miles, then turn left into Fort Ross State Park. Park in the large paved lot. The trail begins at the western end of the lot, where the gravel road continues down around to the left. *DeLorme: Northern California Atlas & Gazetteer:* Page 82, D3.

The Hike

If you stopped most Americans—or Californians, for that matter—on the street and told them about Fort Ross, chances are they would be more than a little surprised to learn that by the time California became a state in 1850, a Russian outpost had already been standing on the Sonoma Coast for nearly forty years.

It was 1812, to be exact, when Russian expedition leader Ivan Alexandrovich Kuskov left his Alaskan base with twenty-five Russians and eighty Native Alaskan hunters, with orders to construct and manage a fortified settlement on a remote and undeveloped stretch of rocky California coastline. At the time the chosen location was well within the boundaries claimed by Spain as its exclusive domain. The territory was so vast, however, that Spain had yet to establish settlements farther north than Santa Rosa. Nevertheless, the Spaniards were aware of Russian

The Russian Cemetery

activities at Fort Ross, and regarded the settlement with strong suspicion, if not outright hostility.

The Russian motivation for the establishment of the Fort Ross colony was the same as what had driven them to conquer the vast reaches of eastern Siberia in the sixteenth and seventeenth centuries—the fur trade. The Russian equivalents of French-Canadian voyageurs and American mountain men were known as *promyshlenniki*. Like their North American counterparts, the *promyshlenniki* hunted fur-bearing animals in huge numbers, constantly moving into new territory as prey became harder and harder to find. By the 1740s this hunger for new hunting grounds brought the Russians to the new world. In Alaska they claimed huge expanses of territory for the czar, eventually establishing permanent outposts on the islands of Kodiak and Sitka. Native Aleutian Islanders with their swift skin kayaks, or *baidarkas*, were recruited to hunt for the abundant fur seals and sea otters, whose high-quality pelts brought exorbitant prices in Europe and Asia. Soon the Russians were exporting upwards of 62,000 pelts a year from Alaska.

Cemetery Trail

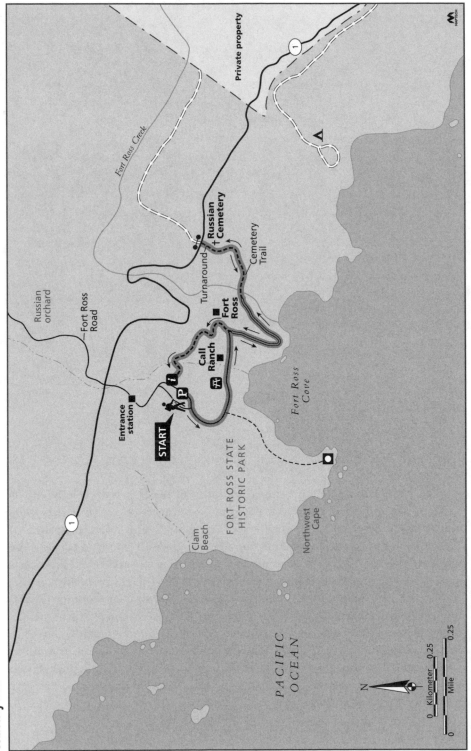

Not surprisingly, numbers of seals and otters quickly began to plummet, and by the turn of the century, the Russians were already casting eager glances south to the abundant sea otter populations of California.

Numerous hunting expeditions led to the establishment of the fort in 1812. The settlement soon grew to include a small village of around 250 men, women, and children, the majority of whom were either Aleuts, local Kashaya Indians, or Russian-Indian Creoles. In its heyday the fort operated a farm, dairy, orchard, and numerous semi-industrial workshops. Still, it was only a matter of time before the economic basis of the colony—sea otters—began to disappear. By 1820 the otters had been hunted nearly to extinction. The colony hung on for another twenty years, relying on ranching for its sparse livelihood, but by 1841 the Russians had had enough. The land and buildings were sold off to California ranchers, beginning an era that lasted until 1962, when the fort became a state park, and restoration of the remaining stockade buildings began.

With such a rich history, it is not surprising that few people come to Fort Ross with hiking in mind. Indeed, there is only one trail to speak of in the park, and that is a short one. Still, the brief hike offers a pleasant diversion from a long road trip up the coast, and is well worth checking out. Beginning at the visitor center parking lot, the trail follows a gravel road down toward the coast through a picturesque tunnel of wind-bent Monterey cypress. Past this is the Call House, headquarters of the Call family's ranch, which operated here from 1873 to 1962. South of the house is the stockade and fort proper, which is an exploration in itself, to be undertaken at leisure, either now or on the way back. The hike continues out to the point, then down to tiny Fort Ross Cove, where the Russians once had a thriving little industrial center, complete with everything from a blacksmith to a cooper, and even a small shipyard. From here a singletrack path follows the creek up to a small grassy meadow, where the fort's cemetery once stood. Wooden crosses in the Russian Orthodox style adorn the small graveyard. Return to the fort along the same trail and proceed to the excellent visitor center via a separate footpath.

Miles and Directions

0.0 Start at the west end of the main parking lot. Follow the gravel road down to the left.

0.1 The road turns to pavement and curves to the left. To the right, a side trail heads down to the point. Continue on the road.

0.2 Picnic area is on the left.

0.25 Call Ranch House is on the left.

0.3 Pass the fort, then follow the road as it curves right.

0.4 At the point, the road switches back to the left, and heads down into Fort Ross Cove.

0.5 The trail reaches the bottom of the cove. Continue more or less straight, crossing the small creek via the footbridge and continuing on singletrack path.

0.7 The trail pops out of trees and curves left.

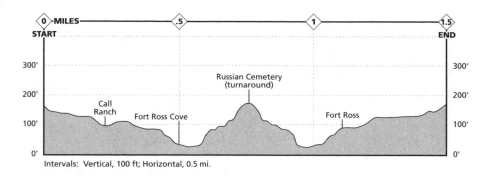

Intervals: Vertical, 100 ft; Horizontal, 0.5 mi.

0.8 Russian Cemetery. Across the ravine, the fort seems deceptively close. Return the way you came to the fort.

1.3 Back at the fort. After exploring the stockade, exit via the north gate, and follow the paved path right, back to the visitor center.

1.5 Visitor center, end of trail.

Hike Information

Local Information
Sonoma County Tourism Program, www.sonomacounty.com.

Local Events/Attractions
Living History Day, held the last Saturday of July, craft demonstrations, period food, etc., Fort Ross State Historic Park; (707) 847-3286; (707) 847-3437.

Jazz on the River, held in early September, Guerneville; (510) 655-9471; www.jazzontheriver.com.

Russian River Blues Festival, held in late June, Guerneville; (510) 655-9471; www.jazzontheriver.com/blues.

Lodging
Salt Point State Park, a few miles north of Fort Ross, has more than 100 campsites; (707) 847-3221.
There is also a small campground just south of the fort.
State park campsite reservations: (800) 444-7275.

Organizations
Stewards of Slavianka, Duncans Mills; (707) 865-0180; www.stewardsofslavianka.org.

31 Two Ridge Loop

A full loop along the two ridges surrounding Armstrong Redwoods State Reserve. This is a challenging hike, especially in summer, when the exposed ridges can get very hot. The views from the top are worth the effort, however. From the summit of Pool Ridge, you have the opportunity to get a rare bird's-eye view of an old-growth redwood forest, not to mention the Russian River Valley beyond. The hike begins and ends in the aforementioned redwood groves.

Start: Pool Ridge trailhead.
Distance: 4.2-mile loop.
Approximate hiking time: 3 to 4 hours.
Difficulty: Strenuous, due to steep trail and elevation gains.
Trail surface: Dirt path, dirt road, and gravel road.
Lay of the land: Second-growth redwood forest, oak forest, and exposed, grassy hillsides.
Other trail users: Equestrians.
Canine compatibility: No dogs allowed.
Land status: State park; state recreation area.

Nearest town: Guerneville.
Fees and permits: $4.00 day-use fee (pedestrians and cyclists free).
Schedule: Open year-round, 8:00 A.M. to one hour after sunset. Visitor center is open from 11:00 A.M. to 3:00 P.M. daily.
Map: USGS map: Cazadero, CA.
Trail contact: Armstrong Redwoods State Park, Austin Creek State Recreation Area, Guerneville; (707) 869-2015; armvs@mcn.org.

Finding the trailhead: From Santa Rosa, head west 6 miles on California Highway 12 to Sebastopol, then north 15 miles on California Highway 116 (River Road) to Guerneville. In town, head north on Armstrong Redwoods Road 2.4 miles to the visitor center, and another 0.5 mile to the picnic area. Park at the picnic area. The trailhead is at the western (left) edge of the picnic area, near the rest rooms. *DeLorme: Northern California Atlas & Gazetteer:* Page 83, D4.

The Hike

If you take a road trip through the Redwood Coast, starting at the Oregon border and working your way slowly south, it becomes very apparent that, with a few notable exceptions, there are fewer and fewer of the ancient trees to be found as you move southward. This was not always so. When Europeans first arrived in the area, they found a huge swath of virgin redwood forest growing just inland from the coast from Oregon to San Simeon. But the pressures of this new civilization hit earlier and harder in the south. Huge tracts of forest were felled for lumber and cleared for agriculture. It was a lucky grove that survived to the present day.

While there are few old-growth redwood groves in Sonoma County, those remaining are all the more precious to visitors and locals alike. Armstrong Redwoods State Reserve is one of these gems, and it protects 805 acres of land containing some

The trail just pass the first saddle

of the last old-growth groves in the area. The oldest tree in the park is the Colonel Armstrong Tree, estimated to be about 1,400 years old. While it may seem strange to name a tree after a person who was born when the tree was already more than 1,200 years old—and whom the tree has since outlived by more than 100 years—given the history of the park, it is understandable. The tree—and the reserve—take their name from a Civil War veteran named James Boydston Armstrong, one of the early settlers in the area, and the man ultimately responsible for saving the reserve's redwoods from the ax. Armstrong set out from his native Ohio in 1874, settling in the young logging town of Guerneville.

▶ **Before it was renamed after leading citizen George E. Guerne, the logging camp of Guerneville was aptly known as Stumptown.**

Aside from his many business interests, which included lumbering and land speculation, Armstrong had a strong interest in botany, and he was a friend and contemporary of the famous horticulturist Luther Burbank. Armstrong, and later his family, worked for nearly forty years to create a park and botanical garden from the 440 acres at the heart of the reserve. It wasn't until 1917 that the dream was finally realized. In that year the land became a county park. In 1934 the state took over, and the reserve took its present form.

The hike begins in the picnic area in the center of the park. From the edge of the old-growth redwoods protected by the Old Colonel's foresight, the hike quickly leaves the shady groves, climbing an old logging road steeply uphill to the saddle on Pool Ridge. From the saddle, hikers have a sweeping view out over the park, looking down on the ancient forest canopy from above. The landscape up here is very different from the lush groves at the trailhead. In the place of towering redwoods, there are aromatic bay laurel and gnarled oaks, clinging tenaciously to the steep slopes amid swaths of parched golden grasses. In spring, wildflowers steal the show, covering the open meadows with constellations of color. The trail heads north along the ridge and soon comes to a scenic detour. This leads left up to a bare knoll, which offers an even better view of the valleys below than the saddle did earlier.

The remainder of the hike circumscribes a large loop through Armstrong and the neighboring Austin Creek State Recreation Area, which protects another 6,000 acres of rolling hills and deep valleys. The return leg drops down off the ridgetop and gradually descends through scruffy second-growth forests. Shortly before returning to the picnic area, the trail climbs down through an impressive old-growth grove, offering a final reward for all the hard work.

Miles and Directions

0.0 Start just to the left of the rest room at the west end of the picnic area. The trail heads steeply up an old dirt logging road called the Pool Ridge Trail.

0.1 The trail begins a couple of switchbacks.

Two Ridge Loop

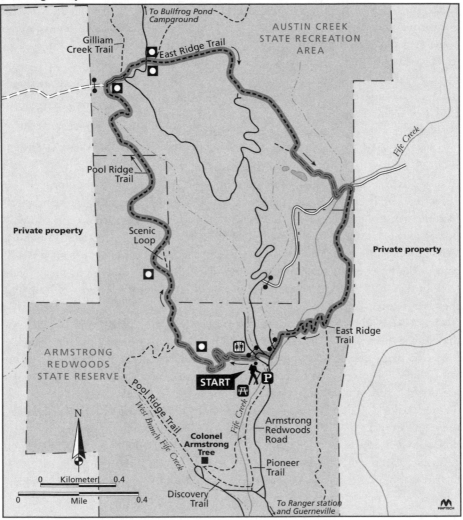

0.2 The trail heads into a narrow ravine, switches back right at the ravine's head, and continues to contour around the hill.

0.4 The trail rounds a knob and switches back again, following the ridge.

0.5 The forest opens on the right, offering a view of the valley far below. A few yards later, the trail tops out at a saddle on the ridge. A trail heads left to the Armstrong Tree, but we continue straight, contouring up along the other side of the ridge.

0.6 The trail reaches another saddle and climbs steeply along the ridge.

0.8 The trail crosses back over to the other side of the ridge, plunging into an oak grove studded with fir.

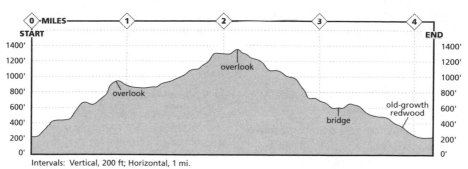

Intervals: Vertical, 200 ft; Horizontal, 1 mi.

0.9 The trail grade mellows out, allowing for a breather. Shortly afterward, a side loop heads up to the left. The detour climbs steeply to a nice overlook, then curves around to the right and rejoins the main trail about 0.1 mile farther up. Take either route.

1.0 The trail starts heading gently downhill, following the right side of the ridge.

1.8 The trail begins to switchback steeply up.

1.9 After topping out on a saddle, the trail ends at a gravel road. A locked metal gate is located several yards to the left. Turn right onto the road and follow it around the bend. You will shortly come to a junction, with two singletrack trails heading down to the left. To the extreme left is the Gilliam Creek Trail. We take the middle route, following the East Ridge Trail.

2.1 The trail arrives at the paved access road, just below a saddle. Cross the road and continue on the path up the other side, which shortly curves right and reaches the saddle. Vistas open up on both sides of the ridge. Continue steeply down the other side of the ridge on the East Ridge Trail.

2.4 The trail crosses a stream, continuing downhill on the left side of the waterway.

2.5 A dirt road heads down to the right toward some old walls and a water tank. Continue straight.

2.6 A spur trail heads right to some private homes. Keep going straight.

2.8 The trail drops down onto a dirt road bed. Turn left, and continue downhill. The trail soon comes to a meadow, with two small reservoirs on the right.

2.9 The trail ducks back into forest at the end of the meadow.

3.0 The trail ends at a gravel road. Turn left onto the road and follow it over the small bridge. On the other side of the creek, turn right onto the resumed trail, continuing downstream. (FYI: If you look back at the bridge from just downstream, you can see that the relatively new metal structure overlies an older wooden span with a pronounced sag. Beneath the gravel of the earlier structure, the original planking can still be seen.)

3.7 The East Ridge Trail continues straight toward the ranger station, but we turn right, heading downhill toward the picnic area via a connector trail. The trail immediately begins several switchbacks.

3.8 A bench is on the knob to the right. A bit later there is a large redwood stump on the left that has an excellent example of curly grain.

3.9 The trail passes through a fine stand of old-growth redwoods.

4.1 The trail crosses a bridge and arrives at the overflow parking lot for the picnic area. Follow the road down to the left to return to the trailhead.

4.2 Trailhead.

Hike Information

Local Information
Russian River Chamber of Commerce and Visitor Center, Guerneville; (877) 644-9001; (707) 869-9000; www.russianriver.com.

Local Events/Attractions
Stumptown Daze Parade and Rodeo, late May–early June; (707) 869-1959.

Jazz on the River, held in early September, Guerneville; (510) 655-9471; www.jazzontheriver.com.

Russian River Blues Festival, held in late June, Guerneville; (510) 655-9471; www.jazzontheriver.com/blues.

Armstrong Woods Pack Station, horse rentals, Guerneville (adjacent to Armstrong Redwoods State Reserve); (707) 887-2939; www.RedwoodHorses.com.

Hike Tours
Stewards of Slavianka, Duncans Mills; (707) 865-0180; www.stewardsofslavianka.org.

Lodging
There is a drive-in campground at Bullfrog Pond in Austin Creek State Recreation Area, Guerneville; (707) 869-2015. Backcountry camping is also possible.

32 Bodega Head Loop

Spectacular views of the ocean, pocket beaches, and rugged cliffs await hikers on this quick loop around Bodega Head. Wildlife lovers with binoculars can observe rare birds, blue and gray whales, and sea lions from the rocky promontory, which juts out into the Pacific.

Start: From the east parking lot.
Distance: 1.7-mile loop.
Approximate hiking time: 1 hour.
Difficulty: Easy, due to level terrain and short length.
Trail surface: Dirt path.
Lay of the land: Coastal headlands, rocky cliffs, and windswept grassland.
Other trail users: Bird-, whale-, and sea lion-watchers.

Canine compatibility: Dogs not permitted.
Land status: State park.
Nearest town: Bodega Bay.
Fees and permits: None.
Schedule: Open year-round dawn to dusk.
Map: USGS map: Bodega Head, CA.
Trail contact: Russian River Area State Parks, Duncan Mills; (707) 865-2391; www.mcn. org/1/rrparks/rrweb.htm.

Finding the trailhead: From Bodega Bay on California Highway 1, turn west onto East Shore Road and drive 0.3 mile before turning right onto Bay Flat Road, which then becomes West Shore Road. Continue 3.5 miles, then take the left fork in the road and drive another 0.4 mile to the east parking lot. The trail leaves from the east end of the parking lot. *DeLorme: Northern California Atlas & Gazetteer:* Pages 92–93, B4.

The Hike

As you begin the loop, the first thing you see will be Bodega Harbor, with its fishing fleet, and the long sand spit of Doran Beach, which partially encloses the harbor. Located at the south end of a 17-mile string of beaches, Bodega Head is a grassy headland surrounded by steep cliffs and pocket beaches. Attentive hikers can see an astounding variety of wildlife along the trail. Be especially attentive in the cliffs and waters surrounding the head, as that is where the bulk of the wildlife is found.

The name of the bay and town is thought to stem from a visit, circa 1775, by Spain's Juan Francisco de la Bodega y Quadra Mollineda. The sailor parked his schooner, *Sonora,* at the south end of the bay, and in those days, simply landing was enough to warrant having a place named after you.

Even earlier, in 1579, Sir Francis Drake passed this way on a voyage of exploration and plunder, before being forced to stop for repairs in a sheltered bay. Most scholars believe Drake's landing point was an estuary on nearby Point Reyes, but some assert the possibility that the English ship anchored here, near the mouth of the present harbor at Campbell Cove. The latter theory gained support in 1962, when utility workers discovered a stone wall fitting the description of a small fort

Cliffs at Bodega Head

that Drake had built during his six-week stay. But the debate surrounding the real Drakes Bay continues.

More recently, Bodega Bay and the town of Bodega, located a few miles inland, achieved a kind of infamy as the filming location for Alfred Hitchcock's classic film *The Birds.* The film, which stars Tippi Hedren, Rod Taylor, Jessica Tandy, and Suzanne

Pleshette, depicts a quiet fishing village suddenly tormented by swarms of hostile birds. The town looks very different now, but movie buffs will find that a few of the buildings seen in the film remain.

There are still a lot of birds here—though you don't have to worry about any mass attacks of gulls. All of the birds around Bodega are people friendly. The natural geology of the headlands and Bodega Harbor provides a variety of habitats ranging from tall rocky cliffs to sheltered salt marshes, providing the birds with both safe nesting sites and direct access to feeding grounds at sea. Aside from the expected seagulls, bird-watchers can find marbled godwits, brown and white pelicans, Hedwicks wrens, northern harriers, and the black-crowned night herons.

▶ Blue whales are the largest animals that have ever lived— including dinosaurs.

The black-footed albatross, looking like a large dark gray seagull with a wingspan of more than 6 feet, occasionally puts in appearances—which is very unusual for a bird that rarely spends time on any land, let alone mainland. Living at sea without fresh water to drink, the albatross consumes more salt than an average bird. To make up for their high salt consumption, albatrosses have developed a special nasal gland that removes excess salt from their blood. Apparently, all birds have this gland—called the salt gland—but evolution has rendered it inactive in most birds. The salt gland converts the salt to a concentrated fluid that is expelled from the nostrils.

Another star of the native bird population is the rhinoceros auklet—so named for the small white horn that grows from the base of its beak during summer. A cousin of the rhinoceros auklet, the tufted puffin, also makes its home here. During the summer months, the tufted puffin has a huge red and yellow bill, a white face, and plumelike eyebrows that sweep back along the side of its head. The bird loses some of its physical pizzazz during the winter months; it sheds the outer layer of its bill, and its plumage turns a somber dark gray.

The region's birds aren't the only wildlife worth watching. Due south of Bodega Head is a rock outcrop that's a favorite haul-out spot for sea lions. And an excellent lookout for gray whales is located to the west as you round the head and reach the west parking lot.

Miles and Directions

0.0 Start at the end of the east parking lot, near the rest room. Follow the Bodega Head Loop around the edge of the bluffs.

0.1 (FYI: The trail offers a good view of Bodega Bay from this spot.)

0.3 (FYI: An offshore rock on the south side of the head is often occupied by loud and boisterous sea lions. Mats of the succulent ice plant grow on the cliff edges here.)

0.5 A shortcut leads back to the parking lot on the right. Continue straight around the edge of the bluffs.

0.6 (FYI: The rocky promontory to the left has a small sea cave at its base.)

0.8 (FYI: Cormorants can often be seen down on the rocks to the right.)

Bodega Head Loop

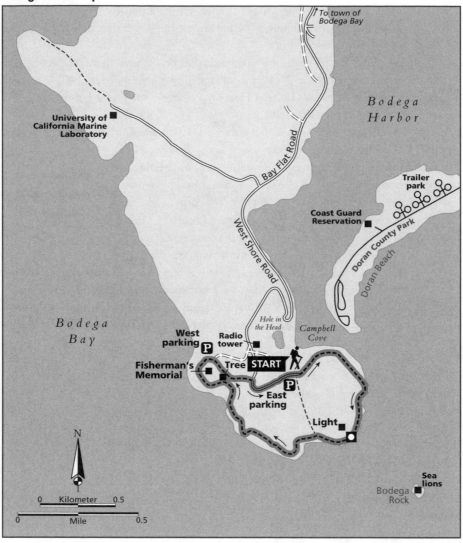

1.1 The trail passes above a sheltered cove and a beach that's impossible to get to safely. (Note: Do the smart thing and enjoy it from afar.)

1.2 (FYI: A memorial to fishermen—shaped like the prow of a ship—can be seen to the right.)

1.3 The trail reaches the west parking lot. (FYI: This is an excellent spot to look for passing gray whales. A nearby interpretive sign tells more about the watery behemoths.) The trail back to the east parking lot heads across the meadow, starting next to the rest room and heading past a clump of windblown cypress on the right.

1.5 The trail reaches the east parking lot access road. Turn right and follow the gravel road back to the parking lot and trailhead.

1.7 Arrive back at the east parking lot and trailhead.

WHALE WATCHING

Although humpbacks, blue whales, and killer whales are all sighted off the California coast, gray whales are most commonly spotted from shore. From November through January, they can be observed as they migrate southward to the warm lagoons of Baja California, where young are born. From February through June, they make their way back to the summer feeding grounds of the Bering and Chukchi Seas, swimming a little closer to shore.

From afar, gray whales can be identified by their heart-shaped spout—which is much smaller than the blue whale's—and by the predictable swimming pattern (usually three to four short dives lasting between 1 and 3 minutes, followed by a longer dive of 5 to 15 minutes). Before a deep dive, whales often raise their flukes high in the air, preparing for a vertical descent that, for gray whales, lasts up to twenty minutes. If you are lucky you may see a whale spyhopping—that is, sticking its head out of the water as if for a better look. Breaching is also seen, although it is much more common in Mexican waters. When a gray breaches, it comes almost straight up, bringing three-quarters of its body out of the water before crashing down on its side with a monstrous splash.

Any high spot along the coast will be good for whale watching, but some of the best locations are Point Reyes, Bodega Head, Mendocino Headlands, beaches along the Lost Coast, and Crescent City.

For those who want to get closer, there are several operators who offer whale-watching boat trips during migration periods. These trips usually depart twice a day and last two to four hours. During peak whale times, knowledgeable members of the volunteer group Stewards of Slavianka visit the park on weekends to talk about whales and to help people spot them.

Hike Information

Local Information
Bodega Bay Area Chamber of Commerce, Bodega Bay; (877) 789-1212; (707) 875-3422; www.bodegabay.com.

Local Events/Attractions
Seafood, Art & Wine Festival, held in August, Bodega Bay; (707) 824-8404.
Taste of Bodega's Crab Cioppino, held in November, Bodega Bay; (707) 875-3422.

Bodega Bay Fisherman's Festival, held in April, boat parade, blessing of the fleet, food and crafts, Bodega Bay; (707) 875-3286.

Lodging
Bodega Dunes—Sonoma Coast State Beach, more than 100 campsites, plus hot showers, Bodega Bay; (800) 444-7275; (707) 875-3483.

33 Sky/Laguna Loop

This is a strenuous hike, but one with plenty of variety. Beginning in dense forest, the trail passes through several native habitats and a recovering burn zone on the way down to the beach on Drakes Bay. The trail makes a stop at the summit of Mount Wittenberg, and a short detour will take hikers to Sculptured Beach. Two hike-in campgrounds and a youth hostel are on or near the route, allowing for easy overnight stays.

Start: From the Sky Trail trailhead.
Distance: 10-mile loop.
Approximate hiking time: 5 to 6 hours (overnight possible).
Difficulty: Difficult, due to steep trails and elevation gain.
Trail surface: Gravel road, partially paved road, and dirt path.
Lay of the land: Bishop pine forests, northern coastal prairie and scrub.
Other trail users: Cyclists, equestrians.
Canine compatibility: Dogs not permitted.
Land status: National seashore.
Nearest town: Olema.

Fees and permits: No entrance fees, but campers must get a permit. Camping costs $12 per site per night for one to six people; more for larger groups. Make reservations, Monday through Friday, 9:00 A.M. to 2:00 P.M., at (415) 663–8054.
Schedule: Open daily from sunup to sundown. Visitor center is open Monday to Friday, 9:00 A.M. to 5:00 P.M.; weekends and holidays, 10:00 A.M. to 4:30 P.M.
Maps: USGS maps: Drakes Bay, CA; Inverness, CA.
Trail contact: Point Reyes National Seashore, Point Reyes Station; (415) 464–5100; www.nps.gov/pore.

Finding the trailhead: From San Francisco, drive north on California Highway 1/U.S. Highway 101 for 7 miles, until the two highways separate north of Sausalito. Follow CA 1 west, then north along the coast, about 26 miles to the town of Olema. At Olema, turn left onto Bear Valley Road and drive north 1.9 miles. Turn left onto Limantour Road and follow it up 3.5 miles before turning left into the Sky Trail trailhead parking lot. The trail begins at the gate on the east side of the lot. *DeLorme: Northern California Atlas & Gazetteer:* Page 93, D5.

The Hike

Considering how close it is to a large urban area, Point Reyes National Seashore has an astoundingly untamed, and varied, character. The high, densely forested eastern side contrasts sharply with the bare, windswept prairies and pastures of the western slopes. And in between lie the fire-dependent Bishop pine stands and vast expanses of coyote brush dominated vegetation, known as northern coastal scrub. The spectacular seashore for which the park is named lies at the outer perimeters of the Point Reyes area. And an impressive list of animals calls this home, including tule elk, bobcat, black-tailed deer, and the larger axis and fallow deer (two exotic species that

Half-tame fox at the visitor center

were introduced in the 1940s). In addition to the wild animals, 45 percent of native North America bird species have been spotted here.

Shaped roughly like an elongated triangle, Point Reyes sits on the part of the earth's crust known as the Pacific Plate, which is steadily moving north along the North American Plate of the mainland at the rate of about 2 inches a year. Along its eastern edge, the triangle is partially separated from the rest of the continent by Tomales Bay, a long, thin arm of the Pacific Ocean that marks the rift zone of the famous San Andreas Fault. South of the point, the fault plunges inland, where it periodically wreaks havoc—most notably in nearby San Francisco.

The well-developed trail system at Point Reyes offers ample opportunity for hikers to mix-and-match routes, thereby creating their own perfect trek. This particular loop was chosen because it sees much less use than the Bear Valley trails and passes through most of the habitat types present in the national seashore. As an added bonus, it stops off at the summit of Mount Wittenberg for a bird's-eye view of Drakes Bay. You also have the option of taking a short detour from Coast Camp down to the beach.

Sky/Laguna Loop

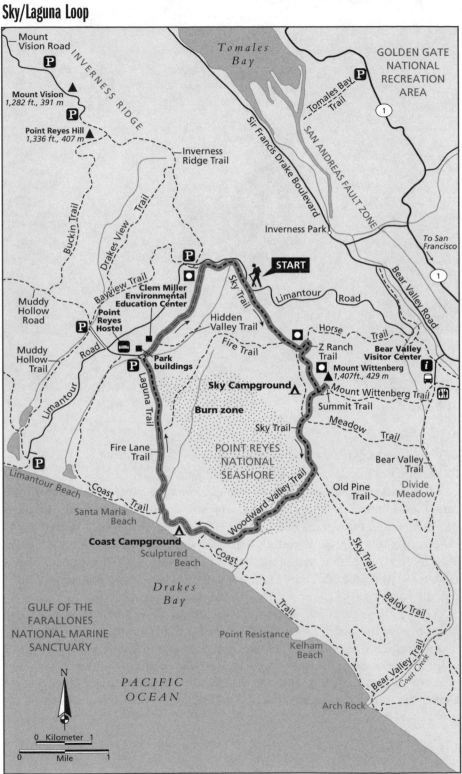

This stretch of coast has been the source of much debate among historians throughout the years. The dissention stems from questions about the exact point of anchorage chosen by English explorer Sir Francis Drake in the year 1579. Drake was in the midst of his "Voyage of Circumnavigation," a multipurpose mission that included searching for a secret northwest passage to the Pacific and raiding Spain's many New World holdings, when his ship, the *Golden Hind,* sprang a leak. Drake turned and headed south, seeking a sheltered place along the uncharted California coast to anchor and repair the ship. Most evidence to date indicates that the spot he chose was the nearby Drake's Estero.

The debate was almost settled in 1936 when a brass plate, reputedly left by Drake at the infamous estuary, was recovered. But the discovery proved to be a hoax. Nevertheless, several fragments of Chinese pottery like those held in the *Hind's* hull have been found at area archeological sites, and anthropologists have confirmed that the sailor's descriptions of native people he encountered depict the area's Coast Miwoks. Scientists recently have suggested that Campbell Cove, near the mouth of Bodega Harbor, is the true location of Drake's stopover. Only time—and more research—will settle the debate.

You may occasionally glimpse the ocean once sailed by the *Golden Hind* as you make your way down from Mount Wittenberg to the coast, but you are more likely to notice the charred trees visible on the edge of the forest. Much of the landscape below looks like it is recovering from some type of major devastation. That something was the Vision Fire, which burned 14 percent of the national seashore in 1995. The youth hostel and the nearby Clem Miller Environmental Education Center were saved from the surrounding destruction by firefighters. Hostel caretakers will be glad to tell the story of how the building was completely covered with fire-retardant foam during the incident. In the end, only one of the hostel's small outbuildings was lost. The fire initially was very destructive to the local wildlife, but the affected plant communities have been regenerating rapidly. And the Bishop pine—whose cones require the intense heat of fire to release seeds—has taken advantage of the opportunity to repopulate several areas previously lost to cattle ranching.

Cattle ranching has a long and prestigious history at Point Reyes. The Gold Rush of 1849 sparked the intensive cattle ranching, which provided the growing San Francisco population with dairy products. The abundance of grass and fresh water combined with the long growing season created optimal conditions for ranching. By 1867 Marin County was producing 932,429 pounds of butter per year—most of it coming from Point Reyes. Several of the old ranches have shut down, but a large portion of Point Reyes is still dedicated to cattle ranching, especially on the western side. Here, the native coastal prairie has largely been replaced with nonnative grasses, sparking a serious erosion problem. Although strides have been made to reduce the impact of grazing on the ecosystem, soil conservation authorities say environmental pressures are still above healthy levels.

From the Coastal Trail, the climb back up to the Sky Trail trailhead via the Fire Lane and Laguna Trails is long and steep. But the views on a clear day are well worth the effort. A short stint along the Bayview Trail, which runs parallel to Limantour Road, brings you back to the trailhead.

Miles and Directions

0.0 Start at the gate on the east side of the Sky Trail trailhead parking lot. Follow Sky Trail as it heads uphill on a paved access road.

0.1 The trail changes from paved road to gravel road.

0.7 Fire Lane Trail goes off to the right. Continue straight on Sky Trail.

0.8 Sky Trail continues straight leading you to Sky Campground. Turn left onto Horse Trail to the left, and follow it east toward Bear Valley.

1.0 (FYI: There is a great view of the valley down to the left from here, weather permitting.)

1.3 Horse Trail continues straight. Turn right onto Z Ranch Trail, heading to Wittenberg Summit.

1.5 (FYI: Half way up the incline, there is a good view on the right of Tomales Bay.)

1.8 Just after entering a grassy alpine meadow, Summit Trail heads up sharply to the left. Mount Wittenberg Trail heads down to Bear Valley on the left, perpendicular to Z Ranch Trail. To the right, Mount Wittenberg Trail heads down to access Meadow Trail, Sky Camp, and Woodward Valley. Turn a sharp left and follow the Summit Trail a short distance to the top of Mount Wittenberg.

2.0 The trail reaches the summit. (FYI: Enjoy aerial views of the surrounding countryside, mostly to the south.) Turn around and retrace Summit Trail to the last junction.

2.2 Back at the junction, turn right following the sign directing you to Woodward Valley. Head down Mount Wittenberg Trail toward Woodward Valley.

2.6 Mount Wittenberg Trail joins Sky Trail. To the left, Meadow Trail heads down to Bear Valley. To the right, Sky Trail heads back to Sky Camp. Continue straight, following Sky Trail to Woodward Valley.

3.3 Sky Trail continues straight. Turn right onto Woodward Valley Trail and continue downhill.

4.1 (FYI: The trail passes through the 1995 burn zone. Plenty of dead and charred trees attest to the ferocity of that blaze.)

4.3 (FYI: There is a nice view of Drakes Bay on the left.)

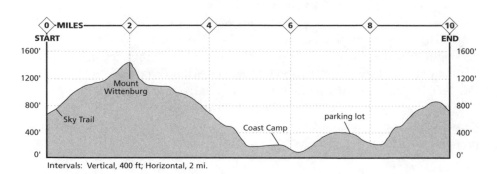

Intervals: Vertical, 400 ft; Horizontal, 2 mi.

4.5 (FYI: As the trail rounds a corner, Limantour Spit can be seen straight ahead.)

4.7 (FYI: The trail now passes through the fire recovery zone, characterized by very brushy vegetation.)

5.1 Woodward Valley Trail ends at the Coast Trail. Turn right onto Coast Trail and follow it toward Coast Camp.

5.7 The trail passes through Coast Camp. (FYI: Reservations have to be made in advance to camp here, but it's also a nice place to break for lunch, as there are several picnic tables. Don't be surprised to see mountain bikes, which are ridden here from the west via Limantour Spit and the Coast Trail.)

5.9 A spur trail branches right and up to access campsites 1 through 7. Continue straight on Coast Trail.

6.0 Coast Trail continues straight. Turn right onto Fire Lane Trail and follow it uphill.

6.4 The dirt road surface of Fire Lane Trail becomes dirt singletrack.

6.7 Junction. Fire Trail heads right. Laguna trail goes left. Go left.

7.5 Junction. A few park buildings and the Laguna parking lot. Take the trail through the trees to the right.

7.7 Junction. The Clem Miller Environmental Education Center is to the left and the Hidden Valley Trail is to the right; straight ahead is our trail.

7.8 Leave the meadow and switchback up. Near the top, the trail becomes gravel as it joins the old road.

8.1 Top out after steep climb.

8.2 After brief decline, climb again.

8.3 On top again, with a nice view of Limantour.

9.3 Junction. Bayview Trail is to the left, Sky Trail is to the right. Go right.

10.0 Arrive back at the trailhead.

Hike Information

Local Information

West Marin Chamber of Commerce, Point Reyes Station; (415) 663-9232; www.pointreyes.org.

Local Events/Attractions

Sand Sculpture Contest, Point Reyes National Seashore; (415) 464-5100.

Strawberry Festival, held in April, celebration of the First Fruits Ceremony of the Coast Miwok people, Kule Loklo; (415) 464-5100.

Habitat Restoration, held at regular intervals throughout the year, call the park for more information; (415) 455-4655.

Adopt a Trail Program, volunteer for trail and restoration work; (415) 663-1092.

Marin Museum of the American Indian, Novato; (415) 897-4064.

Lodging

Point Reyes Hostel, off Limantour Road within the National Seashore; (415) 663-8811. Office hours: 7:30 to 9:30 A.M. and 4:30 to 9:30 P.M.

For camping within the Seashore, call (415) 663-8054 to make reservations.

Public Transportation

Golden Gate Transit, (415) 923-2000; www.transitinfo.org. Bus route #65 serves the Bear Valley Visitor Center from the San Raphael Transit Center on weekends and holidays.

34 North Burma/Cobblestone Loop

This challenging hike climbs steeply up through classic California oak forest, rewarding hikers at the top with a wide meadow and small, rush-hemmed Ilsanjo Lake. After a refreshing foot soak, hikers wander some more through savannalike meadows trimmed with historic rock walls before heading down past an old quarry to the visitor center, and up a level stretch to the trailhead.

Start: North Burma trailhead.
Distance: 6.6-mile loop.
Approximate hiking time: 3 to 4 hours.
Difficulty: Easy to moderate, due to elevation gain and some rough trail.
Trail surface: Dirt path, gravel road, and paved road.
Lay of the land: Oak forests, open, grassy meadows.
Other trail users: Mountain bikers, equestrians.

Canine compatibility: No dogs allowed.
Land status: State park.
Nearest town: Santa Rosa.
Fees and permits: $2.00 day-use fee.
Schedule: Open year-round 9:00 A.M. to sunset.
Map: USGS map: Santa Rosa, CA.
Trail contact: Annadel State Park, Santa Rosa; (707) 539-3911; www.parks.ca.gov.

Finding the trailhead: From U.S. Highway 101 in Santa Rosa, exit the highway at the junction with California Highway 12 and follow CA 12 east 1.3 miles. Follow CA 12 to the left as it curves, becoming Farmers Lane, and continue another 4.7 miles through town. Turn right onto Montgomery Road and follow it 2.8 miles, then turn right onto Channel Drive. Continue another 1.1 miles to the park entrance gate, then 0.5 mile farther to a small turnout on the right side of the road. The North Burma trailhead is the small kiosk on the right. *DeLorme: Northern California Atlas & Gazetteer:* Page 93, A7.

Public Transit: From the Civic Center BART or Transbay Terminal in San Francisco, take Golden Gate #80 to the Santa Rosa Transit. Transfer to the Sonoma bus #30 and ride it to Spring Lake Village. At the village, walk east .25 mile on Montgomery Drive to the footbridge on the south side of the road. Cross the bridge and head left on Channel Drive another 0.8 mile to the trailhead. For more information, call (415) 455-2000 or visit www.transitinfo.org/Outdoors/Annadel_State.

The Hike

It is unusual to find large expanses of open space immediately adjacent to large urban centers, especially those that are crisscrossed with hiking and biking trails and open to the public. Luckily, there is an exception to every rule, and Annadel State Park is Santa Rosa's exception. The park's 5,000 acres and 35 miles of trail are parked firmly up against the city's eastern limits, with residential neighborhoods marching right up to the park's entrance gate. As can be expected, given the circumstances, the

Lake Ilsanjo

park sees a fair bit of use, but the proliferation of trails does a good job of dispersing visitors.

One of the reasons the land was saved from developer's dozers is that up until the 1960s, it belonged to a millionaire tycoon by the name of Joe Coney. Having amassed a fortune in steamships, oil tankers, gold and silver mines, and various other enterprises, Coney bought up the acreage for a vast ranch in the rolling oak woodlands of Sonoma County in 1934. He used it more as a playground than a business venture. Exotic game, such as pheasants and Indian chukar, were brought in to increase the sport of hunting parties. Coney imported prize cattle and horses from Europe, and he experimented with hops production and perlite mining. Borrowing a page from Carnegie and Rockefeller, Coney was also very generous with his holdings,

▶ Santa Rosa is the hometown of two famous illustrators: Robert Ripley, creator of "Ripley's Believe It or Not!"; and Charles Schulz, the cartoonist behind Snoopy, Charlie Brown, and the other "Peanuts" characters.

North Burma/Cobblestone Loop

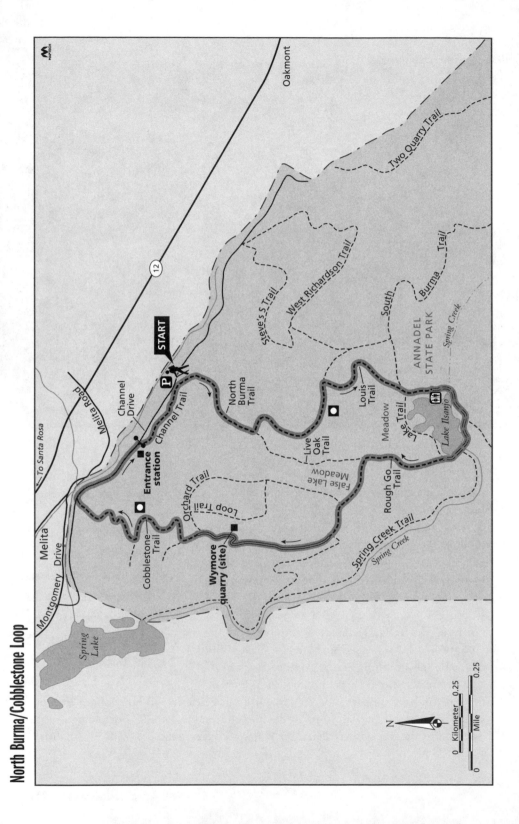

allowing everyone from the Boy Scouts to the Marines to use his land for various purposes.

All that changed in the 1960s, as Santa Rosa's sprawl began to lap against the ranch's boundaries. The land was reassessed as a potential subdivision location, and the taxes skyrocketed. Coney was forced to sell off his holdings to pay the bills. It seemed as if the peaceful hills would soon be suburbanized, but at the last minute the state, helped out by public donations and private grants, jumped in to buy the land for a park.

The hike begins at the North Burma trailhead, a half mile past the park gate along Channel Drive. The singletrack trail heads steeply up into the oak forest, alternating between steep ascents and gentle contouring until it tops out on the ridge. From there the modest grade skirts large, flat meadows that can vaguely resemble African savanna during blazing-hot summer days.

Luckily the trail offers respite from the summer heat in the form of Lake Ilsanjo, a reed-encircled watering hole at the lower end of the large meadow. The lake is part of the Joe Coney legacy. Created in 1956 when Joe and his brother dammed Spring Creek, the lake was stocked with black bass and opened to the public. The rather exotic-sounding name is simply a contraction of Ilsa and Joe, named for Coney and his wife. The inspiration for the invented name may have come from an earlier landowner, Samuel Hutchinson, who coined the name Annadel, probably shortened from "Annie's Dell," and named after his daughter, Annie.

From the lake the trail heads back up toward the ridge along the Rough Go Trail, crossing several more meadows before reaching the park's western ridge, overlooking Santa Rosa. This last leg of the trail explores an earlier era in the land's history: the quarry years. In the 1880s the ridge was the source of cobblestone for the streets of San Francisco, as well as building blocks for several Santa Rosa structures still standing today. Gravity-driven cars carried the blocks down a private railway to the valley below, where Southern Pacific freight trains were waiting to service points south.

The Cobblestone Trail offers plenty of evidence of this early industry, with several quarry pits and piles of stone along the trail. The path roughly follows the course

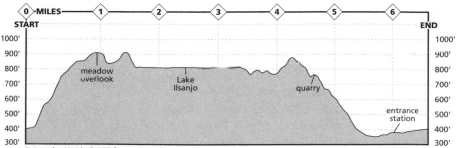

Intervals: Vertical, 100 ft; Horizontal, 1 mi.

of the old railroad tracks, although reroutes have been undertaken in recent years to circumvent fragile meadows.

Once you reach Channel Road, follow it east toward the main gate, and then along the parallel-running Channel Trail to the trailhead.

Miles and Directions

0.0 Start at the North Burma trailhead. The trail heads steeply uphill to the left.

0.2 The trail curves left through a draw, crossing a streambed (dry in summer).

0.3 The trail switches back to the right, following up the edge of a larger drainage.

0.5 A spur trail comes in from the left. Continue straight.

0.6 At the junction, the Live Oak Trail heads straight, but we turn left, following the North Burma Trail.

0.7 The trail tops out and begins heading gently downhill.

0.9 The forest opens up, revealing a large flat meadow below to your right. A spur trail heads downhill to the right, but we continue straight.

1.1 The trail reenters the forest. Another spur trail heads to the right. Continue straight.

1.2 The trail forks. Take the right spur, heading downhill.

1.3 The trail joins an old path in a narrow meadow just below the ridge saddle. Veer right, continuing downhill.

1.4 An expansive view of the meadow opens on the right.

1.5 The trail flattens out on the edge of the meadow, skirting around the forest fringe.

1.8 At the junction, a gravel road heads left and right. Continue straight on the Lake Loop.

2.0 At the fork, the left fork continues around the lake, while the right fork accesses a picnic area, rejoining the main trail 0.1 mile later. Take the left fork.

2.3 A spur trail leads down to the right. Continue straight.

2.4 The spur rejoins the road from the right. Continue straight, crossing a low marshy spot. A few yards later, turn right, following the Lake Trail across the earthen dam.

2.5 At the other end of the dam, the Spring Creek Trail comes up from the left. Keep going straight. Shortly afterward, the trail reaches a section of concrete road. A dirt road continues straight, but we turn right.

2.6 At the junction, the Lake Trail continues to the right, but we go straight, along the Rough Go Trail.

3.1 The trail forks, with the Live Oak Trail going straight, and the Rough Go Trail veering left. Take the left fork. (FYI: You can take the Live Oak Trail if you want a shorter loop. It is 0.8 mile back to the first junction with North Burma Trail, and another 0.6 mile back to the trailhead.)

3.3 (FYI: The trail passes through an old rock wall, running perpendicular to the trail. Notice also that the trail is strewn with volcanic "bombs.")

3.5 At the junction, the Orchard Trail heads right, and Rough Go continues straight, curving left. Take the left trail, crossing a large flat meadow.

3.7 The Rough Go Trail continues straight, dropping down the west side of the ridge, but we turn right onto the Cobblestone Trail. Santa Rosa is visible in the distance to the left.

4.4 The trail switches back to the right, climbing steeply into thicker forest.

4.5 The trail levels out again. A short distance later, it enters a cut in the ridge. The flat area, marked on the right by a shallow pit, is the Wymore quarry. The trail keeps left, passing through another cut in the ridge.

4.6 The Orchard Trail comes in from the right. Continue straight. A deep gully is visible to the right, part of the old quarry.

4.7 A spur trail comes in from the right. Go straight. A few yards later, another spur from the Orchard Trail heads right. Turn left instead, following the Cobblestone Trail. The trail crosses a small meadow, then heads back into the forest.

4.8 A spur trail heads left along the course of the old road to the park's boundary. Continue straight on the dirt path.

5.3 There is a bench on the left, overlooking the town below.

5.4 The trail forks, with the left fork heading west to the park boundary. Take the right fork, continuing on the Cobblestone Trail.

5.6 The trail switches back and heads down into a meadow.

5.8 The trail pops out on the park entrance road. Turn right and head east toward the park entrance station.

6.1 Entrance station. Just beyond the station on the right, the trail leaves the road, following a parallel course along a dirt path.

6.4 A couple of small pits mark the location of past human activity.

6.6 Back at the trailhead.

Hike Information

Local Information

Santa Rosa Chamber of Commerce,
Santa Rosa; (707) 545-1414;
www.santarosachamber.com.

Santa Rosa Convention and Visitors Bureau,
Santa Rosa; (800) 404-7673; (707) 577-8674; www.visitsantarosa.com.

Local Events/Attractions

Two nearby state parks honor famous American authors. Robert Louis Stevenson State Park is roughly 20 miles northeast of Santa Rosa, near the town of Calistoga; (707) 942-4575. Jack London State Historic Park is in Glen Ellen, a quick 10 miles to the southeast on CA 12; (707) 938-5216.

Lodging

Spring Lake Regional Park–Santa Rosa, Santa Rosa; (707) 539-8092.

This adjacent park has numerous tent and RV sites for $16 per night. The campground is open daily from May 1 through September 30, and on weekends and holidays the rest of the year. For reservations call (707) 565-2267 between 10:00 A.M. and 3:00 P.M.

35 Shoreline/Ridge Loop

This hike is a pleasant loop of trails that begins at the remnants of a turn-of-the-century Chinese shrimp-fishing village and explores the dry oak-woodland hills of the San Francisco Bay Area, with plenty of options for longer or shorter hikes. Gorgeous views of San Pablo and San Francisco Bays are the icing on the cake.

Start: From the China Camp Village trailhead.
Distance: 5.7-mile loop.
Approximate hiking time: 2.5 hours.
Difficulty: Easy to moderate, due to some mild elevation gain and good trails.
Trail surface: Dirt path, dirt, and gravel roads.
Lay of the land: Bay shore and rolling, oak-covered hillsides.
Other trail users: Cyclists, joggers, and equestrians.
Canine compatibility: Dogs not permitted.
Land status: State park.

Nearest town: San Rafael.
Fees and permits: $5.00 day-use fee at the China Camp Village area. There are day-use fees at some other park areas as well. Parking along North San Pedro Road is free.
Schedule: Open year-round. Museum exhibit open daily 10:00 A.M. to 5:00 P.M. Concession stand and fishing pier open weekends only.
Maps: USGS maps: San Quentin, CA; Petaluma Point, CA.
Trail contact: China Camp State Park, San Rafael; (415) 456-0766; www.parks.ca.gov.

Finding the trailhead: From San Francisco, drive north 18 miles on U.S. Highway 101 and exit at North San Pedro Road. Head east 5.2 miles on North San Pedro Road, and turn left into the parking lot for the China Camp Village Historic Area. The trailhead is to the left of the rest rooms near the entrance of the parking lot. *DeLorme: Northern California Atlas & Gazetteer:* Page 94, D2.

The Hike

This hike begins with a quick visit to the China Camp Village site, which consists of a few weather-beaten buildings and a long wooden pier. But don't let the old village's ramshackle appearance dissuade you from exploring the historical site—especially the small museum that tells the story of the Chinese-Americans who settled here in the late nineteenth century. These settlers made their living by fishing and processing grass shrimp, mostly for export to the Far East. At its peak the village was home to nearly 500 residents, but a series of racist and repressive laws passed by increasingly hostile European-Americans all but destroyed the town and its industry. The village currently has only one permanent resident—a descendant of the early Chinese settlers.

With so few physical reminders left, it's difficult to picture the thriving community that once existed here. Ironically, it was the same anti-Chinese sentiment that brought the settlers here in the first place that eventually drove them out again. That initial wave of Chinese emigration came in 1848, following the discovery of gold in

Remnants of China Camp

the California hills. There had been a few Chinese merchants living in the state before this time, but the Asian population exploded toward the middle of the century. The Gold Rush was a powerful lure, especially for those Chinese immigrants coming from poorer regions in Canton (Guangdong), most notably an area known as the Four Districts. Conditions there had grown intolerable, largely because of instability brought on by foreign colonial powers and the homegrown opium trade. By the mid-1800s the ruling Qing dynasty was in a shambles. And in 1850 the Taiping Rebellion destabilized the region even further.

This disarray stood in sharp contrast to the glowing handbills proclaiming that riches were waiting in America for enterprising men. By 1852 some 20,000 Chinese were pouring into the state every year. The majority of those arriving in San Francisco—known to the Cantonese as Gam Saan, or "golden mountains"—were landless peasants seeking jobs as mine laborers.

Although quick to take advantage of the cheap labor, many European-Americans soon developed strong anti-Chinese sentiments. This growing racism led to the passage of a Foreign Miner's Tax, as well as the expulsion of Chinese laborers from mining camps. And in 1854 California applied the same discriminatory legislation to

Shoreline/Ridge Loop

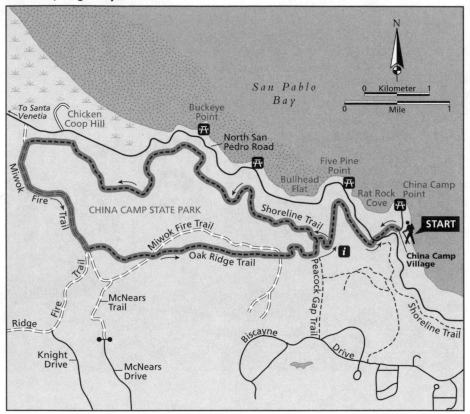

Chinese-Americans that it already had put into place against blacks and Native Americans: That year, the state Supreme Court ruled that no Chinese person could testify against a white person in court.

The Chinese mining industry had virtually dried up by 1870, when most of the easy surface gold deposits were gone. The displaced miners were frustrated, discouraged, and forced to turn to other occupations. Some found jobs on the railroads, as manual laborers charged with the grueling work associated with building train tracks through the mountains. Others turned to the fisherman's trade they had known in their homeland. Small fishing villages began sprouting up around the San Francisco Bay Area, where the Chinese used traditional techniques and sold mainly to other Chinese or overseas markets. But the prejudice that haunted Chinese mine workers followed them into the fishing trade. And by 1911 increasing pressure and resentment from non-Chinese fishermen prompted the passage of laws outlawing the main Chinese fishing methods.

In spite of all these difficulties, most villages continued to function, and the Chinese-Americans tenaciously refused to abandon their new home. Knowledge of the Chinese-Americans' tough history in the state should provide food for thought as you begin the Shoreline/Ridge Loop.

After visiting the China Camp historical site, pick up the trail near the rest rooms at the entrance to the upper parking lot. The path heads west and soon crosses North San Pedro Road to ascend into the oak-shaded hills of San Pedro. The trail then levels out and contours gently around the grassy slopes to offer ample views of San Pablo Bay. After passing the large mound on the shore known as Chicken Coop Hill, turn left onto the Miwok Fire Trail and climb a steep hill for the return trip along the ridge. As you make your way along the Oak Ridge Trail, be sure to take in the breathtaking views over San Rafael and the Richmond–San Rafael Bridge.

These vistas are likely to be enhanced by clear weather and good visibility, a rarity in the Bay Area. Unlike other parts in the region, China Camp State Park averages a stunning 200 fog-free days per year. The mild weather also creates an environment hospitable to beautiful year-round foliage. In late winter the manzanita produces dazzling white blossoms. And wildflowers put on a display in springtime that includes honeysuckle, milkmaids, and shooting stars. Thanks to the mild weather, any time of year can offer a good hike in the park.

Miles and Directions

0.0 Start at the China Camp Village trailhead, near the parking lot entrance, and to the left of the rest rooms. Follow the trail as it heads north parallel to North San Pedro Road.

0.2 An unmarked trail continues north along the road. Turn left, crossing North San Pedro Road, and continuing up the hill on Shoreline Trail.

0.4 Continue straight along the Shoreline Trail.

0.7 The trail arrives at the park headquarters and ranger's office. Cross the gravel road and continue straight on the other side.

0.9 Peacock Gap Trail heads uphill to the left. Continue straight, along Shoreline Trail.

2.2 (FYI: The hill ahead and to the right is called Chicken Coop Hill, one of many colorful names applied to geographic features in the park.)

2.6 The Shoreline Trail continues straight. Turn left instead, and head uphill onto Miwok Fire Trail.

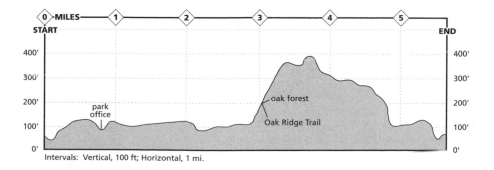

3.1 The Miwok Fire Trail continues straight. Turn left onto Oak Ridge Trail, continuing through the dense oak forest on the narrow dirt path.

3.4 Continue straight on Oak Ridge Trail as it crosses Miwok Fire Trail.

3.7 (FYI: At an opening in the trees, there is a good view to the right of San Rafael and the Oakland Bridge.)

4.0 Continue straight on Oak Ridge Trail as it crosses Miwok Fire Trail again.

4.6 As Oak Ridge Trail joins with Peacock Gap Trail, continue straight on Peacock Gap Trail, heading downhill.

4.8 Peacock Gap Trail intersects with Shoreline Trail. Turn right onto Shoreline Trail and retrace the first part of the hike to the trailhead.

5.7 Arrive back at the trailhead.

Hike Information

Local Information

Marin County Web site: www.marin.org.
Marin County Convention and Visitors Bureau Web site: www.visitmarin.org.

Local Events/Attractions

China Camp Heritage Day, held in September, tours of China Camp Village, children's activities, and historic fishing boats; (415) 456-1236.

Bay Model Visitor Center, a huge scale model of the bay, used for research and planning, complete with tides, Sausalito; (415) 332-3871.

Marin Historical Museum, open Thursday through Saturday 1:00 to 4:00 P.M., San Rafael; (415) 454-8538.

Lodging

China Camp State Park, thirty campsites, plus room for recreational vehicles.
State park campsite reservations: (800) 444-7275.

Public Transportation

Golden Gate Transit: (415) 455-2000; www.transitinfo.org. Bus route #23 runs weekdays from the San Raphael Transit Center to North San Pedro Road and Vendola Drive in Santa Venetia near the west end of the park. From Fisherman's Wharf in San Francisco, the park can also be reached with the Blue and Gold Line's Baylink Ferry; (877) 64–FERRY; (707) 64–FERRY; www.baylinkferry.com.

36 Railroad Grade Trail

Mt. Tamalpais, or Mt. Tam as locals call it, has been attracting wanderers for more than a century. There is a little of everything here, including open grassland, dense laurels, redwood- and fern-filled canyons, and oak knolls. As the name suggests, the trail follows the path of an old railroad grade. Along the way, hikers can even stop at the historical railroad-built West Point Inn for refreshment.

Start: From the Mountain Home Inn.
Distance: 7.6-mile loop.
Approximate hiking time: 3.5 to 4 hours.
Difficulty: Moderate to strenuous, due to elevation gain and steep descent.
Trail surface: Gravel fire road, dirt path.
Lay of the land: Second-growth redwood forest, chaparral, and oak woodland on mountain slopes.
Other trail users: Cyclists, equestrians.
Canine compatibility: Leashed dogs permitted within Marin Municipal Water District but not on state park trails.

Land status: Municipal water district and state park.
Nearest town: Mill Valley.
Fees and permits: $4.00 day-use fee for cars at the summit. Parking at Mountain Home Inn is free.
Schedule: Open 7:00 A.M. to sunset year-round. Visitor center at East Peak open daily in summer, weekends the rest of the year.
Map: USGS map: San Rafael, CA.
Trail contact: Mount Tamalpais State Park, Mill Valley; (415) 388–2070.

Finding the trailhead: From San Francisco, head north on U.S. Highway 101. Five miles north of the Golden Gate Bridge, leave US 101 at the Marin City exit, following signs for California Highway 1 North. Follow CA 1 through Marin City and up the hill 3.1 miles, before turning right onto the Panoramic Highway. Continue another 2.6 miles to Mountain Home Inn. Park in the large lot on the left side of the road. The trail starts across the road and a few yards to the left.

From public transportation: Weekends only, take Golden Gate Transit bus #63 from the Marin City Transfer Center to the Mountain Home Inn. Call (415) 455–2000 for schedule. *DeLorme: Northern California Atlas & Gazetteer:* Page 104, A1.

The Hike

A fascinating history combines with a wide variety of natural habitats to make this hike a treasure. The best feature of this route, though, is undoubtedly the spectacular views. The trail follows the course of the old railroad bed as it snakes its way up the south side of Mount Tamalpais (aka Mount Tam), offering expansive views to the east, west, and south at every turn. With each switchback and the successive gain in elevation, the views get more panoramic and peer farther into the distance. But the trail saves the best for last. At the East Peak, the path shows hikers a sweeping view of the entire northern San Francisco Bay Area.

This region gained popularity in the late nineteenth century when crowds of tourists from Mill Valley flocked to the summit and its Tavern of Tamalpais. At this

View to the north with Lake Lagunitas

point cars were not commonplace, and roads had not yet been built here. So the preferred means for sightseers to reach the summit was via rail. The Mount Tamalpais Scenic Railway was constructed in 1896 to help shuttle the masses of visitors up the mountain. The railroad climbed at a steady 7 percent grade for 8.5 snaking miles to reach the summit, which offered spectacular views of the surrounding lowlands and water bodies—even at just 2,571 feet.

The return trip was a special attraction for visitors, who descended the mountain in individual "gravity cars." These cars—each staffed only with a brakeman—coasted down the steady grade to Mill Valley or Muir Woods in a ride that lasted all of fifteen minutes. To get the gravity cars started, the passengers were asked to rock back and forth until the cars started to roll downhill. That's when gravity took over, and the ride began. To get back up the hill, the gravity cars were towed behind the next locomotive leaving for the summit.

The whole trip was very popular in its day, eliciting praise from celebrities such as Sir Arthur Conan Doyle, who called the railroad, "more exciting than anything like it in the world." Alas, once the use of automobiles became widespread—and the Pantoll and Ridgecrest Roads were built—the railroad became obsolete, and service

Railroad Grade Trail

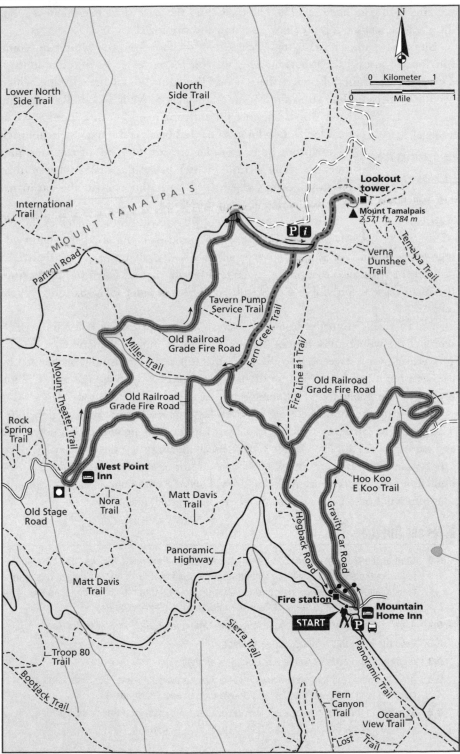

Lower North Side Trail

North Side Trail

International Trail

MOUNT TAMALPAIS

Pantoll Road

Miller Trail

Mount Theater Trail

Rock Spring Trail

Old Stage Road

West Point Inn

Nora Trail

Matt Davis Trail

Matt Davis Trail

Panoramic Highway

Sierra Trail

Troop 80 Trail

Bootjack Trail

Tavern Pump Service Trail

Old Railroad Grade Fire Road

Old Railroad Grade Fire Road

Fern Creek Trail

Fire Line #1 Trail

Old Railroad Grade Fire Road

Hoo Koo E Koo Trail

Hogback Road

Gravity Car Road

Fire station

START

Mountain Home Inn

Panoramic Trail

Fern Canyon Trail

Ocean View Trail

Lost Trail

Lookout tower

Mount Tamalpais
2,571 ft., 784 m

Verna Dunshee Trail

Temelpa Trail

N

0   Kilometer   1

0   Mile   1

was finally discontinued in 1930. The tracks and ties have since been removed, but the grade remains and is used now as a trail and fire road.

Since we cannot travel by rail, we'll set off on foot from the Mountain Home Inn, located just off the Panoramic Highway on the lower slopes of the mountain. The first part of the hike traces the route of the Muir Woods Branch Line, which eventually became known as the Mount Tamalpais & Muir Woods Railway. The Muir Woods line met up with the main line at a spot known as the Double Bowknot, so named because the track switches back on itself four times in order to gain 600 feet of elevation in a short space. This section—which brings the total number of turns on the line to 281—helped earn the railroad the nickname "Crookedest Railroad in the World."

▶ Hoo Koo E Koo is another name for the Coast Miwok people, who are indigenous to this area.

Just above the junction, hikers will find remnants of the old Mesa Station, where trains could pass one another using a siding—described as a short section of parallel track that allowed one locomotive to pull off the main line. Part of the concrete sidewalk that separated the siding from the main track is still visible and provides a reference point for visualizing the old station.

Another relic from the Iron Horse era is the historic West Point Inn, which stands at the westernmost turn of the line. Originally built as a stopover for passengers waiting for a stagecoach to the coast, the still-rustic inn is now maintained by the West Point Inn Association for the hikers and cyclists who use the trail. The inn is open to the public for refreshments and overnight accommodations.

Farther up the mountain, time has been less kind to historic railroad structures. The Tavern of Tamalpais, which originally stood near the present-day visitor center and served as the focal point for tourist mobs during the railroad's heyday, is no longer standing. Plans are under way, however, for a small railroad museum to be built alongside a reconstructed section of track. Along with railroad memorabilia, the museum will house a re-creation of one of the original gravity cars.

Miles and Directions

0.0 Start at the Mountain Home Inn parking lot. Cross the Panoramic Highway and turn left, following the shoulder a few yards, then take the road that forks off to the right. This road forks again immediately; a paved road leads up to the left to the fire station, and two gravel roads split off to the right. Take the middle road (Gravity Car Road).

0.1 Another gravel road heads down to the right. Continue straight on Gravity Car Road.

0.2 Pass the locked gate and continue straight.

0.3 A gravel road heads up to the left. Continue straight.

0.4 (FYI: An opening in the forest allows a good view to the southeast. San Rafael and its bay, San Francisco, and the Oakland Bridge can be seen from here.)

0.9 At a fork in the road, take the left fork. (FYI: A few yards later, the trail passes what is left of the old Mesa Station.)

1.1 (FYI: There is a great view to the southwest and east from here.)

1.2 Gravity Car Road ends at Old Railroad Grade, which switches back to the right, heads downward, and continues straight. Go straight on Old Railroad Grade, climbing steadily.

1.3 Hoo Koo E Koo Trail joins Old Railroad Grade from the left. Continue straight.

1.4 Hoo Koo E Koo Trail splits off again, heading down to the right. Follow Old Railroad Grade up to the left.

2.0 Hogback Road goes down to the left. (You will take this down on the return trip.) For now, continue straight on Old Railroad Grade.

2.3 Fern Creek Trail goes up to the right. Continue straight.

2.5 Miller Trail heads up to the right. Continue straight on the main grade.

2.7 (FYI: A view south along Panoramic Highway opens up, as well as another view of San Francisco.)

3.0 (FYI: From here you can see a panorama stretching from Richmond to the Pacific.)

3.1 The trail reaches the historic West Point Inn. (FYI: There is a picnic area to the left, and refreshments can be had at the inn.) Nora Trail heads down to Matt Davis Trail just below the picnic area. Follow the grade up around behind the inn, where Mount Theater Trail takes off to the left. Continue straight, following the grade.

3.9 Miller Trail crosses the trail. Continue straight.

4.1 Tavern Pump Service Trail heads steeply downhill to the right. Continue straight.

4.5 The trail reaches a locked gate at the junction with Pantoll Road. Turn right onto Pantoll Road and follow it uphill, keeping to the right as it forks a few yards later.

4.7 Fern Creek Trail goes down to the right. Continue straight.

4.8 The road dead-ends at the Tamalpais summit parking lot and visitor center. The trail continues uphill, just to the left of the rest rooms.

5.0 (FYI: There is a good view to the north, as the trail rounds the mountain.)

5.1 The trail ends at Gardener Lookout on the summit of Mount Tamalpais. This is the turnaround point for this leg of the hike. Retrace the trail to the summit parking lot.

5.4 Back at the summit parking lot, head right, crossing the lot. At the west end of the lot, Fern Creek Trail leads down toward Old Railroad Grade. Take this trail downhill through the brushy vegetation.

5.5 Fern Creek Trail crosses the lower branch of Pantoll Road. Continue straight on Fern Creek Trail.

6.0 Tavern Pump Service Trail goes up to the right. Continue straight on Fern Creek Trail.

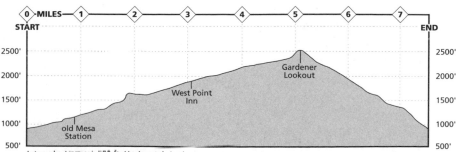

Intervals: Vertical, 500 ft; Horizontal, 1 mi.

6.4 Fern Creek Trail ends at Old Railroad Grade. Turn left onto Old Railroad Grade and head downhill.

6.8 Turn right onto Hogback Road and head steeply downhill. **Option:** As a milder alternative, retrace Old Railroad Grade and Gravity Car Road to the trailhead.

7.0 Hoo Koo E Koo Trail crosses Hogback Road. Continue straight, heading downhill on Hogback Road.

7.2 Hogback Road becomes Throckmorton Trail. Continue straight toward the Throckmorton Fire Station, keeping to the left as you pass a large water tank.

7.4 The trail passes a locked gate, just before reaching Throckmorton Fire Station. Continue past the station, following the paved road down to the left.

7.5 The road ends at Panoramic Highway. Cross the highway and follow the shoulder up to the Mountain Home Inn parking lot.

7.6 Arrive back at the trailhead.

Hike Information

Local Information

Marin County Web site: www.marin.org.
**Marin County Convention and Visitors Bureau
Web site:** www.visitmarin.org.

Local Events/Attractions

Mountain Play, outdoor theater held from May to June on Mount Tamalpais; (415) 383-1100.

Lodging

The West Point Inn, Mount Tamalpais State Park, Mill Valley; (415) 388-9955. They have five rustic cabins practically on the trail, and they're open Tuesday through Sunday. For reservations call (415) 646-0702, twenty-four hours a day. Rooms are $30 for adults, $12 for ages five through twelve, free for ages five and younger. Closed Sunday and Monday nights.
Local camping information: (415) 388-2070; (415) 456-1286.

Restaurants

The West Point Inn, refreshments for hikers, Mount Tamalpais State Park, Mill Valley; (415) 388-9955.

Hike Tours

The Mount Tamalpais Interpretive Association, lead guided hikes regularly, San Rafael; (415) 258-2410; www.mttam.net.

Public Transportation

Golden Gate Transit, bus service; (415) 455-2000; www.transitinfo.org.

Honorable Mentions

North Bay/Wine Country

G Robert Louis Stevenson Trail

This moderate 2-mile out-and-back hike climbs the lower slopes of Mount Saint Helen to the site where the famous author of *Treasure Island* and *Silverado Squatters* once spent his honeymoon in a small cabin. The cabin is now gone, but a small monument marks the spot. From San Francisco, head east 31 miles on Interstate 80 to Vallejo. Exit onto California Highway 29, and head north another 49 miles up the Napa Valley to Calistoga. Turn right in town, and continue north on CA 29 another 7 miles to the large dirt parking area on the ridgetop. The trailhead is on the west side of the road. For more information, contact Robert Louis Stevenson State Park, Calistoga; (707) 942-4575. *DeLorme: Northern California Atlas & Gazetteer:* Page 84, C1.

H Wolf House Trail

This easy 1.16-mile out-and-back hike visits the gravesite and ruined dream house of famous author Jack London. The hike begins and ends at the House of Happy Walls, built by Jack's widow and now functioning as a visitor center and museum. From San Francisco, head north 27 miles on U.S. Highway 101. Exit onto California Highway 37 and drive west 8 miles. Turn left onto California Highway 121 and head north 7 miles to Big Bend. Continue straight on California Highway 116 for 1.5 miles, then go straight again on Arnold Drive for another 7 miles. In Glen Ellyn, turn right onto London Ranch Road. Drive a mile or so to the park entrance, then left to the trailhead. For more information, contact Jack London State Historical Park, Glen Ellyn; (707) 938–5216. *DeLorme Northern California Atlas & Gazetteer:* Page 94, B1.

I Olompali Trail

This easy to moderate 2.6-mile loop trail takes hikers on a walk through about 4,000 years of history, beginning with a Coast Miwok village and continuing through Spanish missionaries, cattle ranchers, and a hippie commune that hosted the Grateful Dead. An interpretive booklet from the visitor center explains everything. From San Francisco, head north 29 miles on U.S. Highway 101. The park entrance is on the west side of the highway and is only accessible from the southbound lane, so you will have to continue north until you can turn around, then come back down. Half a mile up the entrance road is the main parking lot. The trail begins at the west end of the parking lot. For more information, contact Olompali State Historic Park, Novato; (415) 892–3383. *DeLorme: Northern California Atlas & Gazetteer:* Page 94, C1.

J Jepson/Johnstone Loop

This easy 2.6-mile loop explores the topography of the northern Point Reyes area. Along the way the hike passes through one of the last virgin stands of Bishop pine and visits a secluded walk-in beach on Tomales Bay. Starting from the Heart's Desire parking lot, the trail heads uphill through the forest, eventually crossing a private access road and joining the Johnstone Trail. Follow this back down the ridge to Pebble Beach, then back to Heart's Desire along a shoreline connector trail. To reach the park from San Francisco, head north 7 miles on U.S. Highway 101. In Mill Valley, head west on California Highway 1 and continue 27 miles to Point Reyes Station. Turn left onto Sir Francis Drake Boulevard and follow it west 6.6 miles to the fork in the road. Take the right fork (Pierce Point Road) and continue another 1.2 miles. Turn right into Tomales Bay State Park and follow the access road 2.1 miles to its end in the Heart's Desire parking lot. For more information, contact Tomales Bay State Park, Inverness; (415) 669-1140. *DeLorme: Northern California Atlas & Gazetteer:* Page 93, C–D5.

South Bay

With the increased population of the Bay Area comes the increased partitioning of the land into smaller and smaller counties. The five counties of this region could easily fit into the larger Humboldt County up north, but the population of each one would dwarf Humboldt's. Fortunately, the residents of these urban areas are just as fond of wild and open spaces as the folk behind the Redwood Curtain—if anything, even more so. A crazy quilt of public lands blankets nearly every inch of undeveloped land here, creating a wealth of hiking opportunities totally unexpected in such a city-dominated area. State parks, county parks, open-space preserves, a national recreation area, and other agencies manage these lands for the preservation of natural habitat, as well as for the enjoyment of the region's many hikers. The result is a variety of playgrounds that makes it easy to get away from the crowds, even within sight of major cities.

As with the other regions of the Redwood Coast, topography has played a huge role here in deciding where settlements are located, and what land is saved. The great natural harbor of San Francisco Bay plunges southward just east of the city that shares its name, leaving a long, ridge-backed peninsula lying like a Chinese dragon between the quiet waters of the bay and the turbulent Pacific. The steep and unstable nature of this ridge—it is scarred along its full length by the San Andreas Fault—led settlers to build out into the bay rather than develop its upper slopes, and today a string of industrial cities lie sprawled out on the reclaimed land of the South Bay's shores, while the hills behind them are largely left to chaparral and oak forests.

Away to the east, across the sprawling Silicon Valley, rolling hills climb once again, harboring drier, hotter landscapes of grass and oak forest, where cows are more at home than people. The huge Henry W. Coe State Park waits here, occupying former ranching lands and offering true wilderness within day-trip distance of the city.

On the coast a loose string of tiny towns dots the shoreline between San Francisco in the north and Santa Cruz in the south. Separated from the South Bay's urban areas by the crumpled mass of the Santa Cruz Mountains, the coast retains a remote and forgotten atmosphere. Numerous parks and state beaches line the shores here, alongside dairy operations and some of California's specialty crops—brussels sprouts and artichoke among them.

Deep in the mountains, large groves of old-growth redwood can still be found in Big Basin State Park, while smaller groves and thick second growth remain to be explored in several other nearby parks. On the highest ridges, open grasslands and oak woodlands beckon, offering unparalleled views of the surrounding countryside.

37 Sweeney Ridge Trail

This little-known hike is one of the best-kept secrets of local open-space fans. On clear days the ridge offers spectacular bird's-eye views of South San Francisco Bay on the one side and the Pacific coast on the other. The trail, part of the 400-mile Bay Area Ridge Trail, passes by an abandoned Army radar installation on its way south along the ridge. The turnaround point for the hike is the spot where Spanish explorer Gaspar de Portola "discovered" San Francisco Bay in 1769.

Start: At the small overlook parking area of Skyline College.
Distance: 4.2 miles out and back.
Approximate hiking time: 2 to 3 hours.
Difficulty: Moderate, due to some sketchy trail and steep climbing.
Trail surface: Dirt path, gravel road, and paved road.
Lay of the land: Open, grassy ridges.
Other trail users: Cyclists.

Canine compatibility: Dogs allowed, on leash.
Land status: National recreation area.
Nearest town: San Bruno.
Fees and permits: None.
Schedule: Open year-round.
Map: USGS map: Montara Mt, CA.
Trail contact: Golden Gate National Recreation Area, San Francisco; (415) 556-0560; www.nps.gov/goga.

Finding the trailhead: From San Bruno, on Interstate 280, exit at Skyline Boulevard and head north another two stop lights on California Highway 35. Turn left onto College Drive and follow it up 0.6 mile to the college loop. Turn right and drive around the loop 0.3 mile to a small scenic vista parking lot on the right, overlooking the Pacific coast. Park here. The trail heads up along the ridge at the south end of the lot. *DeLorme: Northern California Atlas & Gazetteer:* Page 104, C-D2.

The Hike

Given the stunning views of San Francisco Bay and the Pacific coast from Sweeney Ridge, it is surprising that the trail doesn't see more use—doubly so, considering the high population density in the surrounding urban areas. Then again, the trail isn't exactly well advertised. The northern trailhead is an unsigned dirt path heading off into the bushes from the parking lot of San Bruno's Skyline College—not exactly an irresistible attraction unless you know where it leads.

From the parking lot, the trail climbs steeply up the ridge, briefly joining a paved road leading to a couple of water tanks. (Speaking of water, be sure to bring plenty, since there is no water of any kind to be had on the ridge.) The trail continues up behind the tanks, and the real nature of the trail soon becomes apparent, as stunning views open up on both sides of the ridge. The first real landmark after the water tanks comes when the trail reaches the first of three summits. A small concrete box of a building stands empty and abandoned. Until 1974 this structure

Abandoned Army building on the first summit

was part of the U.S. Army's Nike Missile Site SF-51, charged with protecting the peninsula during the height of the cold war. Together with the larger cluster of buildings on the next summit south, the installation housed radar dishes and other equipment used to track and guide the Nike missiles to enemy aircraft. The missiles themselves were housed in silos on Milagro Ridge, a couple of miles north.

The land on Sweeney Ridge is now dedicated to more peaceful pursuits. As part of the Golden Gate National Recreation Area, the 23,000-acre Sweeney Ridge Unit provides recreational opportunities for hikers, mountain bikers, and wildlife lovers, as well as habitat for the endangered Mission blue butterfly.

From the building the trail heads down into a deep, brushy cut via a long series of stairs. Once at the bottom the trail heads immediately back up the other side, climbing once again to the ridgetop. Upon reaching the main cluster of Army buildings on the second summit, the trail joins a one-lane paved road, once used as an access road for cold warriors. From this point on, there is relatively little elevation change before reaching the trail's turnaround point.

Sweeney Ridge Trail

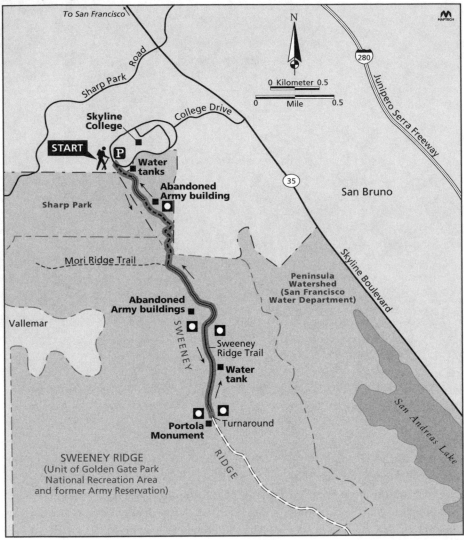

On clear days hikers can enjoy an unparalleled view from the ridge. To the east South San Francisco Bay lies spread out like a giant wading pool, ringed by the grit of urban sprawl. San Francisco International Airport squats on the near shore, sending up or receiving a jumbo jet every few minutes. To the west lies the relatively tranquil San Pedro Valley and the Pacific Ocean, stretching to the horizon.

About 2 miles from the trailhead, the paved road dives down to the east, and the trail continues straight a short distance to the Portola Monument. Two carved granite monuments mark the spot. The reddish stone to the left commemorates the site where Spanish captain Gaspar de Portola led an expeditionary party in October 1769 and became the first European to lay eyes on the harbor of San Francisco Bay. The explorers were actually on an overland mission to map the coast from Baja California north to Monterey Bay, but they overshot the mark by 100 miles or so when the waters off Monterey failed to live up to the sailor's reports of a fine, wind-sheltered harbor. The Spaniard was nevertheless pleased with what he found.

The second monument honors Carl Patrick McCarthy, who labored for many years to have the Portola discovery site officially recognized as a historic landmark. From the monuments, return the way you came.

THE CALIFORNIA MISSION ERA

In the annals of California history, there have been many events that changed the course of history drastically—take the Gold Rush, for example, or the brief war that resulted in American annexation—but the one that changed life in California the most was undoubtedly the founding of the first Spanish mission in San Diego in 1769. Undertaken as a joint military/religious effort by explorer Gaspar de Portola and Franciscan Padre Junipero Serra, the mission was to be the first of several forays into the vast territory known to the Spanish as "Alta California." The missions were intended to be outposts of Christian civilization, firmly establishing Spanish claims to the region and bringing the dual gifts of salvation and civilization to the Native American peoples already living there. Unfortunately, these "gifts" ended up doing more harm than good. Nothing short of the total disruption of Native lives and cultures resulted from Spanish missionization. The slow rate of conversion to the new faith—with its accompanying total immersion in feudal Spanish culture—eventually led to the institution of several dubious practices aimed at increasing Native participation. These included "recruiting" neophytes from Native villages at gunpoint, incarceration in the missions, flogging, and even branding crosses into converts' arms to aid in their retrieval should they escape to their former villages. But as harmful as the missions were to Native societies, it was imported European diseases that did the most damage. Smallpox, syphilis, and other exotic ailments brought by the newcomers played the largest role in decimating Native populations. By the end of the era, the Native population had declined by more than half.

In all, twenty-one missions were established, the last and northernmost being built in Sonoma in 1823. When Mexico achieved independence from Spain in the early nineteenth century, it began a policy of reform that included secularizing the missions, but the damage had already been done. For the Native Americans, life in California had changed forever.

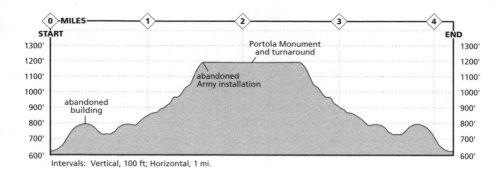

Intervals: Vertical, 100 ft; Horizontal, 1 mi.

Miles and Directions

0.0 Start at the south end of the small scenic overlook parking lot. Head up the ridge along the narrow dirt path.

0.1 Turn right onto the paved road, heading uphill. The road ends shortly, at two large water tanks. Continue around the fence to the right, climbing the faint dirt path up the hill behind the tanks.

0.2 At the junction with the gravel road, turn right, heading south up the ridge.

0.3 The trail is now over the tree line, with excellent views to both sides on clear days.

0.5 The trail arrives at an abandoned Army building on the first peak. Continue down into the saddle on the paved trail to the right of the building.

0.6 Descend into the saddle via a long series of steps.

0.8 The trail reaches the bottom of the saddle and begins climbing up the other side.

1.1 The trail reaches the ridgetop again, just before a junction. To the right, the Mori Ridge Trail heads west down toward Pacifica. Continue to the left on the Sweeney Ridge Trail.

1.4 The trail makes a long S curve, climbing to the top of the second ridge.

1.6 A group of abandoned Army buildings stands open to the right. Continue left, heading south along the straight one-lane paved road.

1.7 The trail passes a water tower on the left.

2.0 The road curves left and heads downhill. Continue straight along the ridge. A few yards later, veer left on the short spur trail to the two small monuments on the ridgetop.

2.1 The monuments are the turnaround point. Return the way you came.

4.2 Trailhead.

Hike Information

Local Information

San Mateo County Convention and Visitors Bureau, Burlingame; (650) 348-7600; www.sanmateocountycvb.com.

Half Moon Bay Coastside Chamber of Commerce and Visitors Bureau, Half Moon Bay; (650) 726-8380; www.halfmoonbay chamber.org.

Local Events/Attractions

San Mateo County Historical Museum, Redwood City; (650) 299-0104; www.sanmateohistory.com.

South San Francisco Historical Society Museum, South San Francisco; (650) 829-3825.

Marine Science Institute, Redwood City; (650) 364-2760.

Lodging

Hostelling International–Point Montara Lighthouse, Montara; (650) 728-7177; www.norcalhostels.org.

Hostelling International–Pigeon Point Lighthouse, Pescadero; (650) 879-0633; www.norcalhostels.org.

Organizations

The Friends of Sweeney Ridge; (650) 871-9478; www.pacificalandtrust.org/ sweeneyridge.

38 Alpine Lake/Ridge Loop

An amazing resource so close to the frantic traffic and urban sprawl of Silicon Valley, the patchwork of public lands that make up the South Skyline Regional Open Space Preserves are crisscrossed with enough trails to make everyone happy. This hike skirts picturesque Alpine Lake before climbing a grass-and-oak-covered ridge to some impressive panoramas of the western Santa Cruz Mountains. This trail is part of the Bay Area Ridge Trail network.

Start: Russian Ridge parking area.
Distance: 2-mile loop.
Approximate hiking time: 1 to 2 hours.
Difficulty: Easy to moderate, due to elevation gain and exposure to the hot sun in summer.
Trail surface: Dirt path, gravel road.
Lay of the land: Open, hilly grassland, interspersed with shady oak groves.
Other trail users: Cyclists, equestrians.
Canine compatibility: Dogs not allowed on trail.

Land status: Open-space preserve.
Nearest town: Los Altos Hills.
Fees and permits: None.
Schedule: Open year-round during daylight hours.
Map: USGS map: Mindego Hill, CA.
Trail contact: Skyline Ridge Open Space Preserve, Midpeninsula Regional Open Space District, Los Altos; (650) 691-1200; www.openspace.org/preserves.

Finding the trailhead: From Palo Alto, head west on Page Mill Road, climbing steeply. From the junction with Interstate 280, it is 8.9 miles up to the ridge and the junction with California Highway 35. At the junction, continue straight (now Alpine Road) and turn right almost immediately into the large gravel parking lot. The trailhead is at the kiosk near the pedestrian tunnel under Alpine Road. *DeLorme: Northern California Atlas & Gazetteer: Page 114, B4.*

The Hike

Let it never be said that the citizens of the South Bay Area do not love their wild lands. Consider the facts: less than 10 miles east—as the crow flies—pumps the heart of Silicon Valley, San Jose, where two-bedroom homes go for well more than $1 million, and people earning $100,000 a year have been known to turn up in homeless shelters. Half that distance to the north lies Stanford University, where the best and brightest of a generation toil amidst an urban sprawl that stretches unbroken up to land's end at the Golden Gate Bridge. Space is clearly at a premium.

And yet right next door to this monstrous monoburb lie thousands of acres of prime real estate, lovingly preserved in their natural state and laced with a network of trails for the enjoyment of all. In the 5-mile radius of land surrounding the Alpine Lake trailhead alone, there can be found no fewer than twenty-two separate parks or preserves, managed by at least six different agencies—for lovers of walks in wild places, a tantalizing prospect.

Alpine Lake/Ridge Loop

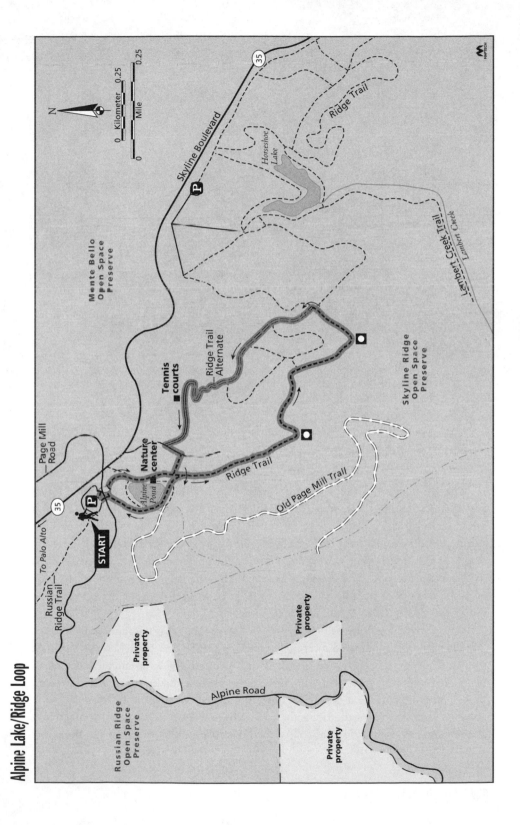

N

0 Kilometer 0.25

0 Mile 0.25

Mente Bello
Open Space
Preserve

Skyline Boulevard

P

Horseshoe
Lake

Ridge Trail

Lambert Creek Trail

Lambert Creek

Page Mill
Road

Tennis
courts

Ridge Trail
Alternate

Skyline Ridge
Open Space
Preserve

Nature
center

Alpine
Pond

Ridge Trail

Old Page Mill Trail

35

To Palo Alto

Russian
Ridge Trail

P

START

Russian Ridge
Open Space
Preserve

Private
property

Private
property

Alpine Road

Private
property

MAPTECH

Alpine Lake

The hike begins in the large gravel parking lot at the junction of Alpine Road and CA 35. Passing through a tunnel under Alpine Road, the trail heads down a broad gravel path to the David C. Daniels Nature Center on the shore of little Alpine Pond. From here the trail climbs up out of the shady forest to the open, grassy slopes of the ridge's west side, where views open up of the thickly forested valleys to the south and west. The drainage directly below the ridge leads south to the old-growth groves of Portola Redwoods State Park. Beyond that, over the next ridge, lie the forests of Big Basin Redwoods State Park.

This part of the hike follows a portion of the Bay Area Ridge Trail, a long-distance route being created to completely encircle the San Francisco Bay Area. At the time of this writing, more than half the planned 400-mile circuit has already been established on existing trails, connecting various public parks and preserves. With volunteer labor and donations, more should be coming online soon.

At the south end of the ridge, the trail swings around to the east, soon arriving at the junction with a dirt fire road. The hike follows this fire road up along the ridgetop, completing the loop through a pleasant pattern of alternating open meadows and shady oak groves. Once back at Alpine Pond, the trail follows around the left side this time, crossing the earthen embankment that contains the small reservoir. On the far end, Old Page Mill Trail heads down the valley, following the course of an old nineteenth-century log-hauling road that serviced William Page's mill, near present-day Portola Redwoods State Park.

Page's wasn't the first road that passed this way. The native Ohlone Indians once followed a trail over this pass that dated back to hundreds or even thousands of years before the arrival of Europeans. During the years of Spanish rule, the route was used as a trail connecting the coastal ranch of San Gregorio with the Rancho San Francisquito—now known as Palo Alto. In 1868 the Menlo Park and Santa Cruz Turnpike Corporation built a toll road along the route of modern day Alpine Road. The venture was less than totally successful, and in 1894 the county took over, creating the road you see today. From Alpine Pond the trail follows a dirt path up to the left, crossing over the historic byway and returning to the trailhead.

Miles and Directions

0.0 Start at the kiosk in the center of the parking lot. Head down the short flight of steps and through the tunnel under Alpine Road.

0.1 A gravel road joins the trail from the left. Continue straight to the nature center.

0.15 At the junction just past the nature center, take the left fork, heading uphill.

0.2 Cross the paved road, continuing straight on the other side. A few yards later, a spur trail heads left to the remnants of an old cattle station. Continue straight.

0.3 An old roadbed heads left and right, crossing the trail. Continue straight. A few yards later, the trail exits the forest into a wide meadow.

0.5 The trail rounds a rocky outcrop, with a great view of the valley to the right.

0.7 A connector trail heads left up to the ridge. Continue straight. Shortly after, the trail rounds another rock outcrop, with another great view.

0.8 The trail passes through a shady oak grove.

0.9 The trail rounds the end of the ridge, heading east. A view to the south opens up on the right.

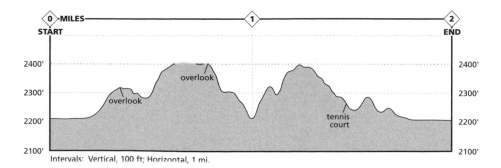

Intervals: Vertical, 100 ft; Horizontal, 1 mi.

1.0 At the junction, turn left onto the dirt fire road, heading uphill.

1.2 An alternate trail heads left. Continue straight.

1.3 Another connector trail heads left. Continue straight.

1.4 An old roadbed joins the trail from the right. Continue straight.

1.5 At the T junction, turn right onto the new dirt road, heading downhill.

1.6 The road surface switches from dirt to gravel, and the road makes a sharp switchback. A tennis court squats inexplicably in the forest to the right.

1.7 At the cluster of buildings, follow the switchback around to the left. Almost immediately, turn right again onto the paved road, following the sign for Alpine Pond.

1.8 End of the ridge-trail loop. At the junction with the singletrack trail, continue straight along the road. A few yards later the pond loop heads right, and the path ahead forks. Take the right fork, passing over the earthen dam.

1.9 At the north end of the dam, continue straight a few yards, passing over the pond's spillway, then take the left fork in the trail, heading uphill.

2.0 Cross Alpine Road and continue the last few yards to the trailhead.

Hike Information

Local Information

San Mateo County Convention and Visitors Bureau, Burlingame; (650) 348-7600; www.sanmateocountycvb.com.

Santa Cruz County Conference and Visitors Council, Santa Cruz; (800) 833-3494; (831) 425-1234; www.scccvc.org.

Santa Clara Chamber of Commerce and Convention and Visitors Bureau, Santa Clara; (408) 244-8244; www.santaclara.org.

Local Events/Attractions

The Tech Museum of Innovation, where Silicon Valley shows off, San Jose; (408) 294-TECH; www.thetech.org.

May Fete Children's Parade, held in early May, Palo Alto; (650) 463-4921.

Moonlight Run, held in October, 5K walk, 10K run, and 5K run, Palo Alto; (650) 326-8210; (650)463-4920; www.PaloAltoOnline.com.

Lodging

Hostelling International–Hidden Villa, Los Altos Hills; (650) 949-8648; www.norcalhostels.org.

39 Castle Rock Double Loop

This hike explores the deep folds and rocky heights of Castle Rock State Park, perched up on the ridge of the Santa Cruz mountain range between the urban centers of San Jose and Santa Cruz. The dense oak forest of the park is studded with large granite outcrops that local rock climbers find irresistible. The park's namesake Castle Rock is marked by strange honeycomb formations, but it is Goat Rock that provides the best views.

Start: Castle Rock trailhead.
Distance: 4-mile double loop.
Approximate hiking time: 2 to 3 hours.
Difficulty: Moderate, due to elevation gain and some steep trail.
Trail surface: Dirt path, gravel road.
Lay of the land: Oak forest, exposed rock outcroppings.
Other trail users: Rock climbers.

Canine compatibility: No dogs allowed.
Land status: State park.
Nearest town: Saratoga.
Fees and permits: $5.00 day-use fee.
Schedule: Open year-round, 8:00 A.M. to sunset (registered campers exempt).
Maps: USGS map: Montara Mtn, CA.
Trail contact: Castle Rock State Park, Los Gatos; (408) 867-2952, www.parks.ca.gov.

Finding the trailhead: From Interstate 280 in San Jose, exit onto Saratoga Avenue and follow it southwest 5 miles to the center of suburban Saratoga. Follow signs for California Highway 9 through town, and continue west on CA 9 another 8 miles to the junction with California Highway 35. Turn left and follow CA 35 south 2.5 miles, then turn right into Castle Rock State Park. Park in the large gravel lot. The trailhead is up near the road, on the south side of the entrance. Three trailheads leave from the parking lot: one by the rest rooms, one at the bottom of the lot next to a kiosk, and one up near the entrance on the left. Take the last one, up to Castle Rock. *DeLorme: Northern California Atlas & Gazetteer: Page 104, C-D2.*

The Hike

From the frenetic big-city bustle of the San Francisco Peninsula, the Santa Cruz Mountains stretch southeast in an unbroken line for some 60 miles, neatly dividing the megalopolis at the southern end of the Bay Area from the string of towns and cities lining Monterey Bay's north shore. Pressed between these two urban centers, the mountains arch skyward in a crumpled mass of bald, grassy ridges and deeply forested valleys. Thanks to a combination of relatively recent population growth and local residents' love of nature, much of this land has been preserved in the form of numerous state, county, and city parks, as well as a patchwork of open-space preserves.

Midway along the knobby spine of the range, perched high on the tallest ridge, lies Castle Rock State Park. Created in 1968 the park encompasses some 3,800 acres of redwoods, mixed conifers, grasslands, and clusters of rare black oak forest. Along with neighboring parks and open-space preserves, the park provides habitat for

Oak forest and meadow on the Ridge Trail

common animals such as black-tailed deer, coyote, red-tailed hawk, acorn wood-pecker, California mountain king snake, and Pacific rattlesnake. Less common species include the golden eagle, Brewer's calandrinia, and steelhead trout. But what sets Castle Rock apart from other nearby public lands are, of course, the rocks.

Throughout the park, hikers will find outcrops of concretelike Vaqueros sand-stone looming unexpectedly from the surrounding vegetation. Unlike many types of sandstone, this variety has a fairly hard and stable exterior surface, with a unique weathering system that results in strange, sculptured formations—attributes that make it very popular with rock climbers. So popular, in fact, that a Castle Rock Climbers Committee has been formed with volunteers from the local climbing community to help deal with climbing-related resource issues in the park. Unless it has been raining, hikers are likely to see climbers at several sites along the hike (rain makes the sandstone softer and more likely to crumble, discouraging climbers dur-ing the wet season).

From the trailhead next to the park's main entrance, the first stop along the hike is at the park's namesake Castle Rock. The trail climbs steeply from the trailhead,

Castle Rock Double Loop

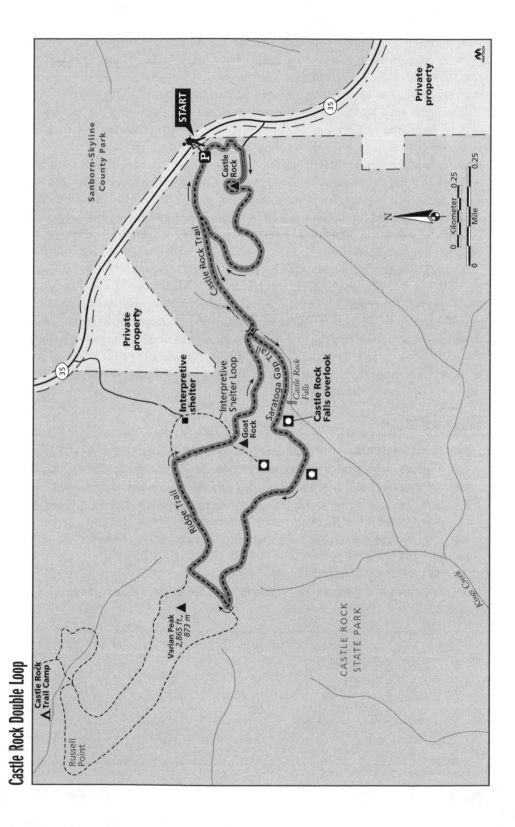

soon joining a gravel road that leads right to the rock. Although it is the highest point in the park, do not expect much of a view from the top—surrounding trees effectively screen the peak from the rest of the scenery. Still, the rock itself is impressive enough, and there are plenty of views later in the hike.

Originally used by Ohlone Indians as a seasonal camp, the land saw little change until well after the California Gold Rush of 1849. The early 1880s brought railroads to the eastern valley, spurring the creation of logging camps and paving the way for settlements in the surrounding mountains. In 1886 a school was opened next to Castle Rock, serving the children of local ranchers. The first schoolmarm, Miss Ida M. Jones, taught an inaugural class of six students, and she lived in a cabin attached to the schoolhouse. Around on the back side of the rock, hikers will find a small cave once used by the young schoolteacher as a temporary dwelling, while her cabin was being built. Honeycomb formations—called fretworks—cover the cave's walls and ceiling.

From Castle Rock the trail heads back down to the Saratoga Gap Trail, following the path downstream to Castle Rock Falls. An overlook at the top of the falls offers hikers the first scenic vista of the hike. If you are lucky, you might see some climbers scaling the sheer rock face directly below the platform. The trail then contours around the upper slopes of the valley, eventually heading uphill and returning along the ridgetop to Goat Rock, home of the best views in the park. The final leg of the journey drops down to the junction just above the falls and returns along the Saratoga Gap Trail to the trailhead.

Miles and Directions

0.0   Start at the trailhead near the parking lot entrance. Follow the singletrack path uphill.

0.1   A spur trail heads down to the right, to a separate trailhead. Continue uphill to the left.

0.2   The singletrack trail ends at a gravel road. Turn right, following the road along the ridge.

0.3   Castle Rock is on the left in the small clearing. The trail continues past the rock, curving around behind it. (FYI: The cave is around the back side of the rock.)

0.4   At the switchback, a spur trail heads straight to a cluster of boulders. Follow the well-signed main trail back to the right.

0.5   The trail dips into a saddle, then up the other side.

0.7   At the junction, turn left onto the Saratoga Gap Trail, heading downhill along the creek.

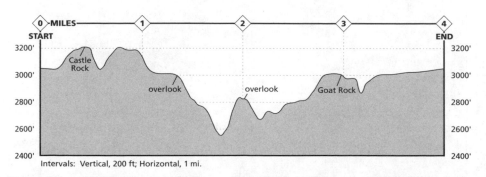

Intervals: Vertical, 200 ft; Horizontal, 1 mi.

1.2 Cross the creek via a small footbridge. On the other side, turn left at the junction, continuing downstream.

1.4 The trail arrives at the Castle Rock Falls overlook. (FYI: The cliff below the platform is a favorite of climbers.)

1.5 (FYI: An excellent view of the valley opens up to the left. Look out over brush for a view of the valley.)

1.7 (FYI: The trail rounds a bend and dives into a gully below Goat Rock. A few yards later, it passes over a low rock outcrop, offering another great view of the valley.)

1.9 The trail dives into another hollow.

2.1 At the junction, turn right onto the cutoff trail, heading up toward the ridge.

2.2 The trail arrives on the ridge. At the junction, turn right onto the Ridge Trail.

2.3 A spur trail heads right to the Emily Smith Bird Observation Point. Continue straight, following the main trail as it makes a sharp bend to the left.

2.5 At the junction, turn right, following the trail to Goat Rock.

2.7 The trail reaches the upper knob of Goat Rock from behind. Just before reaching the outcrop, a spur trail heads right along the meadow toward an overlook (0.1 mile). At the rock, another trail heads left up toward the interpretive shelter. Take the right fork instead, heading steeply downhill along the edge of the outcrop.

2.8 At the bottom of the rock, a climber's spur trail heads right a few yards to the base of the rock face. Follow the main trail left and continue downhill.

3.1 The trail passes under a low overhanging rock.

3.3 End of the Goat Rock loop. At the junction with the Saratoga Gap Trail, cross the footbridge and head left, upstream.

3.8 The trail to Castle Rock heads up to the right. Continue straight toward the parking lot.

3.9 The trail passes a popular climbing boulder on the left.

4.0 Trailhead.

Hike Information

Local Information

Santa Cruz County Conference and Visitors Council, Santa Cruz; (800) 833-3494; (831) 425-1234, www.scccvc.org.

San Mateo County Convention and Visitors Bureau, Burlingame; (650) 348-7600; www.sanmateocountycvb.com.

Santa Cruz Chamber of Commerce, Santa Cruz; (831) 457-3713; www.santacruzchamber.org.

Saratoga Chamber of Commerce, Saratoga; (408) 867-0753; www.saratogachamber.org.

Local Events/Attractions

The Tech Museum of Innovation, where Silicon Valley shows off, San Jose; (408) 294-TECH; www.thetech.org.

Loch Lomond Highland Games, held in October, traditional Scottish games, plus music and crafts, Ben Lomond; (831) 479-1508.

Hakone Festival, held in mid-May, free admission and events at the world-class Japanese gardens, Saratoga; (408) 741-4994; hakone.com.

Lodging

There are two backcountry camps in the park. Call (831) 338-8861 for reservations.

Hostelling International-Sanborn Park Hostel, Saratoga; (408) 741-0166; www.sanbornparkhostel.org.

Hostelling International-Hidden Villa, Los Altos Hills; (650) 949-8648; www.norcalhostels.org.

40 Berry Falls Loop

This much-loved trail leads through the heart of Big Basin Redwoods State Park, the oldest of California's state parks, on a large loop trail. The path follows the courses of fern-carpeted Berry and West Waddell Creeks, with plenty of banana slugs, salamanders, and other slimy critters to keep you company. The highlight of the trail is a series of unusual waterfalls on Berry Creek.

Start: From the Redwood Trail trailhead.

Distance: 10.4-mile loop.

Approximate hiking time: 5.5 to 6 hours.

Difficulty: Moderate, due to good trails, but there are some steep sections.

Trail surface: Dirt path.

Lay of the land: Richly forested hills, dry ridges, and waterfalls.

Other trail users: Hikers only.

Canine compatibility: Dogs not permitted.

Land status: State park.

Nearest town: Saratoga.

Fees and permits: $5.00 day-use fee required.

Schedule: Open year-round 6:00 A.M. to 10:00 P.M.

Maps: USGS maps: Franklin Point, CA; Big Basin, CA.

Trail contact: Big Basin Redwoods State Park, Boulder Creek; CA (831) 338–8860; www.parks.ca.gov.

Finding the trailhead: From San Jose, head south 7 miles on California Highway 17 from the junction of Interstate 280, and exit onto California Highway 9 at the Saratoga exit. Head west 4 miles on CA 9 to the suburb of Saratoga. Follow CA 9 as it turns left and passes through the shopping district before heading out of town. Continue on CA 9 out of Saratoga and up into the Santa Cruz Mountains, climbing 7 miles to the ridge and the junction with California Highway 35. Cross the ridge and continue down the other side another 5.5 miles on CA 9, then take the right fork onto California Highway 236 at the sign for Big Basin Redwoods State Park, continuing another 3.3 miles to the park headquarters and visitor center. Turn right into the day-use area, and park in the first parking lot on the left. The trail starts on the west side of the parking lot.

From Santa Cruz, head north 13 miles on CA 9 to the town of Boulder Creek, and turn left onto CA 236. Follow CA 236 another 10 miles to the park headquarters. Turn left into the day-use area, and left again into the first parking lot. The trailhead is on the west side of the lot.

Public Transportation: Santa Cruz Metro route #35 runs to Big Basin Redwoods State Park from Santa Cruz on weekends only. Call (831) 425–8600 for more information, or check out www.scmtd.com for the current schedule. *DeLorme: Northern California Atlas & Gazetteer:* Page 115, C4.

The Hike

The Berry Falls Loop starts at the Redwood Trail trailhead, just across from the Big Basin Redwoods State Park visitor center on the west side of the parking lot. This

Berry Falls Creek ▶

area is the hub of activity in the park, and there are apt to be crowds on most days. But don't worry. The well-developed network of 80-plus miles of trail helps disperse hikers away from the visitor center. This path follows a short section of the Redwood Trail through a showcase grove of the giant trees before crossing Opal Creek and heading south along the opposite bank.

The trail soon shows its true character. The path begins to climb deeper into the forest via a series of switchbacks, and from here the terrain becomes steeper and the trails more convoluted. The path spends most of its time climbing, descending, or following the contours of hillsides above various creeks. At the junction with the Middle Ridge Fire Road, a sign warns hikers that the trail to Berry Falls is a strenuous one, not suited for a casual stroll. The trail drops down into the West Waddell Creek drainage, first following Kelly Creek then West Waddell Creek downstream to Berry Creek and the falls. Incidentally, Waddell Creek takes its name from early lumberman William Waddell, who, in the 1860s, built a sawmill near the mouth of the creek, on what is now Waddell Beach. While in the area, in the mid 1870s, Waddell was mauled to death by a grizzly bear—this being when grizzlies still roamed the park in abundance.

> San Jose, at the heart of high-tech Silicon Valley, is the eleventh largest city in the United States.

During that same time period, the redwoods enjoyed relative security. As recently as 1875, redwood forests covered 53 percent of the land in Santa Cruz County. Members of a Spanish expedition first spotted the giant trees in 1769, but it was many years before technology had advanced to the point where loggers could profitably harvest the redwoods on a large scale. Even the early 1800s saw lumberjacks milling the logs using a two-person handsaw—a practice that was slow and labor intensive. But the logging industry was revolutionized in 1840 when the first water-powered sawmill was built north of Santa Cruz on the San Lorenzo River. This industrial advance signaled the end of the redwoods' reign. And by the turn of the century, the groves of Big Basin were some of the last old-growth redwood stands in the county.

Of all the redwood parks in the California State Park system, Big Basin is the oldest. In fact, the park, which contains the largest contiguous stand of coast redwoods south of San Francisco, was the first state park in California. Following a fire in the Santa Cruz Mountains in 1899, local conservationists became interested in saving the last large grove of redwoods from the logger's ax—a threat even greater to the redwoods than fire. The campaign was led by poet and writer Josephine Clifford McCrackin, who worked with artist and photographer Andrew P. Hill and other residents to form the Sempervirens Club. The group, aided by the California Pioneer Society and the Native Sons & Daughters, eventually convinced the state legislature to set aside land for a park. And in 1902, 3,800 acres of old-growth redwood forest were designated California Redwood Park. Other parks were subsequently created, so the original California Redwood Park had to be renamed Big

Berry Falls Loop

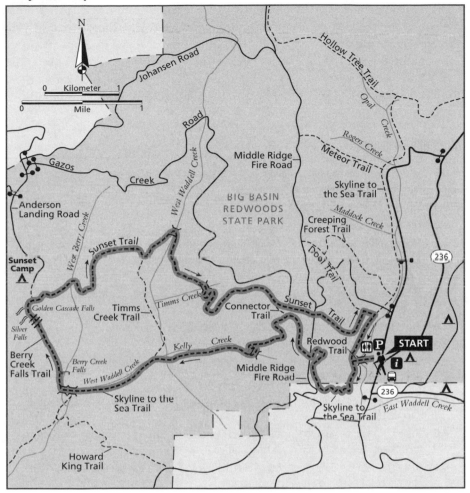

Basin. The park has continued to grow throughout the years and now contains more than 18,000 acres.

Berry Creek Falls, the first waterfall the trail encounters, is arguably the most impressive cascade in the park—although there are many falls along the various waterways that can compete. As the trail makes its way up West Berry Creek, it passes the watery grotto of Silver Falls, climbs stairs up the cliff to the top of the falls, and continues onward to Golden Cascade Falls. This third waterfall is a series of plunges over slickrock shaped like a theme-park waterslide. The rock base is stained red and orange from minerals in the surrounding earth.

Leaving the waterfalls and West Berry Creek behind, the trail climbs to the ridge, where the vegetation changes drastically. Knobcone pine, buckeye, and chinquapin, better suited to the dry climate on the ridge, replace the humid shadow of redwoods and Douglas fir. For a brief stretch, even this airy forest gives way to chaparral as the trail passes over an outcropping of pale, near-white sandstone. But the trail quickly descends again into deep forest, where the path contours around the upper slopes of the park on the Sunset Trail. The trail eventually drops down into the basin of the park's hub—emerging on Opal Creek just upstream of the visitor center and following the waterway down to the first bridge you crossed on this hike. From here it's just a short jaunt back to the trailhead.

Miles and Directions

0.0 Start at the Redwood Trail trailhead. Follow Redwood Trail straight past the rest rooms and across Opal Creek via the footbridge.

0.1 Turn left onto Skyline to the Sea Trail.

0.2 The trail veers away from Opal Creek and begins to climb the hill to the right.

0.8 Skyline to the Sea Trail crosses Middle Ridge Fire Road, which runs along the ridge to the left and right. Go straight, continuing down on Skyline to the Sea Trail toward Berry Creek Falls.

1.3 The Sunset/Skyline to Sea Connector Trail heads off to the right. Continue straight on Skyline to the Sea Trail.

2.0 Cross Kelly Creek via a wooden footbridge and continue downstream.

2.2 A short alternate trail goes off to the right. Continue straight.

2.4 The alternate trail rejoins the main path. Continue straight, heading downstream.

2.8 Timms Creek Trail heads right. Continue straight on Skyline to the Sea Trail.

3.7 (FYI: On the other side of the boulder, to your right, is a 40-foot sheer drop. It's worth a look, but be careful.)

4.0 The trail descends on wooden steps to West Waddell Creek and crosses the creek on two footbridges. Veer left on the other side, and continue downstream.

4.1 Turn right onto the Berry Creek Falls Trail. (Skyline to the Sea Trail continues left to Rancho del Oso.) Continue uphill toward the falls.

4.2 The trail climbs a little to the Berry Creek Falls overlook. (FYI: Berry Creek Falls is just more than 60 feet tall.) From here, follow Berry Creek Falls Trail as it continues upstream.

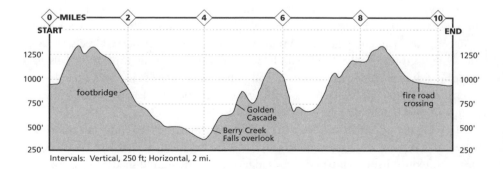

Intervals: Vertical, 250 ft; Horizontal, 2 mi.

WHERE'S THE BEAR?

Grizzly Flats, Grizzly Creek, Bear Valley. Place-names like this are common throughout California, but the beast that inspired them is unfortunately gone forever.

It has been estimated that there were as many as 10,000 California grizzly bears *(Ursus californicus)* roaming the Golden State when the first Spanish missionaries arrived. Run-ins with grizzlies were so common during the mission era that caballeros often lassoed the animals and brought them in for use in special bullfights. These bear versus bull battles are the origin of the modern stock-market terms for up-turning and down-turning markets.

When American settlers took over the state in 1846, the grizzly was still so plentiful that it was chosen as the symbol of the fledgling "Bear Flag Republic." To this day a grizzly graces the Californian state flag.

But the new Californians were not kind to their mascot; within a period of seventy-five years, it had been driven to extinction by trapping, poisoning, and hunting. The last grizzly to be shot in California was taken by a hunter in 1922. A few isolated sightings were reported until 1924, but the last bears, unable to find mates, died out soon after. In 1953 the grizzly was designated the official state animal of California.

4.6 The trail reaches Silver Falls, which is not quite as tall as Berry Creek Falls, but still impressive. (FYI: The creek is an unusual color due to oxidized minerals in the ground.) Follow the trail as it climbs wooden stairs to the top of the falls.

4.7 The trail passes Golden Cascade. (FYI: This waterfall gets its name from the reddish yellow color of the rock and the waterslide shape that plunges down in a series of consecutive small drops.) Above the Golden Cascade, the trail climbs to the drier forest on the ridge.

5.1 A short trail to Sunset Camp heads left. This junction marks the end of Berry Creek Falls Trail and the beginning of Sunset Trail. Continue straight along Sunset Trail.

5.3 The trail crosses a small outcropping of white sandstone, surrounded by chaparral.

7.0 Timms Creek Trail heads right at a fork in the trail. Continue to the left, on the Sunset Trail.

9.1 Sunset/Skyline to the Sea Connector Trail heads right at a fork in the trail. Take the left fork, continuing on Sunset Trail.

9.5 The trail crosses Middle Ridge Fire Road. Continue straight on Sunset Trail toward park headquarters.

9.9 Sunset Trail dead-ends into Dool Trail. Turn right and follow Dool Trail to Opal Creek.

10.0 Dool Trail dead-ends into Skyline to the Sea Trail at Opal Creek. Turn right onto Skyline to the Sea Trail and follow it downstream.

10.3 The trail reaches the junction with Redwood Trail. Turn left onto Redwood Trail and cross over the bridge. Retrace the first 0.1 mile of the hike to the trailhead.

10.4 Arrive back at the trailhead and parking lot.

Hike Information

Local Information

San Jose Downtown Association, San Jose; (408) 279-1775; www.sj-downtown.com.
San Jose Convention and Visitors Bureau, San Jose; (888) SAN-JOSE; www.sanjose.org.
Santa Cruz Chamber of Commerce, Santa Cruz; (831) 457-3713; www.santacruzchamber.org.
Santa Cruz County Conference and Visitors Council, Santa Cruz; (800) 833-3494; (831) 425-1234; www.scccvc.org.

Local Events/Attractions

Roaring Camp, take a ride on one of two historic railroads, Felton; (831) 335-4484.
Loch Lomond Highland Games, held in October, traditional Scottish games, plus music and crafts, Ben Lomond; (831) 479-1508.
Mountain Man Gathering, held in October, living-history event reenacts an 1830s trapper gathering, with demonstrations and trading posts, Roaring Camp, Felton; (831) 335-4484.

Lodging

Big Basin Redwoods State Park. For camping reservations, call (800) 444-PARK. (There are nearly 150 campsites within the park.) For concessionaire tent cabins, call (800) 874-TENT.

Hike Tours

Ranger-led walks are offered in season. Contact park headquarters for up-to-date information.

Public Transportation

Santa Cruz Metro, bus service; (831) 425-8600; www.scmtd.com.

41 Año Nuevo/Six Bridges Loop

Out-of-the-way Butano State Park is a great place to go to escape the urban hustle without spending half your weekend in the car. Ranching activity going back 150 years has changed the park environment, but Mother Nature is proving herself as a competent healer. The hike takes a tour of several plant communities now thriving within the small park's borders.

Start: Año Nuevo trailhead.
Distance: 3.3 mile loop.
Approximate hiking time: 2 to 2.5 hours.
Difficulty: Moderate, due to a steep climb and elevation gain.
Trail surface: Dirt path, gravel road.
Lay of the land: Mixed conifer forest, riparian forest.
Other trail users: None.
Canine compatibility: No dogs allowed.

Land status: State park.
Nearest town: Pescadero.
Fees and permits: $4.00 day-use fee.
Schedule: Open year-round; day-use hours vary according to season.
Map: USGS map: Franklin Point, CA.
Trail contacts: Butano State Park, Pescadero; (650) 879-2040; Bay Area District Headquarters, San Francisco; (415) 330-6300; www.parks.ca.gov.

Finding the trailhead: From 280 at Palo Alto, head west up Page Mill Road 8.9 miles to the junction with California Highway 35. Continue straight on Alpine Road 7 miles, then turn left onto Pescadero Road and follow it another 10 miles almost to the town of Pescadero. Turn left onto Cloverdale Road just before town and drive 4.2 miles to Butano State Park. Turn left onto the park entrance road and follow it 0.3 mile to the entrance station. Park here. The trail begins at the small Año Nuevo Trail sign on the south side of the entrance road, just a few yards to the left. *DeLorme: Northern California Atlas & Gazetteer:* Page 114, C3.

The Hike

If you happen to be in the market for a quiet weekend far away from the madding crowds of city life, Butano State Park is the place for you. Seen from the air, the 2,200-acre park may seem to be practically in the backyards of the nearby metropolitan areas. On the ground, however, it is a very different story. Santa Cruz and the string of towns along the northern shore of Monterey Bay are only 20 miles away along winding Coast Highway 1, but the narrow road and lack of development seem to be enough to keep the crowds away. Tucked back a couple of miles off the highway, Butano seems to while away the time little changed from the days when the last settlers scratched a living from these rolling hills.

Although the land was originally used seasonally by the native Ohlone people, the name Butano first shows up in the history books around the time of the Mexican land grants. In the year 1835, the young nation of Mexico began a program of privatizing and redistributing lands formerly controlled by the Californian missions.

The old road, heading down from the ridge

Most of this redistribution took the form of enormous land grants, given to influential citizens or in lieu of payment to those owed money by the government. Some of these ranchos were so huge that most of present-day San Mateo County was contained within only two such parcels. One of the last land grants was tiny by comparison, being only a single square league in size. It was named *Butano,* although whether the name (Spanish for *gas*) came from a natural seepage or had something to do with the nearby Arroyo de los Frijoles is not entirely clear.

The grantee did not enjoy his rancho for long, however. Following a brief but decisive war with Mexico, the United States took control of California in 1848, and by 1860 several American settler families were calling the area around the canyon home. Most of the original old-growth redwood groves in the valley were soon felled, forever altering the face of the land. By the 1940s the Pacific Lumber Company was moving to log the last of the giant redwoods. The Loma Prieta chapter of the Sierra Club objected, however, and set in motion a process that led to the dedication of Butano State Park in 1961. Today the park is home to a variety of habitats, including riparian alder forest, redwood/Douglas fir groves, and oak woodlands. This hike visits all three of these plant communities as it makes a loop from the valley floor to the ridge, and back again.

The trail begins at the entrance station/visitor center. A small sign on the south side of the entrance road marks the spot where the Año Nuevo Trail plunges into the lush growth along Little Butano Creek. The trail climbs steeply along the first leg of the hike, quickly ascending to the ridge via a series of several switchbacks. With the gain in elevation comes an equally rapid shift in vegetation, as the forest changes from moist riparian alder forest to drier conifer-dominated slopes. Once the trail reaches the ridge, the grade mellows considerably, and the next stretch of the hike finds you wandering pleasantly along the ridgetop through dense forest, although the thick canopy does not allow for much of a view.

After the strenuous climb, the journey back down to the valley floor is tame by comparison. From the ridge the hike follows the course of a gravel fire road, which descends at a reasonable grade down to the creek. The final leg of the hike is along the aptly named Six Bridges Trail. Following a course roughly parallel to the entrance road, the trail meanders through white alder trunks and several kinds of wild berry plants, frequently crossing the small stream via the trail's namesake bridges, before finally arriving back at the trailhead.

Miles and Directions

0.0 Start at the Año Nuevo Trail sign on the south side of the park entrance road. Follow the trail down toward the creek. At the small stream, the trail crosses via a little footbridge and curves left on the other side. At the junction, turn right, heading uphill on the Año Nuevo Trail.

0.1 The trail curves left and heads steeply uphill.

0.2 The trail climbs several wooden stairs.

Año Nuevo/Six Bridges Loop

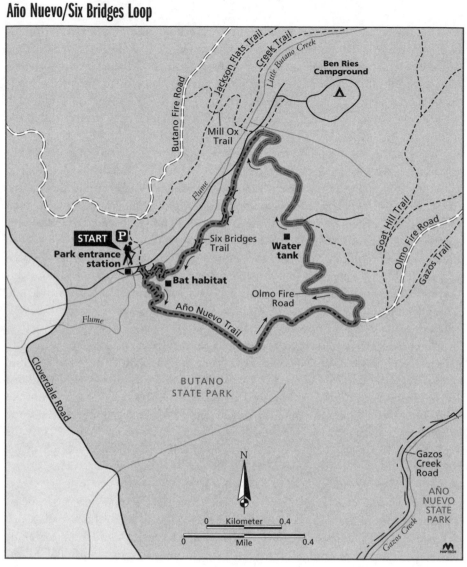

0.3 One of the few scenic vistas on the trail opens to the north, looking out over the valley. The trail begins switchbacks.

0.4 The trail climbs a few steps.

0.5 A spur trail heads right to a bench. Continue straight, following the trail as it veers left.

0.6 The trail levels out, following the ridge.

0.8 The trail drops into a saddle, veering left on the other side.

1.0 Head down into another saddle.

1.1 The trail drops into a third saddle, shifting to the left side of the ridge as it climbs the other side.

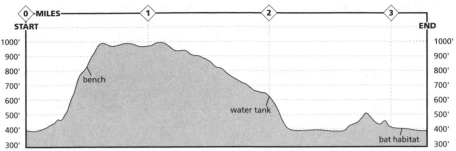

Intervals: Vertical, 100 ft; Horizontal, 1 mi.

1.3 At the junction, the Año Nuevo Trail dead-ends onto the gravel Olmo Fire Road. Turn left, heading downhill on the road.

1.8 The road crosses a small creek via a culvert, climbing slightly on the other side.

1.9 The singletrack Goat Hill Trail joins the road from the right. A few yards later, the road ends at a T junction. Turn left, following the new road downhill.

2.0 The trail passes a water tank on the left. (FYI: The forest has shifted to second-growth redwood.)

2.3 The road makes a long switchback to the right, then back again at the base of the canyon.

2.4 Turn left onto the singletrack Six Bridges Trail, heading uphill.

2.6 The trail levels out and begins contouring around the ridge, about 100 to 150 feet above the park access road, visible off to the right.

2.7 The trail crosses a gravel road leading to an employee residence. Continue straight, dropping down and crossing the first bridge.

2.8 The trail offers a nice view over the marshy riparian area before switching back and heading down into it. At the bottom, cross the second bridge.

3.0 At the fork in the trail, veer left. A few yards later, cross bridge three.

3.1 A spur trail heads left a few yards to a man-made bat habitat. Shortly after, the trail veers left and crosses bridge four. Bridge five follows soon after that.

3.2 The trail reaches the end of the loop. Turn right, passing over the final bridge, and return to the trailhead.

3.3 Reach the trailhead.

Hike Information

Local Information

San Mateo Area Chamber of Commerce, San Mateo; (650) 341-5679; www.sanmateo ca.org.
Half Moon Bay Coastside Chamber of Commerce and Visitors Bureau, Half Moon Bay; (650) 726-8380; www.halfmoonbay chamber.org.

Local Events/Attractions

Pigeon Point Lighthouse, one of the tallest lighthouses in the United States, built in 1872 and now a hostel, Pescadero; (650) 879-0633.
Pescadero Marsh Natural Reserve, one of the largest marshes in California, Pescadero; (650) 726-5202.

Johnston House, a "saltbox" house, built in 1853, now a museum, Half Moon Bay; (650) 726-7084.

Lodging

There is a well-developed campground in the park.

State park campsite reservations: (800) 444-7275.

Hostelling International–Pigeon Point Lighthouse, Pescadero; (650) 879-0633; www.norcalhostels.org.

Restaurant

Arcangeli Grocery Company/Norm's Market, artichoke breads, garlic breads, and other gourmet specialties, Pescadero; (650) 879-0147.

42 Año Nuevo Point Trail

Año Nuevo State Reserve is home to a large population of elephant seals, the largest pinniped in the ocean. The seals come ashore at various times of the year to molt, mate, and occasionally wage bloody battles for breeding rights. An easy day hike leads you out along the Año Nuevo headlands to the scene of all this natural drama: broad sandy beaches nestled up against the dunes of the point. A limited number of visitors are allowed in each day. Call in advance for season-specific information and reservations.

Start: Año Nuevo Point trailhead.
Distance: 3.2 to 3.4 miles, depending on optional routes.
Approximate hiking time: 2.5 to 3 hours
Difficulty: Easy, due to wide trails and little elevation gain.
Trail surface: dirt path, gravel path, sand, and boardwalk.
Lay of the land: Coastal wetland, coastal scrub, and sand dunes.
Other trail users: None.

Canine compatibility: No dogs allowed.
Land status: State reserve.
Nearest town: Davenport.
Fees and permits: $5.00 day-use fee; permit required for seal viewing (available at entrance station).
Schedule: Main park: Open 8:00 A.M. to sunset. Wildlife Protection Area times vary.
Map: USGS map: Año Nuevo, CA.
Trail contact: Año Nuevo State Reserve, (650) 879-2025.

Finding the trailhead: From Santa Cruz, head north on California Highway 1 20 miles to Año Nuevo State Reserve. Turn left into the park entrance and drive 0.2 mile to the large parking lot. Park here. The trailhead is in the southwest corner of the lot. *DeLorme: Northern California Atlas & Gazetteer:* Page 114, C-D3.

The Hike

Año Nuevo State Reserve is a park with only one thing on its mind: elephant seals. The hike out to the point and back is a pleasant enough outing in its own right, but it is the lounging, birthing, bathing, and sometimes battling behemoths at trail's end that make this place so memorable.

The point was given the name Año Nuevo (New Year) by the chaplain of a passing Spanish vessel on January 3, 1603. At the time the area was a seasonal home for the Quroste people, an offshoot of the local Ohlone Indians, who harvested fish, mussels, and abalone from the sea. During the Spanish mission era, the Indians were forced to relocate to Mission Santa Cruz, and ranchers began using the area for beef and dairy production. After World War II, the area east of the Wildlife Protection Area even served a stint as a brussels sprout farm. The state bought the lighthouse island and the strip of beach in 1958, in an effort to protect critical habitat for the elephant seals. At that time the animals were finally beginning to recover from

Molting elephant seals on the beach

decades of hunting that had taken the species to the brink of extinction. The reserve provided a safe haven for seals. The land up to the highway was added to the fledgling reserve in 1971.

The elephant seal gets its name from the large, droopy proboscis that develops on mature males, although their size alone would be reason enough for the comparison. Female elephant seals weigh in at a very respectable 800 to 1,800 pounds, but the largest old bulls can top the scale at nearly 5,000 pounds—roughly the equivalent of two midsize cars! While they are impressive on land, recent advances in marine science have shown them to be even more astounding underwater. We now know that elephant seals are deep-diving specialists, sometimes going as deep as 5,000 feet, on dives lasting as long as two hours. Pressure at that depth is enormous, but the seals cope by allowing their lungs to shrink almost to the size of apples. These animals command respect, especially when seen up close, as they often are at the reserve.

From the trailhead at the large asphalt parking lot, the wide gravel trail heads west across a wide, flat plateau covered with shoulder-high brush. The junction with

Año Nuevo Point Trail

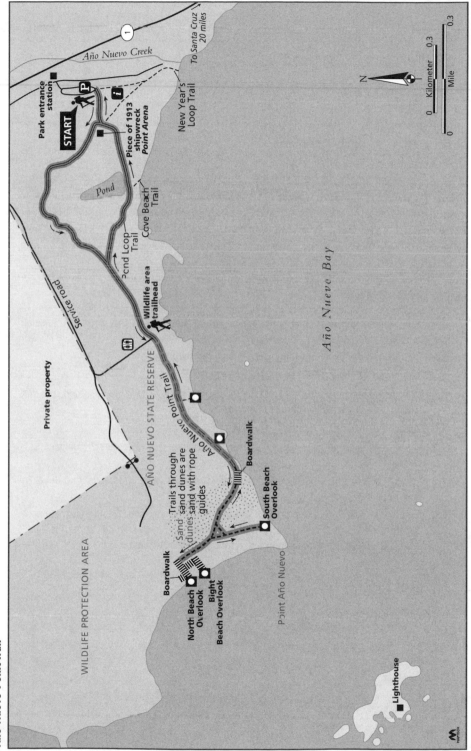

the return portion of the loop trail is marked by a large chunk of the wooden ship *Point Arena,* which ran afoul of the offshore rocks here in 1913. This was in spite of the five-story lighthouse that had been installed on a small island just offshore twenty years earlier. The trail continues out to a small checkpoint, perched above the rocky cliffs to the south.

From here, how (even *if*) you proceed depends upon the time of year and what the elephant seals happen to be doing. From December 1 through December 14, there is no public access at all, to allow female seals to give birth in peace. After December 15 the public is allowed in only on limited tours, guided by volunteer docents. This is the time of year when mating occurs, accompanied by violent battles, as the huge males fight for mating rights, leaving behind bloody scars on the necks of their rivals. From April through November, restrictions ease up a bit, and hikers are allowed unsupervised access with a special day-use permit. Three fenced observation points out in the dunes allow visitors to see the seals lounging on the beach, often only a few feet away. Trained docents are frequently on hand to answer questions and make sure seal-watching etiquette is maintained.

Miles and Directions

0.0 Start at the southwest corner of the parking lot, at the trailhead sign. At the first junction, continue straight, heading due west.

0.6 The trail forks at a shipwreck monument. Take the right fork.

0.8 End of the Pond Loop Trail. Continue straight.

0.9 Wildlife Protection Area trailhead. Continue straight past the little guard station (but only during the self-guided season, and only with a permit).

1.0 A spur trail loop heads left to an overlook. Continue straight.

1.2 A nice teak bench is on the left, overlooking the ocean. The trail enters the dunes and becomes soft sand.

1.3 The trail crosses a short section of boardwalk, then turns right and heads up a dune. Follow the guard ropes.

1.5 End of the main trail. Spur trails lead to three observation points. South Beach Overlook is to the left 0.1 mile. Bight Beach Overlook and North Beach Overlook are to the right, also 0.1 mile. After checking them out, return the way you came.

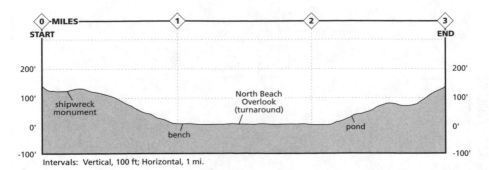

Intervals: Vertical, 100 ft; Horizontal, 1 mi.

2.2 Take the right fork this time, following Pond Loop Trail.

2.3 The pond is on your left. The Cove Beach Trail heads down to the right. Stay on the Pond Loop Trail, continuing to the left.

2.4 A trail heads right to New Year's Beach. Continue straight, arriving back at the shipwreck monument a few yards later. Turn right and return to the trailhead.

3.0 Back at the trailhead.

Hike Information

Local Information

Santa Cruz County Conference and Visitors Council, Santa Cruz; (800) 833-3494; (831) 425-1234; www.scccvc.org.

Santa Cruz Chamber of Commerce, Santa Cruz; (831) 457-3713; www.santacruzchamber.org.

Local Events/Attractions

Santa Cruz Blues Festival, held in late May, Santa Cruz; (831) 479-9814; www.santacruzbluesfestival.com.

Migration Festival, held in February, a celebration of migrating coastal animals including whales, salmon, songbirds, and Monarch butterflies, Natural Bridges State Beach; (831) 423-4609.

Monarch Festival, held in October, Natural Bridges State Beach, Santa Cruz; (831) 423-4609.

Santa Cruz Surfing Museum, Santa Cruz; (831) 429-3429.

University of California at Santa Cruz, Long Marine Lab, Santa Cruz; (831) 459-2883.

Lodging

Hostelling International–Pigeon Point Lighthouse, Pescadero; (650) 879-0633; www.norcalhostels.org.

Hostelling International–Santa Cruz, Santa Cruz; (831) 423-8304; www.hi-santacruz.org.

Hike Tour

Docent-led tours from the wildlife protection area trailhead to the seal-viewing areas are available December 15 through March 31 (reservations required): (800) 444-4445; recorded information: (650) 879-0227. Docents are often on hand at other times to answer questions.

43 Frog Lake Loop

With more than 80,000 acres, Henry W. Coe State Park is the largest state park in California. This hike explores one corner of this vast semiwilderness, once the working cattle ranch of the park's namesake. The high rolling hills and deep, forested ravines are home to abundant wildlife, including the unexpected tarantula, which is honored with a festival in the park each October. The hike offers a cross section of the park's varied landscapes, climbing a ridge to tiny Frog Lake and returning via the forested valley on the Flat Frog Trail.

Start: At the paved road heading up to the east from the parking lot.
Distance: 4.6-mile loop.
Approximate hiking time: 3 hours.
Difficulty: Moderate, due to some steep sections.
Trail surface: Dirt path, gravel road, and brief paved road.
Lay of the land: Rolling grasslands interspersed with oak and manzanita forests.
Other trail users: Cyclists, equestrians.
Canine compatibility: No dogs allowed.

Land status: State park.
Nearest town: Morgan Hill.
Fees and permits: No day-use fee. Permits required for overnight camping in the backcountry.
Schedule: Open year-round. Visitor center is open weekends from 8:00 A.M. to 4:00 P.M. During spring and summer, open 8:00 A.M. to 8:00 P.M. Friday, Saturday, and Sunday.
Map: USGS map: Mt Sizer, CA.
Trail contact: Henry W. Coe State Park, Morgan Hill; (408) 779-2728; www.coepark.org.

Finding the trailhead: At San Jose from the junction of Interstate 280 and U.S. Highway 101, head south 11 miles on US 101 to the town of Morgan Hill. Take the Downtown/East Dunne Avenue exit, turn left at the stoplight, and follow East Dunne Avenue 3.2 miles to a fork in the road. Take the right fork (still East Dunne Avenue) and continue another 12.7 miles to the park. Park in the small gravel parking lot just above a small cluster of red ranch buildings (now the park visitor center). The trail heads up the paved road opposite the parking lot. *DeLorme: Northern California Atlas & Gazetteer:* Page 116, C2.

The Hike

If your first impression as a visitor to Henry W. Coe State Park is that it looks like somebody's ranch, you may be forgiven. Until 1953 that is exactly what it was. In that year Sada Sutcliffe Coe (Henry's daughter) donated the land to Santa Clara County as a park. A few years later the land was passed on to the state to form the heart of a larger park. As a matter of fact, with more than 80,000 acres, Henry W. Coe is the largest park in the California system. More than 250 miles of trail crisscross rolling hills and deep valleys that form the landscape here. Oak, madrone, and manzanita forests are interspersed with the typical golden grasslands of California.

Dead trees in Frog Lake

Frog Lake Loop

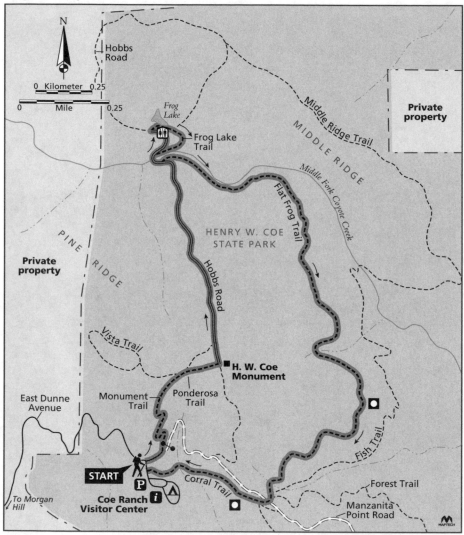

A native of San Jose, Henry Coe (known as Harry to his friends) began his ranching career in 1880, when he and his brother Charles began buying land from homesteaders in the wild backcountry southeast of the city. The brothers grazed cattle on the land, gradually expanding their herds and holdings over time. By 1895 they had some 500 head of cattle grazing 6,000 acres. In time Harry bought out his brother's share and became sole owner of the land, managing the day-to-day activities of his hired hands from the little red ranch house high on Pine Ridge. The house, built in 1905, still stands, and it serves as part of the visitor center complex in today's park. Several other buildings remain, including a blacksmith shop, bunkhouse, hay barn, and stone cool-house.

Outside of the ranch headquarters, the land is still much as it always was, with more than 23,000 acres managed as official wilderness. Even that land outside the wilderness zone has a serene, unspoiled quality to it. And with more than sixty back-country campsites spread out around the park, there is plenty of quiet to go around.

Our hike starts at the small parking lot above the visitor center, heading east up a steep paved road to a locked gate. Leaving the road, the trail climbs up through grassy meadows and the occasional patch of shade to old Harry's memorial. Following his death in 1943, Harry's son Henry S. Coe sold the ranch to the Beach Land and Cattle Company, which built the network of dirt roads now running through the nonwilderness parts of the park. It wasn't long, however, before Sada Coe bought the land back and worked it again as a cattle ranch until 1951. Sada passed on in 1979, and she is buried in nearby Morgan Hill.

From the monument the path follows an old four-wheel-drive track along the ridge, eventually dropping you at a small campsite above Frog Lake. The lake is actually a small reservoir, as attested by the dead trunks of several oak trees that still stand in the shallow black water. Anglers may try their luck here, since bass, crappie, sunfish, and bluegill are all abundant in the park's pond and lakes. From the lake the trail follows a narrow singletrack path back toward the trailhead, contouring around the hillsides through shady forests. Manzanita, which normally takes the form of a large shrub, grows to tree-size here, and several beautiful specimens can be found growing along the trail. The dark burnt-sienna color of the manzanitas' smooth skin contrasts dramatically against the pale grass, providing plenty of subjects for amateur nature photographers.

The trail tops out on Pine Ridge for some excellent vistas of the surrounding landscape before ducking back into the forest and contouring around to the trailhead.

Miles and Directions

0.0 Start at the visitor center parking lot. Head up steep (paved) Manzanita Point Road just across from the gate.

0.1 At the locked gate, veer left, following the dirt trail.

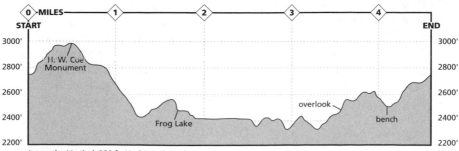

Intervals: Vertical, 200 ft; Horizontal, 1 mi

0.2 The trail crosses a meadow, then enters oak forest and begins climbing switchbacks.

0.4 Junction. To the left, a spur trail heads north 0.2 mile to Vista Point. Turn right, following the Ponderosa Trail to the H. W. Coe Monument.

0.5 The trail crosses a dirt road (Hobbs Road Trail). Straight ahead is the monument. Turn left onto Hobbs Road.

0.6 The Monument Trail joins Hobbs Road from the left. Continue straight. Begin descending.

0.8 The road becomes steep here.

1.4 The road drops down into a saddle. At the bottom, Frog Lake Trail and Flat Frog Trail both head right. Continue straight.

1.5 As the road curves left, turn right and follow the singletrack path past the outhouse and down the hill.

1.6 Frog Lake. Turn right, cross the earthen dam, and continue straight down the narrow dirt path (Frog Lake Trail).

1.8 Back at the Hobbs Road junction. Turn left, then left again onto Flat Frog Trail.

2.2 Giant Manzanita plants reach tree-size here.

2.9 The trail dives into a deep gorge, dropping a series of steps and climbing again on the other side.

3.3 The trees open, revealing a nice panorama.

3.5 The trail rounds the point, heading west again.

4.0 Manzanita Point Road goes left and right. Head straight across the road and down a few yards, then turn right onto the Corral Trail.

4.1 A bench on the left surveys the landscape.

4.4 The trail enters a deep ravine. At the top of this, a nice waterfall can be seen in the wet season.

4.6 Back at the visitor center. Turn right and head up the road a few yards to the parking lot and trailhead.

Hike Information

Local Information
Santa Cruz County Conference and Visitors Council, Santa Cruz; (800) 833-3494, (831) 425-1234; www.scccvc.org.
Santa Clara Chamber of Commerce and Convention and Visitors Bureau, Santa Clara; (408) 244-8244; www.santaclara.org.

Local Events/Attractions
TarantulaFest, held the first weekend in October, Henry W. Coe State Park; (408) 779-2728; www.coepark.org.

Gilroy Garlic Festival, held in late July, Gilroy; (408) 842-1625.

Lodging
There are twenty drive-in campsites located near the visitor center, in addition to more than sixty backcountry hike-in sites scattered around the park. Contact the California Department of Parks and Recreation, 1416 9th Street, Sacramento; (800) 777-0369; (916) 653-6995; www.parks.ca.gov.
State park campsite reservations: (800) 444-7275.

44 Loma Prieta Loop

This hike follows the course of a logging railroad that ran during the heyday of logging in the valley, from 1883 to 1923. The tracks are long since gone and the scars of logging are healing nicely, but many reminders of the past still remain. Railroad ties and historic ruins can be seen in several spots along the way, as the trail climbs gently through second-growth redwood forests before dropping to lush Bridge Creek for the return loop.

Start: At the Porter family picnic area.
Distance: 7.8-mile double loop.
Approximate hiking time: 4 to 5 hours.
Difficulty: Moderate, due to some steep parts and a few sections of rough trail.
Trail surface: Dirt path, gravel road, and old railroad grade.
Lay of the land: Second-growth redwood forest, riparian forest.
Other trail users: Cyclists.

Canine compatibility: No dogs allowed on trails.
Land status: State park.
Nearest town: Aptos.
Fees and permits: $4.00 day-use fee.
Schedule: Sunrise to sunset.
Map: USGS map: Laurel, CA.
Trail contact: The Forest of Nisene Marks State Park, Aptos; (831) 763-7062; www.parks.ca.gov.

Finding the trailhead: From Santa Cruz, head east 6 miles on California Highway 1 to Aptos. Exit at State Park Drive and head north (away from the ocean) a couple of blocks. Turn right onto Soquel Drive and follow it 0.5 mile before turning left onto Aptos Creek Road. Follow this up 1.6 miles to the entrance station, then continue another 2.2 miles to the locked gate at the Porter family picnic area. Park here. The trailhead is at the gate. (Note: During winter months the entrance road is closed beyond the winter gate, which is located 1 mile back toward the entrance station. This will add 2 miles to the hike, round-trip.) *DeLorme: Northern California Atlas & Gazetteer:* Page 115, D6.

The Hike

Tucked away as it is behind the little town of Aptos, the Forest of Nisene Marks State Park is not one that tourists and passersby stumble on by chance. There is little in the way of signage announcing the park's presence until you arrive at the entrance gate, some 1.6 miles up a narrow winding road. It may be that the close proximity of so many other state parks and beaches distracts from Nisene Marks' 10,000-odd acres of convoluted topography and 40 miles of trails, but it may just as well be the case that the local outdoorsy types simply want to keep this little gem to themselves. Local joggers love the mild incline of the railroad grade trails, while cyclists simply enjoy cruising up and down beneath the mature second-growth redwood forest on fire roads that stretch the length of the park. Hikers come for the varied trails, abundant history, and semiwild landscape.

Loma Prieta Loop

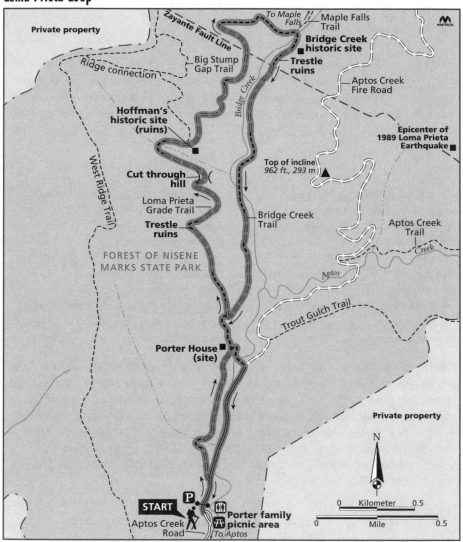

Our hike begins at the Porter family picnic area, 2.2 miles in from the entrance station. (Note: In winter a gate is locked 1 mile farther down, effectively adding 2 miles to the round-trip hike.) Heading past the locked gate, the trail continues along the gravel road a short distance, then veers left onto the gently climbing Loma Prieta Grade, following the course of a logging railroad operated by the Loma Prieta Lumber Company during a forty-year logging period that lasted from 1883 to 1923. While it was in use, the railroad clung precariously to the steep slopes of the Bridge Creek watershed, leaping over the numerous small side creeks via wooden trestles. The latter are now largely gone, with only a few scattered timbers and the remaining grade to show where they once stood. At these spots the trail leaves the railroad grade, contouring around the side draws via singletrack trails and footbridges, and returning to the smoother, wider grade on the other side.

Although the large trestles can no longer be seen and the wounds of large-scale logging are rapidly healing, small reminders abound of the heavy industrial activity that once took place here. Steel rails have been removed, but the wooden ties that once supported them can still be seen along several portions of the trail, sometimes sticking out dramatically into thin air where time and erosion have caused the outside edge of the grade to fall away. Additionally, the hike passes by four historic sites, some containing ruins of buildings and structures associated with the logging era.

▶ The Forest of Nisene Marks State Park is named for a Danish immigrant who farmed in the area and owned this land in the post-logging days. The land was donated to the state by her family in 1965.

If the name Loma Prieta seems vaguely familiar to you, it may be because the 1989 Loma Prieta earthquake that caused extensive damage from Santa Cruz up to the Bay Area had its epicenter near Loma Prieta Peak, roughly a mile due east of Hoffman's historic site. The epicenter lies along a parallel offshoot of the San Ardeas Fault called the Zayante Fault, which bisects the park in a northwest to southeast line, crossing our hike in two places. The quake, which measured around 7.0 on the Richter Scale, caused 66 deaths, nearly 4,000 injuries, and more than $10 billion in property damage. In addition to destroying downtown Santa Cruz, it also razed San Francisco's Marina district and caused part of an elevated freeway and a section of the upper deck of the San Francisco–Oakland Bay Bridge to collapse.

The hike follows the grade up about 3 miles, almost to the ridge, then plunges down a steep ravine to the Bridge Creek historic site. Turning right, the trail follows another old railroad grade hugging the banks of Bridge Creek, which has washed out large portions of the grade, now replaced by singletrack.

The trail eventually rejoins the Loma Prieta Grade just north of the Porter House site, and you retrace your steps to the historic site, where you head left down a short connector trail to Aptos Creek Road, which takes you back to the trailhead.

Miles and Directions

- **0.0** Start at the locked gate.
- **0.1** The road passes through a deep cut.
- **0.2** Take the left fork, passing through the wooden gate and following the Loma Prieta Grade.
- **0.3** The trail leaves the old grade to cross a gully, then returns to it.
- **0.9** The trail passes some large second-growth redwoods, and a few railroad ties can still be seen on the grade.
- **1.0** Porter House site. A connector trail goes straight past the bench and kiosk. Turn left instead, and follow the Loma Prieta Grade uphill.

1.1 The trail gets steeper, having left the grade.

1.3 The trail rejoins the grade, then arrives at a fork. Take the left fork. A few yards up, an old road or grade crosses the trail from right to left. Continue straight on the singletrack.

1.4 The trail delves into a gully, then rejoins the grade.

1.5 The trail leaves the grade to cross a gully, then returns to it.

1.6 The trail narrows where the outside edge of the grade has slid off, leaving railroad ties sticking out into space.

1.7 The trail briefly leaves the grade again.

1.8 The trail crosses another gully. The ruins of the old trestle can still be seen below.

1.9 A small tree is down across the trail, but still growing. Two new trunks are shooting up. Step over it and continue straight.

2.0 The trail narrows, due to slides.

2.1 The grade dives into a deep gully, makes a fairly sharp right turn (for a train), and heads back out again.

2.2 The grade makes a sharp left through a deep cut in the hillside.

2.4 To the right is a long drop. The grade heads back up into a deep ravine, then out again.

2.5 Cross another smaller ravine.

2.6 Hoffman's historic site. At the fork in the trail, take the lower (right) fork. The trail passes some ruins on the right.

2.8 The trail curves right and crosses a bridge over a washed-out area.

3.1 The trail leaves the grade and dives into a couple of shallow hollows.

3.5 The trail heads up to the head of a deep side ravine. Here it leaves the grade and starts descending.

3.6 Begin a series of switchbacks down into a narrow gully.

3.9 The trail pops out onto Bridge Creek. Cross the creek via stepping stones. Bridge Creek historic site. Turn right on the Bridge Creek Trail and follow the grade downstream.

4.0 The trail drops down to creek and crosses a flat. On the left are remains of an old trestle made of whole redwood logs.

4.3 The trail passes through a redwood grove.

4.7 The trail crosses Bridge Creek again, via stepping stones.

4.9 The trail passes under an overhanging cliff.

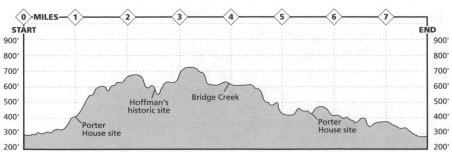

Intervals: Vertical, 100 ft; Horizontal, 1 mi.

5.0 During the wet season, there is a nice waterfall on the right.

5.3 The trail crosses a wide, flat area and a partially collapsed log culvert.

5.4 End of the upper loop. Continue straight on the Loma Prieta Grade, retracing your steps to the Porter House site.

5.7 Porter House site. Turn left onto the connector trail, and follow it down to the creek.

EARTHQUAKE!

California is a state in motion . . . literally. The famous San Andreas Fault—running across western North America from Baja California, Mexico, all the way up to southern Mendocino—marks the boundary between the North American Plate and a section of the ocean's crust that is slowly dragging California's western edge northward at a rate of 2 inches per year.

Most California Indians knew Earthquake as a supernatural man, or brothers, who shook the earth by running. The earthquake that shook a Spanish Californian expedition in 1769 became the first to enter the history books, but there have been several more since then.

December 8, 1812: An earthquake demolishes Mission San Juan Capistrano, killing forty.

November 22, 1852: San Francisco's Lake Merced drops 30 feet after a quake.

October 8, 1865: An earthquake shakes San Francisco. Mark Twain is on hand to witness the spectacle.

April 18, 1906: The Great Earthquake and Fire in San Francisco. The city is ruined. Jail inmates are moved to Alcatraz Island for safekeeping.

March 27, 1964: Crescent City is struck by tsunamis (tidal waves) generated by an Alaskan earthquake. Eleven are killed and downtown is destroyed.

April 14, 1969: Psychics predict an earthquake will cause California west of the San Andreas Fault to fall into the ocean. Ronald Reagan and other politicians arrange to be out of the state, but nothing happens.

February 9, 1971: The San Fernando Earthquake. Sixty-five die, and there is half a billion dollars in damage.

October 17, 1989: The Loma Prieta, or "World Series," Earthquake. Santa Cruz and other Bay Area cities are hard hit. San Francisco Bay Bridge is severely damaged, as are other bridges and overpasses.

April 25, 1992: The Cape Mendocino Earthquake. Fortuna and nearby towns experience damage, especially in old Victorian buildings.

October 16, 1999: The Hector Earthquake (near Los Angeles). Twenty cars of an Amtrak train are derailed and there are blackouts in Los Angeles.

5.9 Cross the creek via a footbridge, then turn right onto Aptos Creek Road.

7.3 The Loma Prieta Mill site is on the right. Some foundation timbers can still be seen.

7.5 Cross Aptos Creek via a bridge.

7.6 Back at the first junction. Continue straight.

7.8 Back at trailhead.

Hike Information

Local Information

Aptos Chamber of Commerce, Aptos; (831) 688-1467; www.aptoschamber.com.
Santa Cruz County Conference and Visitors Council, Santa Cruz; (800) 833-3494, (831) 425-1234; www.scccvc.org.
Santa Cruz Chamber of Commerce, Santa Cruz; (831) 457-3713; www.santacruzchamber.org.

Local Events/Attractions

Santa Cruz Blues Festival, held Memorial Day Weekend, Aptos; (831) 479-9814; www.santacruzbluesfestival.com.
World's Shortest Parade, held July 4, Aptos; (831) 688-1467.
Aptos History Museum, Aptos; (831) 688-1467.

Seacliff State Beach Visitor Center, "The Palo Alto Cement Ship," plus exhibits on natural history and marine and plant life, Aptos; (831) 685-6444.
Capitola Wharf, public fishing pier, Capitola.

Lodging

There is one trail camp in the park, with sites available on a first-come, first-served basis. Contact Santa Cruz State Parks District Office, 303 Big Trees Park Road, Felton; (831) 429-2850; www.santacruzstateparks.org.
State park campsite reservations: (800) 444-7275. There are also campgrounds at the nearby state beaches along CA 1.
Hostelling International–Santa Cruz, Santa Cruz; (831) 423-8304; info@hi-santacruz.org; www.hi-santacruz.org.

Honorable Mention

South Bay

K Ridge Peak Loop

This moderate 3.1-mile loop visits second-growth redwoods, oak forests, and some residual old-growth redwoods. From the Old Tree trailhead, the hike heads east on the Old Tree Trail to the first junction (a short 0.25-mile trail straight ahead brings you to the big tree). Head left on the Slate Trail, heading steeply up to the summit, then down the other side on the Summit Trail. The return loop follows along the bluffs above Pescadero Creek. From Interstate 280 near Palo Alto, head west 8.9 miles on Page Mill Road to the junction with California Highway 35. At the junction, continue straight on Alpine Road and head west 5 miles. Turn left onto Portola State Park Road and drive 4.1 miles to the park headquarters. Continue across a bridge and turn right at the next side road. Park in one of the day-use lots. For more information, contact Portola Redwoods State Park, Cupertino; (650) 948–9098; www.santacruzstateparks.org. *DeLorme: Northern California Atlas & Gazetteer:* Page 114, B4.

Monterey

T he large size of Monterey County in relation to those of the San Francisco Bay Area should be a clue to travelers of the demographics in this region. Most of the area's residents live in the major population centers at the county's northern and southern ends, and to a lesser extent in the small agricultural cities that line U.S. Highway 101 farther inland. But in between these comparatively small urban areas lies a vast stretch of rugged, lonely coastline known as the Big Sur Coast.

As in the northern counties of Sonoma and Mendocino, the rough topography of Monterey's coast forces US 101 inland, where it follows the wide Salinas River Valley in a line parallel to the coast. Likewise as up north, the coast here is serviced by the sinuous two-lane California Highway 1, which in this case wasn't completed until 1937. The two highways are separated by 30 miles of jumbled mountains known as the Santa Lucia Range, which are largely contained within the Los Padres National Forest and Ventana Wilderness Area. The thin strip of coast that remains is occupied by nearly as many state parks as small towns, with trails tempting hikers to all the best spots. Overall, the atmosphere is one of seclusion and solitude—an attribute that has made the area a favorite hideaway of artists and authors, whose ranks include the likes of Henry Miller and Jack Kerouac.

At the northern end of all this wildness sits a cluster of small cities centered around the city of Monterey, a Spanish colonial town with plenty of historic attractions. In the twentieth century, Monterey's fisheries inspired John Steinbeck's novel *Cannery Row,* and the neighborhood is now a thriving tourist draw, along with the nearby Monterey Bay Aquarium. The rich waters and deep submarine canyon just off the coast of Monterey Bay make the area one of the nation's most productive fisheries—a fact attested to by the abalone cannery and whaling station that once operated out of nearby Point Lobos State Reserve.

At the southern end of the Big Sur Coast—and marking the final, southernmost stretch of the Redwood Coast—lie the quiet sandy beaches and rolling hills of San Simeon. Here hikers can enjoy the kinder, gentler side of this coast and ponder the forgotten history of the Native Americans who inhabited this land long ago.

45 Whalers Knoll Loop

A lively jaunt around the rocky headlands of Point Lobos State Reserve, where deep coves and offshore rocks teem with marine life. Due to its proximity to the submarine Monterey Canyon, the reserve's waters are especially rich in aquatic animals, making it as attractive for modern scuba divers as it was for whalers and abalone divers a century ago. The Whalers Cabin houses a museum that interprets much of this history.

Start: At the information station parking lot.
Distance: 2.9-mile loop.
Approximate hiking time: 2 hours.
Difficulty: Easy to moderate, due to a short steep section.
Trail surface: Dirt path, paved road (briefly).
Lay of the land: Grassy coastal bench, cypress forest.
Other trail users: None.
Canine compatibility: No dogs allowed.
Land status: State reserve.

Nearest town: Carmel Highlands.
Fees and permits: $6.00 day-use fee, includes park map.
Schedule: Open year-round; day-use 9:00 A.M. to 5:00 P.M. in winter, 9:00 A.M. to 7:00 P.M. in summer; Sea Lion Point Information Station open 9:00 A.M. to 4:00 P.M.
Map: USGS map: Monterey, CA.
Trail contact: Point Lobos State Reserve, Carmel; (831) 624–4909.

Finding the trailhead: From Monterey, drive south 7.2 miles on U.S. Highway 101 to Point Lobos State Reserve. Turn right (west) onto the park entrance road, drive 0.1 mile to the entrance station, and continue another 0.7 mile to Sea Lion Point parking area. The trailhead is on the north edge of the parking lot, next to the information station. *DeLorme: Southern and Central California Atlas & Gazetteer:* Page 18, D3.

The Hike

Point Lobos is one of those special places where a host of diverse human cultures and histories seem to converge on a single spot, interacting and mixing until it is hard to separate the tale of one group from that of the next. At one time or another, Native Americans, Spanish missionaries, Chinese fishermen, Portuguese and Japanese whalers, and even Hollywood directors have all found themselves drawn to this spot. At the center of all these stories is the land, or rather the place where the land meets the sea—because the sea is the true source of all the commotion. Just offshore is one of the richest marine habitats in the state. Just north of the reserve, the floor of Carmel Bay drops off suddenly, plummeting to a depth of 1,000 feet just a mile north of the point. Six miles offshore, this submarine canyon joins the even larger Monterey Canyon at a depth of 7,000 feet. Strong prevailing winds push the surface water seaward during the spring and summer, bringing up cold, nutrient-rich seawater from the bottom of the ocean to fill the void. The result is a concentration

The Veteran Cypress

and overlap of sea life from several different habitats in one spot. Animals from shallow coastal waters can be found alongside deep-water creatures, feeding on the same bounty. For marine biologists it is an ideal study area. Today the waters surrounding Point Lobos are part of an underwater ecological reserve, protecting the diversity for future generations.

From the trailhead at Sea Lion Point parking area, our hike follows North Shore Trail across a scrub-covered meadow to the coast. Here, a short spur trail leads to a view of the Veteran Cypress, a gnarled old mammoth of a tree perched dramatically above the rocky cliff. The path then skirts the convoluted edge of Point Lobos peninsula's northern edge, arriving at last at Whalers Cabin. This historic structure is now used to house the reserve's whaling museum, but its construction actually predates the whaling days.

The cabin was built sometime in the 1850s by Chinese fishermen as part of a small fishing village that survived here for several years. The small community was soon joined by Portuguese whalers, who were attracted to the area by the deep, rich offshore waters that lured whales in close to land. That proximity meant the whalers

Whalers Knoll Loop

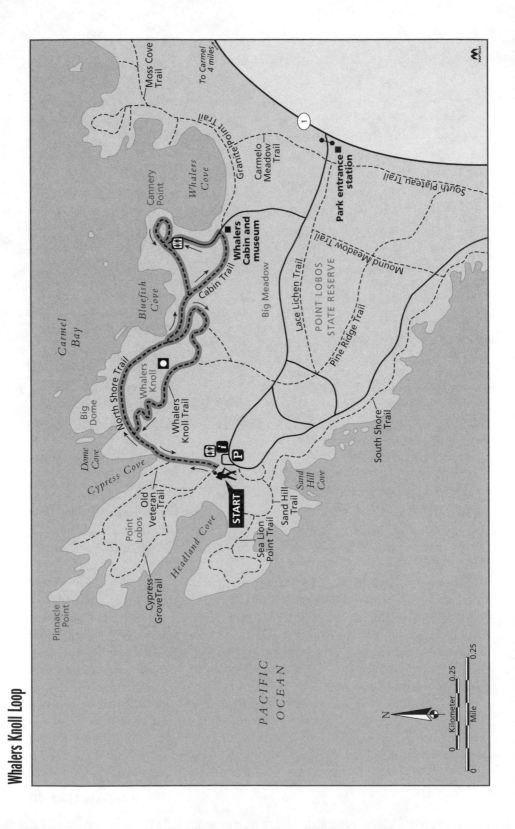

could send their small harpoon boats out directly from shore. The dead behemoths were then rowed back to the cove and hoisted onto land for slaughter. It seemed like easy pickings for the whalers, but the introduction of cheap petroleum-derived kerosene around 1880 ruined the market for whale oil. After a brief Japanese attempt to revive the industry in 1897, whaling ceased for good on Point Lobos.

From the cabin the trail follows the paved road north to Cannery Point, where an abalone cannery operated from 1902 to 1930. Although the cannery buildings are long gone, the trail around the point is still littered with glittering fragments of crushed abalone shell, also known as mother-of-pearl. Cannery Point is also the entry point for scuba divers, who can get permits to dive in this portion of the underwater reserve. Whalers Cove harbors a thriving kelp forest, where 70-foot-tall Giant kelp fronds provide habitat for countless fish, invertebrates, mollusks, and sea lions, as well as the occasional cute and cuddly sea otter.

From Cannery Point the trail heads back along the North Shore Trail to the junction with Whalers Knoll Trail, then follows the latter up to the exposed knob where spotters once signaled directions to whaling-boat crews below. Enjoy the view for a while, then return to the trailhead via the rest of Whalers Knoll Trail and the first segment of North Shore Trail.

Miles and Directions

0.0 Start at the trail next to the information station. At the first junction, take the right fork (North Shore Trail).

0.2 The Old Veteran Trail heads right 0.1 mile to a view of the Veteran Cypress. Continue straight.

0.3 Whalers Knoll Trail heads up to the right. Continue straight.

0.5 Nice view to the north of Monterey Peninsula.

0.8 The trail descends several steps to the next cove. A bench is on the left. Follow the trail to the right.

0.9 Whalers Knoll Trail heads up to the right. Continue straight.

1.0 A spur trail heads left to a bench and overlook. Continue straight.

1.1 The North Shore Trail continues straight, but we veer right onto the Cabin Trail.

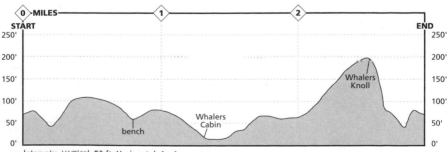

Intervals: Vertical, 50 ft; Horizontal, 1 mi.

1.3 Whalers Cabin and museum. Well worth a look. Turn left onto the paved road, heading north.

1.5 The road ends at a small parking lot. Climb the stairs at the north end to the bluffs, then head right around the short Cannery Point loop.

1.6 At the end of the loop, head west on the North Shore Trail, climbing several steps. At the top, a spur trail goes straight to an overlook. Turn left and follow the North Shore Trail around. On the ground are crushed fragments of abalone shell from the old cannery.

1.8 Cabin Trail heads left. Continue straight, retracing your steps to the next junction.

2.0 This time, turn left onto Whalers Knoll Trail, climbing up the hill.

2.2 The Pine Ridge Trail heads straight. Curve right instead, following the Whalers Knoll Trail.

2.3 A connector trail leads back to the Pine Ridge Trail. Continue straight.

2.5 Whalers Knoll. A bench marks the historic overlook. Head straight down the hill.

2.6 Turn left onto North Shore Trail and retrace the first leg to the trailhead.

2.9 Trailhead.

Hike Information

Local Information

Monterey County Convention and Visitors Bureau, Monterey; (888) 221–1010; www.montereyinfo.org.

Pacific Grove Chamber of Commerce, Pacific Grove; (800) 656–6650; (831) 373–3304.

Local Events/Attractions

Monterey Bay Aquarium, world-famous aquarium complex, run by a nonprofit organization, Monterey; (831) 648–4800; www.montereybayaquarium.org.

Whalefest, held in mid-January, whale watching, exhibits, etc., Monterey; (831) 784–6464.

Annual Sea Otter Classic, held in mid-April, billed as a four-day bicycle circus, with rides, racing, and an expo, Monterey; (530) 661–9500; www.seaotterclassic.com.

Monterey Jazz Festival, held the third weekend in September, Monterey; (925) 275–9255; www.montereyjazzfestival.org.

Taste of Carmel, held in October, a showcase of local cuisine, Carmel; (831) 624–2522.

Lodging

Hostelling International–Monterey, Monterey; (831) 649–0375; www.montereyhostel.org.

46 Whale Peak Loop

This short loop offers more than a mile of wave-blasted coastline, complete with sea caves and offshore stacks. The return leg includes a chance to climb the trail's namesake peak, for a gull's-eye view of the rugged Big Sur Coast. A lucky few may even catch a rare glimpse of the playful but elusive sea otter.

Start: At an unmarked turnout just north of Whale Peak.
Distance: 2-mile loop.
Approximate hiking time: 1 hour.
Difficulty: Easy, due to short length and little elevation gain.
Trail surface: Dirt path.
Lay of the land: Coastal bench meadow, cypress forest (briefly).
Other trail users: Whale-watchers.

Canine compatibility: No dogs allowed.
Land status: State park.
Nearest town: Carmel Highlands.
Fees and permits: None.
Schedule: Open year-round.
Map: USGS map: Soberanes Point, CA.
Trail contact: Garrapata State Park, Monterey Sector, Monterey; (831) 649-2888, www.parks.ca.gov.

Finding the trailhead: From Monterey, take U.S. Highway 101 south 8 miles to Carmel Highlands, then continue another 2.5 miles south to the unmarked turnout just north of the small cone-shaped peak (Whale Peak) located on the west side of the highway. Park here. The trail starts at the locked gate (signed #8) on the west side of the road. *DeLorme: Southern and Central California Atlas & Gazetteer:* Page 30, A3.

The Hike

Imagine for a moment you are an eighteenth-century Spanish explorer. You have been marching for weeks, your men are tired, plagued by illness and injury, and paranoid about Natives. You arrive at a new canyon, and, casting about for a name to scrawl on the hand-drawn map of your travels, you notice an unwelcome little pest crawling up your pants leg. . . .

Whoever the poor soul was that named this place—Garrapata is Spanish for "tick"—he certainly was not focusing on the land's more positive aspects. Which is a shame, really, since there are quite a few things that make the park worth visiting. Most obvious from the trailhead, perhaps, is the sculpted coastline. Here, meadows laden with wildflowers and waving grasses end abruptly at low bluffs. Sea caves and offshore rocks provide plenty of habitat for otters, seals, and a variety of marine birds, not to mention the fish and tide-pool inhabitants. A low peak offers a seagull's-eye view of the whole, while more adventurous folks can head inland, up a deep canyon to the foothills of the Santa Lucia Mountains. And if there are a few ticks, then at least you were warned beforehand.

Whale Peak

At a little less than 3,000 acres, Garrapata State Park is on the small side, as hike-able state parks go, and almost totally undeveloped. Without even a sign to identify itself as a park, Garrapata seems to be hiding in plain sight—thousands of tourists drive through on California Highway 1 without even knowing it's there. The fortunate few in the know, however, locate their favorite spot with the small numbered signs marking the various gates at park turnouts.

The Whale Peak Loop hike begins at the #8 gate, on the west side of the highway just north of the hard-to-miss grassy cone of Whale Peak. The trail heads south through a little clump of trees, where one of the park's few amenities is hidden—a small outhouse, off to the left of the trail. Continuing south across a brushy meadow, hikers arrive at the first brush with the coast, as a deep cove stretches inland nearly to the flanks of the peak. Wildflowers and scruffy plants of nearly every color crowd the coastal bench on the edge of the cliffs here, and the narrow trail winds through the vegetation, sticking close to the shoreline for the next mile or so of the hike. Keep your eyes peeled along this stretch of the trail, because this piece of coast is

Whale Peak Loop

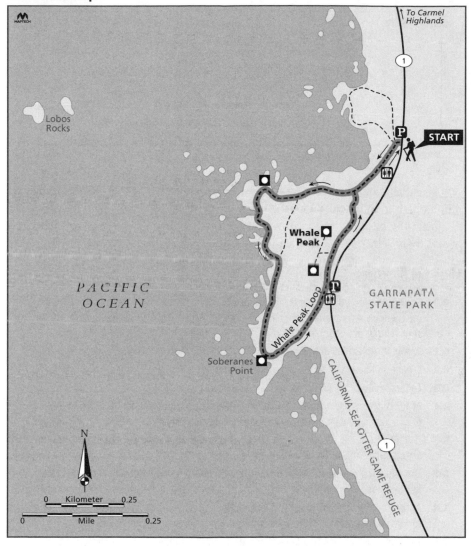

one of the few spots where you have a good chance of spotting rare and endangered sea otters. This water-loving member of the weasel family can often be seen floating on its back, working away on its dinner, or just hanging out in the waves. If you are fortunate enough to spot an otter, count yourself lucky, and take it as a hopeful sign that these playful mammals are making a slow recovery.

The return loop of the hike passes close by the highway, climbing up over the flank of Whale Peak where the highway department has cut a deep gouge for the roadway. A short spur trail here heads left up to the peak's dual summits. From the top the coastline is spread out before your feet in a panorama much more

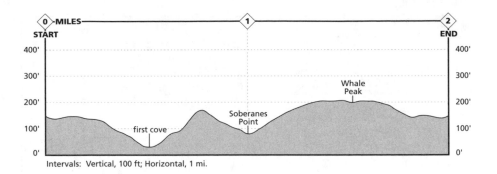

Intervals: Vertical, 100 ft; Horizontal, 1 mi.

dramatic than you would expect from such a small peak. The view is worth the easy climb up, although the wind on the summit may drive you back down fairly quickly.

From the peak the trail returns through the meadow to end the loop, returning to the trailhead along the first leg of the hike.

Miles and Directions

0.0 Start at the locked #8 gate on the west side of the highway. The trail heads down into the meadow. A few yards later, turn left onto the Whale Peak trail, heading toward the small clump of trees.

0.1 An outhouse is hidden in the little forest. Continue straight, making toward the peak.

0.2 A faint trail heads off to the left. Continue straight.

0.3 The trail rounds the upper edge of a small cove.

0.4 At the junction, hikers have a choice between heading right, along the edge of the cliffs, or continuing straight along a more direct route. Head right.

0.5 (FYI: From the point, offshore sea stacks, sea caves, and wave-pounded rocks can be seen.) Follow the trail around to the left.

0.7 The side loop rejoins the main trail; turn right, crossing a railed section of trail over a washed-out cliff.

1.0 At the south end of the headland (Soberanes Point), the trail curves left, heading inland toward the highway. (FYI: The cliffs here are a good place to spot sea otters.)

1.3 The trail turns left and heads north, running parallel to the road.

1.4 A small parking lot is on the right. Continue straight. The trail climbs up the flank of the peak, still running parallel to the highway.

1.5 At the junction, a spur trail heads left up to the top of Whale Peak's twin summits junction. Continue straight.

1.6 Another parking area is on the right. Continue straight, heading across the meadow.

1.8 End of the loop. At the junction, turn right onto the first leg of the trail and return the way you came to the trailhead.

2.0 Trailhead.

Hike Information

Local Information

Monterey County Convention and Visitors Bureau, Monterey; (888) 221-1010; www.montereyinfo.org.

Pacific Grove Chamber of Commerce, Pacific Grove; (800) 656-6650; (831) 373-3304.

Local Events/Attractions

Monterey Bay Aquarium, world-famous aquarium complex, run by a nonprofit organization, Monterey; (831) 648-4800; www.montereybayaquarium.org.

Whalefest, held in mid-January, whale watching, exhibits, etc., Monterey; (831) 784-6464.

Movie on the Beach, held in mid-June, Carmel-by-the-Sea; (831) 626-1255; www.carmelcalifornia.com.

Living History Day in Old Monterey, held July 4, Monterey; (831) 647-6204; www.monterey.org.

Butterfly Parade, held in October, celebrates the return of the Monarch migration, Pacific Grove; (831) 646-6540; www.pacificgrove.org.

Lodging

Hostelling International-Monterey, Monterey; (831) 649-0375; www.montereyhostel.org.

47 River/Ridge Loop

Andrew Molera State Park is a remnant of the historic Rancho El Sur, a Mexican land grant from the early nineteenth century. The land remained in the same family until it became a park in 1968. The hike follows a large loop through the 7.4-square-mile park, exploring several different landscape types along the way. Beginning in the riparian forest on the banks of the Big Sur River, the hike makes stops on a beach, coastal bluffs, and a low mountain ridge before returning along the sandy flats of the river, farther upstream.

Start: At the north end of the large gravel parking lot.
Distance: 3.8-mile loop.
Approximate hiking time: 2.5 to 3.5 hours.
Difficulty: Moderate, due to elevation gain and some steep, rough trail.
Trail surface: Dirt path, sandy beach, and gravel road.
Lay of the land: Riparian woodland, oak forest, beach, and grassy coastal bluffs and ridges.
Other trail users: Equestrians.
Canine compatibility: No dogs allowed.

Land status: State park.
Nearest town: Big Sur.
Fees and permits: $5.00 day-use fee.
Schedule: Park is open to day use from a half hour before sunrise to a half hour after sunset. (Note: The hike requires wading the mouth of the Big Sur River, possible only in summer. At other times of year, a variation of the hike is still possible.)
Map: USGS map: Big Sur, CA.
Trail contact: Andrew Molera State Park, Big Sur; (831) 667-2315; www.parks.ca.gov.

Finding the trailhead: From Monterey, take California Highway 1 south 26.6 miles to Andrew Molera State Park (4.4 miles north of the town of Big Sur). Turn right (west) onto the park entrance road and drive 0.2 mile to a big white gate and a fork in the road. Turn right into the entrance station, and park in the large gravel lot. The trailhead is at the far northern end of the parking lot. *DeLorme: Southern and Central California Atlas & Gazetteer:* Page 30, B4.

The Hike

When Mexico gained independence from Spain early in the nineteenth century, the fledgling nation began a new land policy in its northernmost region, the wild golden land of Alta California. The government began granting huge tracts of land to well-placed dons, mainly for use as cattle ranches—the basis of the Californian economy at the time. One of these grants, encompassing nearly 9,000 acres between the Little Sur River and present-day Cooper Point, was granted to a young elite named Juan Bautista Alvarado in 1834. Alvarado would later come to fame as California's first native-born governor during a short-lived attempt at independence from Mexico, but not before he sold the ranch to his uncle Juan Bautista Rogerio (JBR) Cooper.

Cooper Cabin

Born John Roger Cooper, this salty sea captain had sailed round the horn from New England in 1923, arriving in Monterey at an opportune time. Cooper sold his ship *Rover* to the governor, became a naturalized citizen, changed his name, became a Catholic, and married a beautiful daughter of the influential Vallejo family. Not bad for a first visit.

Cooper spent the majority of his time in Monterey, but he did oversee ranch operations on the land. The cabin he had built on the north shore of the Big Sur River still stands today, just west of the campground. From the trailhead at the north end of the parking lot, the cabin is reached by following the Beach Trail west, along the north bank of the Big Sur. The trail soon joins a gravel fire/access road and heads through the open meadows of Trail Camp. Once the scene of massive outdoor partying on holiday weekends, this campground has been tamed in recent years for health and safety reasons, and occupancy is now limited to twenty-four small parties. At the far end of the campground is a grove of eucalyptus trees, which shelter the historic Cooper Cabin. Built in 1861, it is one of the oldest surviving buildings

River/Ridge Loop

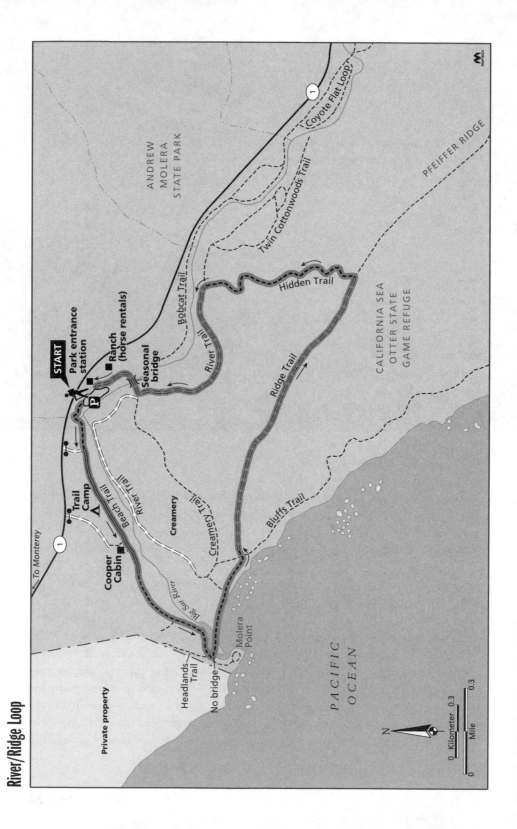

on the Big Sur Coast. From November through March, the eucalyptus trees harbor another attraction as well—Monarch butterflies, which rest in the grove during their long migration up the coast.

Rancho El Sur stayed in the Cooper family for many years, eventually passing to Andrew Molera, JBR Cooper's grandson. Molera ran a successful dairy operation in what is now the park and began the first large commercial production of Monterey Jack cheese, which he brought to market in Monterey along the bumpy coastal wagon roads. When he passed away in 1931, he had no children to take over the operation, and his sister, Frances Molera, also childless, sold 4,800 acres of the land to the Nature Conservancy in 1968, shortly before her death. In 1972 the land became a state park.

From the Cooper Cabin, the hike continues west along the gravel road to the mouth of the Big Sur River. If there is no seasonal bridge in place, hikers will have to wade the stream, but this is not as difficult a chore as it sounds. In summer the river belies its name, and the crossing near the beach is no more than a few inches deep. Once on the other side, the hike follows the beach south to where the bluffs begin, following the narrow trail up the edge of the bluffs to the grassy benchlands above.

The hike soon leaves the Bluffs Trail, heading inland and climbing the Ridge Trail to the first summit. From the ridge—a last coastal outlier of the Santa Lucia Mountains—a fine panorama is laid out below you, taking in the full view of the lower Big Sur River and the adjacent headlands. To the north the remaining lands of the historic Rancho El Sur can be seen stretching into the distance.

The final leg of the trail drops down the steep and narrow Hidden Trail to the sandy flats of the riverbank, crossing via a seasonal footbridge and returning along a gravel road to the parking lot and trailhead.

Miles and Directions

0.0 Start at the north end of the long gravel parking lot. Follow the well-signed trail into the forest.

0.1 The trail makes a quick switchback and descends some steps, then crosses a footbridge, heading downriver.

0.2 The trail joins a gravel road. Turn left, following the road a few yards to the campground.

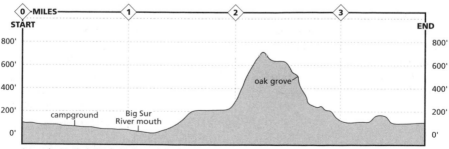

Intervals: Vertical, 200 ft; Horizontal, 1 mi.

0.5 At the western end of the campground, a spur trail heads right to the Cooper Cabin. Continue straight.

0.7 A spur trail goes right to a small building. Continue straight. A few yards later the brush opens to reveal the river on the left and the headlands ahead.

0.8 A spur trail heads left. Continue straight.

1.0 At the junction, the Headlands Trail heads up to the right. Go straight.

1.1 The trail arrives at the mouth of the Big Sur. Wade the shallow water (only in summer), heading left down the beach on the other side.

1.3 At the south end of the main beach, turn left, heading inland at the small trail sign. Almost immediately, turn right onto the Bluffs Trail, heading uphill.

1.4 (FYI: The trail pops out of the brush onto the bluff. There is a great view of the coast behind and to the right, and of the mountains to the left.)

1.5 At the junction, turn left, heading inland.

1.55 At the junction, head right on the Ridge Trail.

1.8 (FYI: About halfway up the slope, another great view opens up behind you.)

1.9 The trail levels out on the ridge and curves left.

2.1 The trail begins to climb again.

2.3 The trail tops out on the highest part of the ridge and begins a gradual descent.

2.4 At the junction, turn left onto the Hidden Trail, heading steeply downhill.

2.6 Pass through a small oak grove.

2.7 At a bend in the trail, the parking lot at the trailhead is visible far below.

3.1 Hidden Trail dead-ends onto the wider, flatter River Trail. Turn left, heading north.

3.2 The trail pops out on the left edge of a meadow.

3.4 A spur trail heads left to a songbird research project. Continue straight, heading back into the forest.

3.5 At the junction, the Beach Trail heads right and left. Turn right, toward the river, crossing it via a seasonal bridge a few yards later. On the other side, the trail meets a gravel road. Turn left onto the road heading downstream.

3.7 At the big white gate, turn left past the park entrance booth toward the parking lot and trailhead.

3.8 Trailhead.

Hike Information

Local Information

Monterey County Convention and Visitors Bureau, Monterey; (888) 221-1010; www.montereyinfo.org.
Big Sur Chamber of Commerce, Big Sur; (831) 667-2100; www.bigsurcalifornia.org.

Local Events/Attractions

Big Sur International Marathon, held the third week in April, a marathon along CA 1 from Big Sur to Carmel; (831) 625-6226; www.bsim.org.
Annual Bird-a-thon, held in early May, bird count and fund-raiser for the Big Sur Ornithology Lab, Big Sur; (877) 897-7740; www.VentanaWS.org.

Big Sur JazzFest, held the first weekend in May, Big Sur; (831) 667-1530; www.bigsurarts.org.

Big Sur River Run, held in late October, a 10K foot race and 5K walk to benefit local charities, Big Sur; (831) 624-4112; www.bigsurriverrun.org.

Lodging

Trail Camp, near the trailhead, has twenty-four campsites. Contact Andrew Molera State Park, Big Sur; (831) 667-2315; www.parks.ca.org. Larger campgrounds can be found at Pfeiffer–Big Sur State Park, a few miles south.

State park campsite reservations: (800) 444-7275.

48 Valley View Loop

Pfeiffer–Big Sur State Park is the unofficial capitol of the Big Sur Coast. The hike follows a gentle trail up through shady redwood groves to 60-foot Pfeiffer Falls, then climbs a challenging grade up to the Valley View overlook, where visitors have the rare chance of seeing North America's largest bird, the California condor, soaring in its natural habitat.

Start: Pfeiffer Falls trailhead.
Distance: 1.9-mile loop.
Approximate hiking time: 1 to 1.5 hours.
Difficulty: Moderate to strenuous, due to some steep, uneven trail.
Trail surface: Dirt path.
Lay of the land: Mature second-growth redwood, old-growth redwood, and oak forest.
Other trail users: None.

Canine compatibility: No dogs allowed.
Land status: State park.
Nearest town: Big Sur.
Fees and permits: $5.00 day-use fee.
Schedule: Open year-round, a half an hour before sunrise to half an hour after sunset.
Map: USGS map: Big Sur, CA.
Trail contact: Pfeiffer–Big Sur State Park, Big Sur Lodge, Big Sur; (831) 667-2315.

Finding the trailhead: From Monterey, take California Highway 1 south 31 miles to Pfeiffer–Big Sur State Park. Turn left (east) into the park entrance and continue past the entrance station 0.5 mile to a four-way stop. Turn left and head uphill 0.3 mile to the small parking lot just above the Ernst Ewoldsen Memorial Nature Center. The trailhead is at the upper end of the parking lot. *DeLorme: Southern and Central California Atlas & Gazetteer:* Page 31, B4.

The Hike

If the wild and rugged stretch of coast between Monterey and San Simeon were a country, Pfeiffer–Big Sur State Park would be its undisputed capitol. The place certainly looks the part—spread out along the lower slopes of the Big Sur River Valley, the park sports a host of lodges, monuments, and other official structures. Undoubtedly the most developed of the coast's parks, Pfeiffer–Big Sur is also home to well more than 200 campsites and a small city of rental cabins perched above the gurgling Pfeiffer Redwood Creek.

Fortunately, the valley's deep redwood forests are able to swallow all of this urban-rustic development without too much trouble. A few minute's hike can take you out of the worst crowds and back into the serene wilderness for which Big Sur is famous.

Our hike begins in the small parking lot above the Ernst Ewoldsen Memorial Nature Center. Starting at the large wooden kiosk, the trail heads upstream along Pfeiffer Redwood Creek, amongst groves of second-growth and residual old-growth redwoods. For anyone familiar with the great ancient redwood groves up north, the

Old-growth redwoods near the trailhead

trees here will be less than awe-inspiring, but they are still impressive reminders of what once was.

About half a mile upstream, the trail ends at Pfeiffer Falls, where the creek takes a 60-foot plunge over a moss-covered cliff. The park and falls are named for the Pfeiffer family, who were the first permanent white settlers on the Big Sur Coast. Michael and Barbara Pfeiffer settled just south of the present-day park, near the mouth of Sycamore Canyon, in 1869. Fifteen years later, their son John homesteaded a parcel on the north bank of the Big Sur River, building himself a cabin that still stands today. By the early twentieth century, tourism had already taken hold, and John and his wife, Florence, set up a resort on the site of today's Big Sur Lodge. The state purchased the resort and much of the surrounding land in 1933, and the park was born.

Just below the base of the falls, the hike heads left onto the Valley View Trail, climbing steeply up the hill to the north. The redwoods are quickly left behind as you switchback up, replaced by drier vegetation dominated by oaks, chaparral, and

Valley View Loop

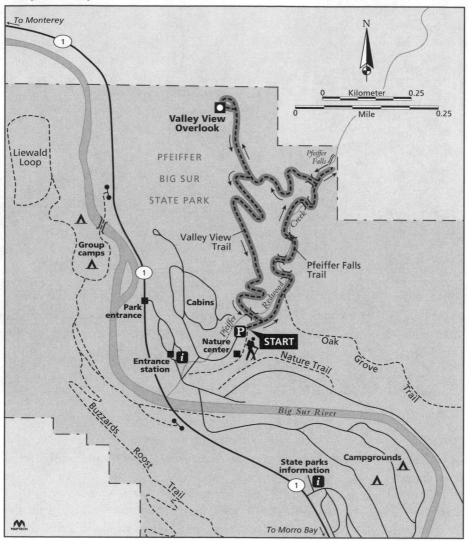

California laurel. At the summit the effort of the climb is rewarded with an expansive view of the lower Big Sur River Valley. Below, the river flows through its narrow forested canyon, separated from the ocean by the long ridge west of the overlook. To the north clear skies will reveal the grassy lowlands of Andrew Molera State Park, and the gray-green of the ocean beyond. Spend a few minutes here before heading down. If you are lucky, you will witness a spectacle that was impossible for nearly 100 years.

Plagued by years of poisoning and shooting, wild condors had completely disappeared from the Big Sur area by the start of the twentieth century. After the last few birds were removed from the wild in 1987, an intensive captive-breeding program worked for a decade to bring the population back up to a sustainable level. In January 1997 the Ventana Wilderness Society released the first of these captive-bred condors back into the wild, right here in Big Sur. Today it one of the few places where people have a decent chance of seeing North America's largest bird in its natural habitat.

From Valley View Overlook, the hike returns to the last junction and heads down the western side of the ridge, rejoining the Pfeiffer Falls Trail near the trailhead.

A SECOND CHANCE FOR THE CONDOR
Half a million years ago, no human had ever laid eyes on North America. The continent was filled to the brim with life, including beasts so strange and, well, *big*, that it's hard to imagine. Among the prehistoric *megafauna* stalking America were mammoths, saber-toothed cats, lions, camels, and a giant relative of the sloth that stood over 10 feet and weighed nearly two tons! When these creatures died, they left a lot of carcass to clean up, and this was where the condor came in. Large carrion required large carrion feeders, and with a wingspan of up to 9 feet, the condor fit the bill.

Fast-forward to about 10,000 years ago, when the first humans arrived in the New World. Whether from climate change or human hunting, most of the megafauna soon died out, but the condor hung on with a reduced range. It wasn't until Europeans arrived in North America that the real trouble began for the condor. The birds ate carrion that had been poisoned by settlers, or consumed lead bullets along with hunters' kills. Often the birds were intentionally killed by ranchers and farmers who (falsely) thought the condors were killing their stock. The constant loss of habitat took its toll as well.

At any rate, by the beginning of the twentieth century, the condor was on the decline, with its range reduced to the coastal mountains of south-central California and a few spots in Mexico. By the 1980s the species was down to just twenty-six birds.

With little hope left of a natural recovery, wildlife authorities took the drastic step of removing all the birds from the wild and beginning an intensive captive-breeding program. By 1997 ten years after the last wild condor had been captured, the condor population was back up to more than one hundred, and the first birds were released back into the wild. To date the program has continued to be successful. The condor population continues to rise, and several subsequent releases are bolstering the bird's chances in the wild.

With a little luck, and a lot of love, the condor will continue to soar in California's skies for generations to come.

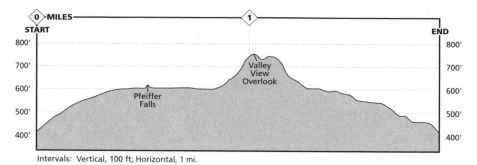

Intervals: Vertical, 100 ft; Horizontal, 1 mi.

Miles and Directions

0.0   Start at the Valley View trailhead. The trail heads up the broad dirt path through the red-woods.

0.1   The Valley View return loop comes in from the left. Continue straight, toward Pfeiffer Falls.

0.2   The trail climbs a few stairs, arriving at a junction. Oak Grove Trail heads right. Continue straight.

0.3   Cross the bridge over the creek, then back over on another bridge a few yards up.

0.4   (FYI: The big redwood on the right has some nice examples of burl growths.)

0.5   At the junction, Valley View Trail heads up to the left. A short spur trail continues straight a few yards to Pfeiffer Falls. Check out the falls, then take the left fork up to Valley View. The trail immediately crosses two bridges and begins climbing steeply.

0.7   The grade mellows somewhat, and the trail arrives at a junction. The return loop heads left down to the left. Continue up the right fork to the overlook.

0.8   The trail switches back, climbing steeply again. A view of the valley opens to the west.

0.9   A short spur trail heads left to an unofficial viewpoint. Continue straight. The trail becomes narrower and rocky.

1.0   The trail forks, beginning a little loop around the overlook. Follow either one the last few yards to the Valley View Overlook. From here, turn around and retrace your steps to the last junction.

1.3   At the junction, take the lower fork this time, heading downhill to the right.

1.4   The trail passes a bench.

1.5   The trail begins switchbacks.

1.6   The trail splits, then rejoins a few yards later.

1.7   An unofficial spur trail heads right. Continue on the main trail.

1.8   The trail crosses the creek via a small footbridge and rejoins the Pfeiffer Falls Trail. End of loop. Turn right, and return the way you came to the trailhead.

1.9   Trailhead.

Hike Information

Local Information

Monterey County Convention and Visitors Bureau, Monterey; (888) 221-1010; www.montereyinfo.org.

Big Sur Chamber of Commerce, Big Sur; (831) 667-2100; www.bigsurcalifornia.org.

Local Events/Attractions

Big Sur International Marathon, held the third week in April, a marathon along CA 1 from Big Sur to Carmel, (831) 625-6226; www.bsim.org.

Annual Bird-a-thon, held in early May, a bird count and fund-raiser for the Big Sur Ornithology Lab, Big Sur; (877) 897-7740; www.VentanaWS.org.

Big Sur JazzFest, held the first weekend in May, Big Sur; (831) 667-1530; www.bigsurarts.org.

Big Sur River Run, held in late October, a 10K foot race and 5K walk to benefit local charities, Big Sur; (831) 624-4112; www.bigsurriverrun.org.

Lodging

There are more than 200 campsites in the park, plus a lodge. Call (800) 444-7275 for campsite reservations; (800) 424-4787 or (831) 667-2171 for Big Sur Lodge.

Organizations

Ventana Wilderness Society, working to save the condor, among other creatures, Salinas; (831) 455-9514; www.ventanaws.org.

49 Partington Point Trail

A short gem of a hike, perfect for stretching the legs on a long Big Sur road trip. The trail is easy to miss, but well worth finding. Beginning at a small dirt turnoff along California Highway 1, the trail heads down into Partington Canyon, then heads straight through 100 feet of rock, thanks to a historic tunnel built in the late nineteenth century by enterprising settlers. The tunnel grants access to a tiny cove once used by ranchers and rumrunners to load and unload cargo.

Start: At the unmarked gate on the west side of the highway.
Distance: 1 mile.
Approximate hiking time: 1 hour.
Difficulty: Easy to moderate, due to short length, but steep trail.
Trail surface: Dirt road, dirt path.
Lay of the land: Deep coastal stream valley, rocky cove.
Other trail users: Abalone divers.

Canine compatibility: No dogs allowed.
Land status: State park.
Nearest town: Big Sur.
Fees and permits: None.
Schedule: Open year-round, from half an hour before sunrise to half an hour after sunset.
Map: USGS map: Partington Ridge, CA.
Trail contact: Julia Pfeiffer Burns State Park, Big Sur; (831) 667-2315; www.parks.ca.gov.

Finding the trailhead: From Monterey, head south 37 miles on CA 1 (6 miles south of the town of Big Sur and 2 miles north of Julia Pfeiffer Burns State Park's main entrance) to a point where the highway dives inland around a side canyon. Pull off the road and park at a small dirt turnout. The trail begins at the locked gate with the sign for no dogs allowed. *DeLorme: Southern and Central California Atlas & Gazetteer:* Page 31, C5.

The Hike

Driving along the winding miles of CA 1, perched high on wild and rugged coastal cliffs, it is easy to miss the trailhead of this hike, even if you are looking for it. For one thing, the narrow, snaking road demands total concentration of anyone who doesn't want to end up in the crashing Pacific Ocean surf far below. And the trailhead isn't exactly well-signed. The narrow dirt road that forms the first part of the Partington Point Trail is marked only by a twisted steel gate that bars auto access and a small square sign with a red line through a stylized dog figure. Parking is limited to a small dirt turnoff on either side of the road, and the whole thing finds itself in one of hundreds of nearly identical small side canyons that break up this stretch of coastline. The best way to find it is really to keep a close eye on the odometer as you approach from easily identifiable landmarks from the north or south (see Finding the trailhead, above). In spite of (or perhaps partly because of) this trail's hidden-in-plain-sight quality, it is well worth the effort to find and hike.

Partington Point Trail as seen from the trailhead

The first part of the hike follows the dirt road down into the canyon, where rocky side walls funnel the creek through a surprisingly lush patch of riparian forest. Here, spur trails head upstream into the woods and downstream to a truly tiny gravel beach used as an entry point for divers. Our trail follows the beach spur for a few yards before heading across the creek on a small footbridge, where it runs up against the face of a rocky knob. At this point the trail reveals the first of its magic moments: A few yards to the right, a tunnel has been cut straight through the rock. At 6 feet wide, 8 feet tall, and roughly 100 feet long, the tunnel seems designed for the comfort of modern hikers, but the aged heavy timbers and planks that line and support the tunnel attest to its true age.

Built in the 1880s by a settler named John Partington and his business partner, Bert Stephens, the tunnel allowed loads of tanbark to be brought down to tiny Partington Cove, where it could be loaded onto small vessels and shipped to San Francisco. Tanbark was valued as a source of tannins, used to cure leather in the days before synthetic substitutes. The oak forests that grew up-canyon yielded an abundant supply of bark, provided the men could find a way to get it onto ships.

Partington Point Trail

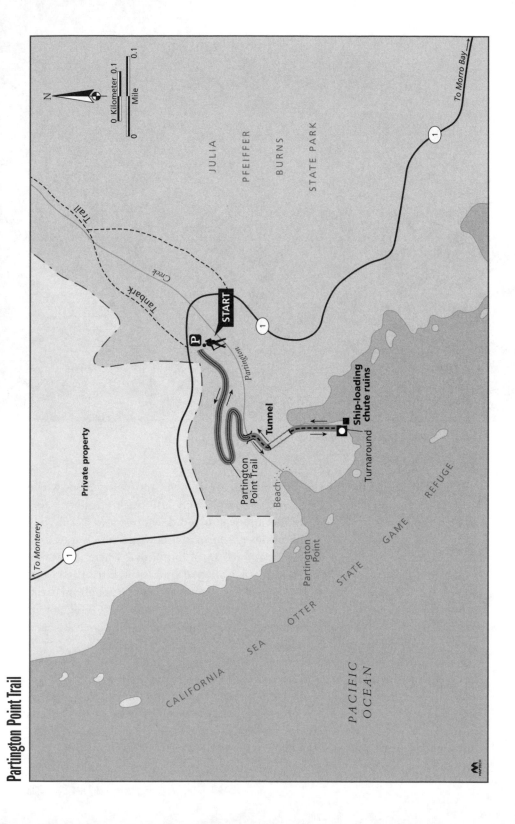

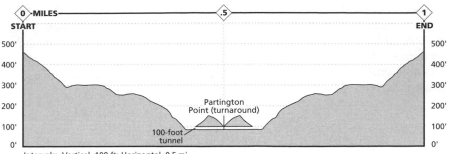

Intervals: Vertical, 100 ft; Horizontal, 0.5 mi.

At the opposite end of the tunnel, the trail emerges into a scene straight out of a pirate movie. The wind and waves have conspired to create a small cove that seems not so much a port as a sort of aquatic garage. Tall overhanging cliffs surround the narrow inlet on three sides, and crystal-blue water shelters a waving kelp forest. At the end of the point, near the cove's opening, the ruins of an old hoist stanchion mark the spot where cargo was loaded and unloaded from the small sailing vessels daring enough to brave the treacherous offshore rocks and enter the cove.

In later years overlogging and shifting industrial needs caused the tanbark trade to dry up, but local residents supported themselves with ranching, exporting meat, hides, and dairy via the cove until CA 1 was finally built in 1937. Rumor has it that during the Prohibition era, Partington Cove was a favorite put-in for smugglers of hard liquor. Not surprising, given the cove's rugged, romantic nature.

From the ruins in Partington Cove, turn around and return the way you came.

Miles and Directions

0.0   Start at the locked gate on the west side of the highway. Follow the dirt road downhill.

0.1   There is a good view of the canyon to your left.

0.2   The view now is of the small beach below.

0.3   The trail reaches the bottom of the canyon. Turn right at the kiosk, then immediately left, crossing the creek via a short footbridge. On the other side, turn right.

0.4   The trail passes through a 100-foot tunnel.

0.5   Partington Point. Ruins of the old hoist are on the left. Turn around and return the way you came.

1.0   Back at the trailhead.

Hike Information

Local Information
Monterey County Convention and Visitors Bureau, Monterey; (888) 221–1010; www.montereyinfo.org.
Big Sur Chamber of Commerce, Big Sur; (831) 667–2100; www.bigsurcalifornia.org.

Local Events/Attractions
Big Sur International Marathon, held the third week in April, a marathon along CA 1 from Big Sur to Carmel; (831) 625–6226; www.bsim.org.

New Camoldoli Hermitage, held on Christmas, Christmas mass with Big Sur monks, Lucia; (831) 667-2787.

Big Sur JazzFest, held the first weekend in May, Big Sur; (831) 667-1530; www.bigsurarts.org.

Lodging

There are campgrounds at Julia Pfeiffer Burns State Park to the south and Pfeiffer–Big Sur State Park to the north.

State park campsite reservations: (800) 444-7275.

50 Limekiln Trail

This short hike makes for an interesting diversion on a road trip up the Big Sur Coast. Tiny Limekiln State Park hosts an excellent beach and some fine second-growth redwood groves, but the real attraction are the four rusting behemoths that give the park its name. Used in the 1880s to convert local limestone to industrial lime, the kilns still serve as a reminder of the lengths to which people went to make a living in this wild land.

Start: At the small ranger station below the upper campground.
Distance: 1 mile out and back.
Approximate hiking time: 1 hour.
Difficulty: Easy, due to short length and good trail.
Trail surface: Dirt path.
Lay of the land: Mature second-growth redwood forest.
Other trail users: None.

Canine compatibility: No dogs allowed.
Land status: State park.
Nearest town: Big Sur.
Fees and permits: $5.00 day-use fee.
Schedule: Open year-round, half an hour before sunrise to half an hour after sunset.
Map: USGS map: Lopez Point, CA.
Trail contact: Limekiln State Park, Big Sur; (831) 667-2403; www.parks.ca.gov.

Finding the trailhead: From San Luis Obispo, drive north 84 miles on California Highway 1 to Limekiln State Park. Turn right into the park entrance and head down 0.2 mile to the entrance station. Park in the day-use parking area up to the right above the entrance station. The trail starts to the left of the brown ranger station, at the lower end of the upper campground. Limekiln State Park is located 42 miles north of San Simeon and 23 miles south of the town of Big Sur. *DeLorme: Southern and Central California Atlas & Gazetteer:* Page 32, D6–7.

The Hike

Dedicated in 1995, Limekiln State Park is one of the youngest parks in the system, and at a little more than 700 acres, it is also amongst the smallest. Nevertheless, the little park has charm, perched as it is between the lonely ocean and the deep shade of second-growth redwood groves. Tucked into a narrow valley along the rugged and serene Big Sur Coast, the park exudes the atmosphere of an isolated hermitage, cozy and self-contained. This quality may be what drew Camoldolese Benedictine monks to establish a monastic retreat in the hills next door in 1958. Today the New Camoldoli Hermitage has more interaction with the surrounding community than you might expect. Aside from hosting Christmas mass open to the public, the brothers offer retreat rooms and trailers (single occupancy only, of course) for those needing to get away from it all. They also operate a small bookstore on the premises, and they even have a Web site (see Local Events/Attractions below).

One of the namesake kilns

Ironically, the history of Limekiln State Park is in stark contrast to the spirit of quiet contemplation embodied by the community of monks next door. The march of progress and the smoke of heavy industry were the order of the day in the 1880s, when the park's namesake limekilns were kept burning around the clock.

The hike begins at the upper end of the campground, where a footbridge crosses the creek, leading into the dark forest beyond. The short trail follows the banks of babbling Limekiln Creek and its tributaries up the narrow canyon. About halfway up, a side trail leads up to the very nice Limekiln Falls.

At trail's end four looming iron hulks mark the spot where the Rockland Cement Company once burned locally mined limestone in these huge wood-fired kilns. Rusted and heavily weathered, the kilns are nevertheless in pretty good shape for having been abandoned more than 100 years ago. They stand as a monument to the determination of early settlers to carve out a living among the wild hills and unforgiving coastline of Big Sur.

When heated for several hours at around 1,800 degrees Fahrenheit, limestone (calcium carbonate) undergoes a chemical change, as the carbon dioxide in the rock is burned off. What's left is calcium oxide—also known as lime. In the nineteenth century, lime was used for all sorts of things, from food processing (think "dutched" cocoa) to the manufacture of mortar and cement. It can also be used to make soaps, fertilizers, bleaching agents, and to kill termites in infested buildings. As the West Coast boomed in the wake of the Gold Rush, lime was in great demand, and the Rockland operation's location had several advantages. A good supply of calcareous rock was on hand for conversion to lime. The redwood forests delivered plenty of firewood for stocking the kilns, as well as lumber to build casks for shipping the lime. Finally, the little point of land south of the mouth of Limekiln Creek made an excellent site for loading the lime onto waiting schooners for shipment to San Francisco and other points along the coast.

Alas, competition was fierce, and the Rockland Cement Company was eventually bought out by a rival named Henry Cowell (namesake of another state park north of Santa Cruz), who shut down the Big Sur operation, thus eliminating the competition. The site languished for years, until it was acquired by the Save-the-Redwoods League in 1994, for the purpose of forming the basis of a state park. The industrial history was secondary to the league—they were interested primarily in the canyon's fine second-growth and residual old-growth redwood groves, which form the lush and verdant backdrop for this hike.

From the limekilns, return the way you came to the trailhead.

Miles and Directions

0.0 Start at the brown building at the upper end of the parking area. Head past it on the left, heading up through the campground.

Limekiln Trail

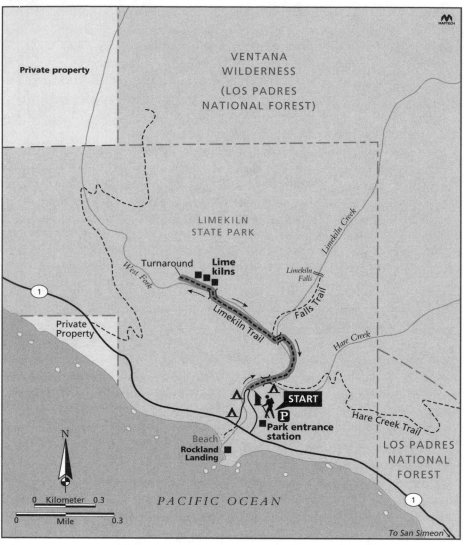

0.1 At the kiosk, cross the bridge, following the trail upstream. A few yards up, the Hare Creek Trail heads right. Take the left fork, heading up the Limekiln Trail.

0.2 Cross the creek via a small bridge. Shortly after, the Falls Trail heads right. Continue straight, upstream.

0.4 Cross over a larger footbridge.

0.5 The trail passes through a narrow pass, then comes to the lime kilns. This is the turn-around point. Return the way you came.

1.0 Trailhead.

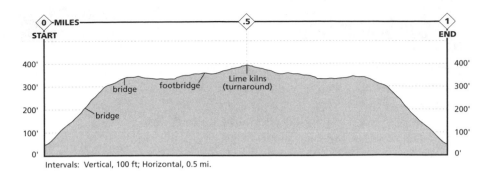

Intervals: Vertical, 100 ft; Horizontal, 0.5 mi.

Hike Information

Local Information

Monterey County Convention and Visitors Bureau, Monterey; (888) 221–1010; www.montereyinfo.org.

Pacific Grove Chamber of Commerce, Pacific Grove; (800) 656–6650; (831) 373–3304.

Big Sur Chamber of Commerce, Big Sur; (831) 667–2100; www.bigsurcalifornia.org.

Local Events/Attractions

New Camoldoli Hermitage, held on Christmas, Christmas mass with Big Sur monks, Lucia; (831) 667–2787; www.contemplation.com.

Big Sur International Marathon, held the third week in April, a marathon along CA 1 from

Big Sur to Carmel; (831) 625–6226; www.bsim.org.

Annual Bird-a-thon, held in early May, a bird count and fund-raiser for the Big Sur Ornithology Lab, Big Sur; (877) 897–7740; www.VentanaWS.org.

Lodging

The park's campground has more than forty campsites, a short walk from the beach and the trailhead.

State park campsite reservations: (800) 444–7275.

51 San Simeon Loop

This mellow hike is a great way to relax while exploring the landscape of the Central California coast. Located just a stone's throw south of the famous Hearst Castle, the park is largely overlooked by tourist crowds. Along the way the hike passes through several habitat types, including seasonal wetland, riparian forest, open grassland, and a rare stand of Monterey pine.

Start: Washburn Day-Use Area.
Distance: 3.6-mile loop.
Approximate hiking time: 2 to 3 hours.
Difficulty: Easy, due to smooth trails and little elevation gain.
Trail surface: Dirt path, boardwalk.
Lay of the land: Seasonal wetland, riparian woodland, and pine forest.
Other trail users: None.

Canine compatibility: No dogs allowed.
Land status: State park.
Nearest town: Cambria.
Fees and permits: No day-use fee.
Schedule: Open year-round.
Map: USGS map: Cambria, CA.
Trail contact: San Simeon State Park, Cambria; (805) 927-2020; www.parks.ca.gov.

Finding the trailhead: From San Luis Obispo, take California Highway 1 north 31 miles to the town of Cambria, and continue north another 2 miles to the Washburn Day-Use Area of San Simeon State Park, located just south of the San Simeon Creek Bridge. Turn right into the day-use area and follow the road 0.1 mile to its end at a small parking lot. The trail starts at the boardwalk on the north edge of the lot. *DeLorme: Southern and Central California Atlas & Gazetteer:* Page 44, D2.

The Hike

When it comes to visitors, San Simeon State Park is consistently outshined by the nearby Hearst Castle, a lavish 165-room Mediterranean Revival mansion built in the 1930s through 1940s by newspaper magnate William Randolph Hearst. Now a state park in its own right, the famous mansion attracts hordes of tourists each year. The far less flashy San Simeon park—located 6 miles south of the castle—is easily overlooked by comparison. Which is a shame, because the park is really a nice place to go for a short hike, explore a variety of local habitats, and just generally enjoy the sun and sea breezes of California's central coast.

San Simeon is an important landmark for several reasons. First of all, it designates the approximate extent of the once-great redwood forest's southernmost groves. Today travelers can see the last of these groves just a few miles to the north, in the moist canyon bottoms along the banks of Salmon Creek.

For drivers heading north on coastal CA 1, the park marks the unofficial beginning of the Big Sur Coast, a wild and largely undeveloped stretch of rocky coastline

Boardwalk through the wetlands near the trailhead

extending north all the way to Monterey. Offshore marine resources are protected along the same stretch of coast in both the Monterey Bay National Marine Sanctuary and the California Sea Otter Game Refuge.

The hike begins at the Washburn Day-Use Area, located about a quarter-mile south of the park's main entrance, on the south shore of San Simeon Creek. The trail follows a wooden boardwalk inland across a seasonal wetland to the Washburn Campground access road, then heads south around the wetlands to a stand of Monterey pine. This stand, located on a low bluff on the southern edge of the park, is one of only five native groves of Monterey pine known to exist.

Continuing the ecological tour, the hike heads down off the bluff, across a swath of lush riparian woodland habitat, and up onto the broad, open grasslands that form the heart of the park. Passing the Washburn Campground in the center of the meadows, the trail continues north to an inconspicuous but enigmatic area designated only by a small interpretive sign on a short spur trail. Underlain by a layer of hardpan soil that prevents effective drainage during the wet season, the area is home to

San Simeon Loop

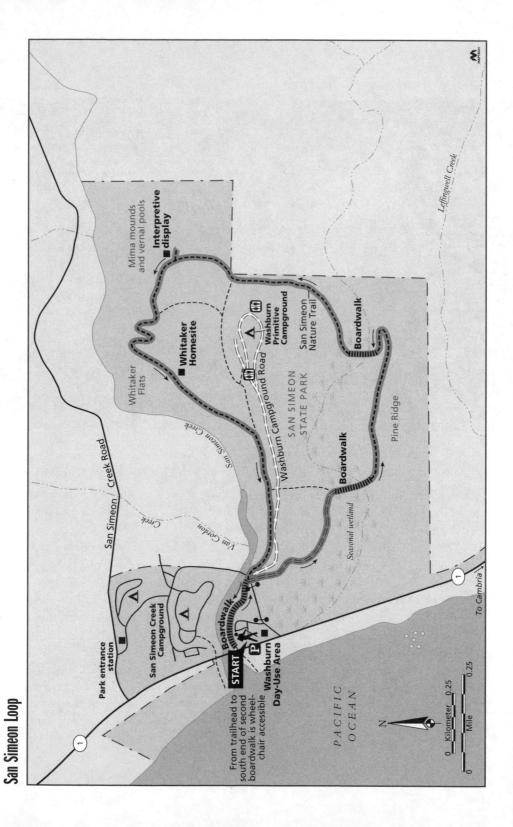

several vernal pools—seasonal ponds inhabited by unique plants and animals. But the most interesting feature of the meadows was only discovered in recent years, when scientists began looking more closely at aerial photos of the park.

Although almost invisible from the ground, the aerial shots revealed that the meadows are covered with strange symmetrical patterns of low circular mounds. These formations are called Mima mounds after the best known example of the phenomenon, the Mima Prairie of Washington state's south Puget Sound. Up to thirty separate theories have been developed as to how the mounds formed. The current favorites include activities of prehistoric pocket gophers, erosion between clumps of ground anchored by trees or other vegetation, and seismic vibrations from earthquakes. In the end no one is really certain, and the origin of the mounds remains a riddle.

From the Mima meadows, the trail continues west around the bluffs to Whitaker Flats, site of an old homestead. Little remains of the farmhouse today, but the grove of eucalyptus trees and other exotic vegetation on the site leave little doubt as to where it once stood. The final leg of the trail completes the loop, returning to the junction on the campground access road and returning to the trailhead along the boardwalk.

Miles and Directions

0.0   Start at the northern end of the Washburn Day-Use Area parking lot. Turn right onto the boardwalk, heading inland.

0.2   The trail crosses a defunct access road and continues on the other side. The Washburn Campground access road runs parallel to the trail on the left.

0.6   At the junction, a cutoff trail heads left to the access road. Continue along the main trail, heading south across a long boardwalk.

0.7   At the south end of the boardwalk, the trail heads uphill on a dirt path.

0.8   An unofficial trail heads right. Continue straight.

1.0   Another volunteer trail heads right. Go straight. A few yards ahead are a bench and interpretive sign. Shortly after that, the trail heads downhill to the left.

1.3   The trail crosses another boardwalk through a riparian zone.

1.4   At the other end of the boardwalk, the trail heads right, climbing up onto a grassy meadow.

1.7   A bench is on the left, overlooking the mountains off to the east.

2.0   At the junction, a spur trail heads left to the campground. Head right, passing through a gap in the fence, toward Whitaker Flats.

2.2   At the junction, a spur trail heads right a few yards to a bench and interpretive sign. Turn left, heading gently downhill.

2.4   A spur trail heads off to a rocky knob on the right. Continue straight.

2.5   A connector trail leads left toward the campground. Go straight, heading downhill.

2.6   The trail bottoms out on a low flat spot, then heads left into the eucalyptus grove.

2.7   Whitaker Homesite. Continue straight.

2.9 The trail crosses a short boardwalk, and a bench on the left.

3.0 At the T junction, turn right, following the trail parallel to the campground access road.

3.1 The cutoff trail to the wetland heads left. Go straight, heading toward the ocean.

3.4 The trail drops down onto the access road. End of loop. Continue straight across the road and return to the trailhead along the first section of boardwalk.

3.6 Trailhead.

Hike Information

Local Information

San Simeon Chamber of Commerce,
San Simeon; (800) 342-5613;
www.sansimeonsbest.com.
Cambria Chamber of Commerce, Cambria;
(805) 927-3624; www.cambriachamber.org.

Local Events/Attractions

Hearst Castle State Historic Park, San
Simeon; (800) 444-4445; recorded info:
(805) 927-2000; www.hearstcastleinfo.com.

Cambria Art & Wine Festival, held in January,
Cambria; (805) 927-3624.
East Meets West, held in June, a celebration
of Cambria's Chinese history at the Guthrie-
Bianchini House and the Chinese Temple,
Cambria; (805) 927-2964

Lodging

The park's campground has one hundred-plus
campsites in two campgrounds.
State park campsite reservations: (800)
444-7275.

52 High Peaks Loop

This hike is the closest a wilderness walk is likely to get to a theme-park roller-coaster ride. The pinnacles themselves are impressive enough, rising unexpectedly from the surrounding gentle hills in giant knobs and towers of rock. But the High Peaks Trail, built in the 1930s and 1940s by Civilian Conservation Corps (CCC) crews, makes optimum use of this bizarre topography. The CCC crews drilled, chipped, and carved until they had the trail climbing, dipping, and clinging to the rock in the unlikeliest of places.

Start: Juniper Canyon trailhead.
Distance: 4.3-mile lollipop.
Approximate hiking time: 2.5 to 3 hours.
Difficulty: Strenuous, due to steep and rocky trail.
Trail surface: Dirt path, bare rock.
Lay of the land: Rocky spires and arid, brushy slopes.
Other trail users: Rock climbers.
Canine compatibility: No dogs allowed.

Land status: National monument.
Nearest town: Soledad.
Fees and permits: $5.00 entrance fee for cars; $2.00 for bikes, motorcycles, or walk-ins.
Schedule: Open from 7:30 A.M. to 9:00 P.M. daily, year-round.
Map: USGS map: North Chalone Peak, CA.
Trail contact: Pinnacles National Monument, Paicines; (831) 389-4485; www.nps.gov/pinn.

Finding the trailhead: From Salinas, drive south 25 miles on U.S. Highway 101. Exit the highway at Soledad and turn left at the junction onto California Highway 146 (Front Street). Continue 0.5 mile on CA 146 and follow the signs as it turns right onto East Street, then, 3 blocks later, right again onto Metz Road. Drive 2.1 miles on Metz Road (still CA 146) and turn left, still following the signs for CA 146. Continue another 7 miles to the entrance of Pinnacle National Monument, and 2.4 miles beyond that to the ranger station and parking lot at the end of the road. The trailhead is in the southwest corner of the parking lot. *DeLorme: Southern and Central California Atlas & Gazetteer:* Page 32, A2.

The Hike

If the monument were named anything other than Pinnacles, it would come as a bit of a shock to see the rocky spires rising up suddenly from the surrounding hills. The long drive in to the monument's west entrance certainly does little to prepare you for the spectacle awaiting at road's end. The landscape of the low Gabilan Range is fairly typical for Central California east of the coastal zone. The smooth, rolling hills are covered with parched, golden grasses and a liberal sprinkling of gnarled oaks and chaparral. But when the road finally dead-ends at the Chaparral Ranger Station, you find yourself staring up at jagged peaks straight out of the Sierra Nevada.

Not that anyone's complaining, mind you. The monument's 24,000 acres provide important habitat for a variety of plant and animal species, and 30-plus miles of trails lead hikers on a roller-coaster ride through the stony wonderland. But hikers aren't

The Pinnacles

the only ones who find themselves drawn to the monument's fantasy landscape. Rock climbers in particular are especially fond of the area, since it provides the only decent climbing opportunities for hundreds of miles around. Numerous large boulders in the Balconies area give climbers a chance to hone their skills for the more technical routes on the smooth walls of Chalone Creek Canyon.

The hike heads southeast from the Chaparral parking lot, following the Juniper Canyon Trail up an increasingly narrow valley. Several spur trails head off to boulders frequented by climbers, but the main trail climbs swiftly to the base of the monument's namesake pinnacles. Soon the path seems to gain more ground vertically than horizontally, as it winds up between knobs of pale gray rock to higher elevations. This is where all the hard work begins to pay off. Spectacular vistas open up at each new turn, and the looming rock formations constantly change as the trail wends its way between and around them. If you are lucky, you may even spot the largest bird in North America—the endangered California condor. The monument is one of a handful of sites chosen for releasing captive-bred condors back into the wild. With a wingspan of 9 feet or so, they should be easy enough to spot. One naturalist has claimed the flapping of their wings can be heard half a mile away! If things go well, condors could once again be nesting and raising young amongst the towering pinnacles.

When the trail finally tops out on the summit, it is the hiking equivalent of that first big hill on an amusement-park thrill ride. The Civilian Conservation Corps built most of these trails in the 1930s and early 1940s, and they seem to have had a lot of fun doing so. The mile and a half loop around the High Peaks is a real piece of work. At times the trail is reduced to a narrow ledge chiseled into the side of a smooth rock face, complete with steel handrails polished by decades of white-knuckled tourists. In one spot the route heads straight up a near-vertical slope via alternating footholds, each one hacked into the living rock. On the north side, numerous examples of renowned CCC rock walls buttress the trail against the side of the mountain. These fine examples of dry-stone masonry still look as solid as the day they were built. But the pride of the corps had to be the grand finale of the High Peaks loop—a 100-foot tunnel carved straight through a flank of the mountain. And they did it just for you.

Return to the trailhead along the Juniper Canyon Trail.

Miles and Directions

0.0 Start at the southwest corner of the Chaparral parking lot. A few yards past the kiosk, turn right onto the Juniper Canyon Trail.

0.1 Sign-in register for climbers. A spur trail heads right to the ranger station. Turn left and follow the trail up the canyon.

0.2 A spur trail heads left to a boulder. Continue straight.

0.7 The canyon narrows and the trail becomes steeper.

1.0 A bend in the trail affords a nice view of Juniper Canyon.

1.1 The trail hits the ridgetop and follows it up to the right.

High Peaks Loop

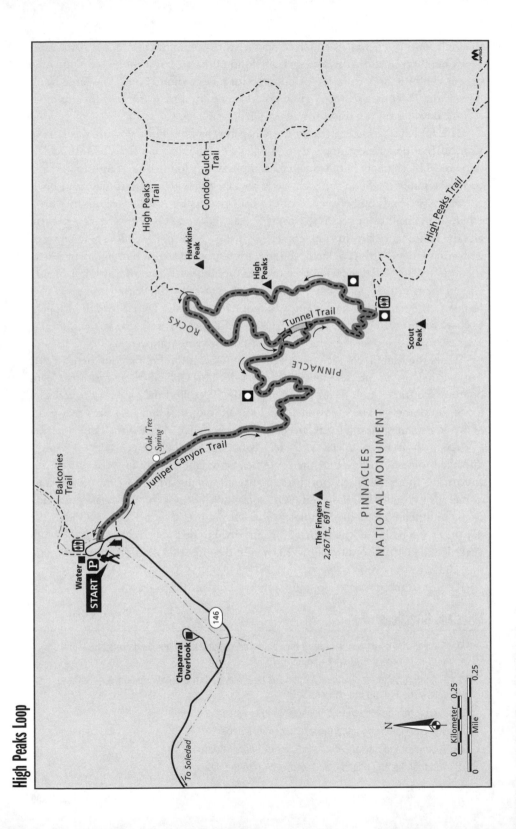

High Peaks Trail

Condor Gulch Trail

Hawkins Peak ▲

High Peaks ▲

PINNACLE ROCKS

Tunnel Trail

Scout Peak ▲

High Peaks Trail

Oak Tree Spring

Balconies Trail

Juniper Canyon Trail

The Fingers ▲
2,267 ft., 691 m

PINNACLES
NATIONAL MONUMENT

Water ■
START
P

Chaparral Overlook ■

146

To Soledad

N

0   Kilometer   0.25

0   Mile   0.25

MAPTECH

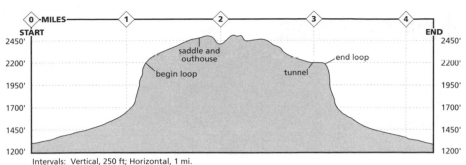

Intervals: Vertical, 250 ft; Horizontal, 1 mi.

1.2 At the base of the Pinnacles, the Tunnel Trail heads left. Continue straight (right).

1.3 The trail passes over the ridge through boulders and spires.

1.5 Great view of the canyon below, and to the west and north.

1.8 The trail reaches the saddle. Excellent views all around. To the right is an outhouse and the trail to Bear Gulch. Turn left onto the High Peaks Trail, heading up.

1.9 The trail crosses over to the south side of the High Peaks and begins dropping down switchbacks.

2.0 The trail climbs a steep staircase chiseled out of solid rock.

2.3 A rock massif overhangs the trail. A few yards later, you descend steps to the saddle.

2.5 Junction. Turn left onto the Tunnel Trail. An old rock drill bit is stuck in the rock to the left, followed by another a few feet later.

2.6 Two more drill bits are sticking out of the boulder on the left.

2.8 Rock walls built by the CCC in the 1930s support the trail here.

2.9 At a bend in the trail, there is a great view of the Pinnacles, and the bridge and tunnel ahead.

3.0 The trail crosses a concrete footbridge and enters the 100-foot tunnel.

3.1 End of the loop. Turn right and follow the Juniper Canyon Trail back to the trailhead.

4.3 Reach the trailhead.

Hike Information

Local Information

San Benito County Chamber of Commerce, Hollister; (831) 637–5315; www.sbccc.org.
Monterey County Convention and Visitors Bureau, Monterey; (888) 221–1010; www.montereyinfo.org.

Local Events/Attractions

Hollister Independence Rally, held Fourth of July weekend, Harleys and assorted mayhem, Hollister; (831) 634–0777.
Civil War Days, held in late August, historical battle re-enactments, Salinas; (831) 751–6978.

Annual Steinbeck Festival, held in August, four days of fun celebrating author John Steinbeck, native son of Salinas, National Steinbeck Center, Salinas; (831) 775–4737; www.steinbeck.org.
Salinas Valley Fair, held in mid-May, King City; (831) 385–3243; www.salinasvalleyfair.com.
California Rodeo Salinas, held in July, top pro rodeo, with steer wrestling, bull riding, calf roping, etc., Salinas; (800) 771–8807; www.carodeo.com.

Honorable Mention

Monterey

└ Asilomar Beach Trail

This easy 2-mile trail parallels a postcard-perfect beach around the headlands of the Monterey Peninsula. Excellent tide pools can be accessed at several points along the trail, just blocks away from a densely populated residential area. Those wishing for a longer hike can continue another 3 miles around the headlands through beachfront parklands to Monterey's famous Cannery Row, home of the world-class Monterey Bay Aquarium. From California Highway 1 at Monterey, head west 4.5 miles on California Highway 68 (which becomes Sunset Drive in the city of Pacific Grove). Once it reaches the beach, the road parallels the trail for its entire length. Start and stop at any of the turnouts. For more information, contact Asilomar State Beach, Pacific Grove; (831) 372–4076. *DeLorme: Northern California Atlas & Gazetteer:* Page 18 C–D5.

Appendix: Hiking Clubs and Trail Groups

California Coastwalk
Sebastapol, CA
(707) 829–6689
www.coastwalk.org
As the name suggests, this group is into hiking on the coast.

The Trail Center
3921 East Bayshore Road
Palo Alto, CA 94303
(650) 968–7065
info@trailcenter.org
www.trailcenter.org
Outings and info for the South Bay Area.

California Alpine Club
P.O. Box 2180
Mill Valley, CA 94942-2180
www.calalpine.org

Sierra Club
National Headquarters
85 Second Street, 2nd Floor
San Francisco, CA 94105
(415) 977–5500
Fax: 415-977-5799
www.sierraclub.org
Most regional chapters offer regular outings.

East Bay Barefoot Hikers
www.unshod.org/ebbfhike
Hiking barefoot and loving it.

North San Francisco Bay Barefoot Hikers
www.barefooters.org/hikers/north_bay
More barefoot hikers.

Friends of Pinnacles
208 Woods Street
Santa Cruz, CA 95062
www.pinnacles.org
Focusing on Pinnacles National Monument.

LandPaths
(707) 524–9318
LandPaths-outings@sonic.net
www.hikenorthbay.com/landpaths
This is a nonprofit organization "dedicated to fostering a love of·the land through public access, environmental education, and land stewardship." They do outings in the North Bay Area.

Bay Area Ridge Trail Council
San Francisco, CA
(415) 561–2595
www.ridgetrail.org

Bay Trail
Association of Bay Area Governments
(510) 464–7900
www.abag.ca.gov/bayarea/baytrail
Creating a continuous low-elevation trail around the bay.

Greenbelt Alliance
530 Bush Street, Suite 303
San Francisco, CA 94108
(415) 398–3730
Fax: (415) 398–6530
info@greenbelt.org
www.greenbelt.org

Santa Cruz Mountain Trails Association
P.O. Box 1141
Los Altos, CA 94023
MHD@slac.stanford.edu
www.stanford.edu/~mhd/trails

California Hiking And Outdoor Society (CHAOS)
www.uc-hiking-club.berkeley.ca.us
A loose network of hikers who organize regular outings in the Bay Area.